Architektur des medizinischen Wissens
Eine Kulturgeschichte der Medizinischen Universität
Wien und des AKH Wien

Herausgegeben von
Markus Müller, Stefan Oláh und Ulrike Matzer
Mit Fotografien von Stefan Oláh
und einem Essay von Ulrike Matzer

Architecture for Medicine
A Cultural History of the Medical University of Vienna
and University Hospital Vienna

Edited by
Markus Müller, Stefan Oláh, and Ulrike Matzer
With Photographs by Stefan Oláh
and an Essay by Ulrike Matzer

Birkhäuser
Basel

Wien ist die lebenswerteste Stadt der Welt. Die ausgezeichnete medizinische Versorgung der Bevölkerung stellt einen wichtigen Parameter für diesen in zahlreichen renommierten internationalen Studien konstatierten Befund dar. Einen wesentlichen Beitrag dazu leistet das Universitätsklinikum AKH Wien, eines der bedeutendsten medizinischen Zentren Europas und das größte Krankenhaus Österreichs, gemeinsam mit der Medizinischen Universität Wien, einer der traditionsreichsten medizinischen Ausbildungs- und Forschungsstätten Europas sowie der größten fachlichen Ausbildungsstätte im deutschsprachigen Raum.

Die vorliegende Publikation *Architektur des medizinischen Wissens* der Kunsthistorikerin Ulrike Matzer und des Fotografen Stefan Oláh dokumentiert aus kulturwissenschaftlicher Perspektive die traditionsreiche Geschichte und medizinhistorisch bedeutsame Rolle des AKH Wien und der MedUni Wien. Aspekte der Stadtentwicklung, der Geschichte der Institution und der Bautypen im Gesundheitsbereich sowie nicht zuletzt die jeweils vorherrschende Formensprache nahmen und nehmen in unterschiedlicher Intensität wesentlichen Einfluss auf das Konzept dieses das Wiener Stadtbild prägenden Bauensembles.

Stefan Oláhs fotografische Bestandsaufnahme der markanten Außen- und Innenarchitektur illustriert gemeinsam mit seinen Detailaufnahmen die Qualität der einzelnen Baukörper und medizinischen Apparate. Gleichzeitig legt er dabei die jeweiligen Spielräume der Architekten offen.

Ich danke dem Rektorat der Medizinischen Universität Wien für die Initiative zu diesem Forschungs- und Buchprojekt und gratuliere Ulrike Matzer und Stefan Oláh sehr herzlich zu ihrer beeindruckenden kulturwissenschaftlichen und künstlerischen Aufarbeitung der Geschichte und Gegenwart des wichtigsten

---

Vienna is the world's most livable city. The excellent medical care available to its population is one of the key parameters of this conclusion, which has been drawn by a number of prestigious international studies. A major contribution to this is made by University Hospital Vienna, one of Europe's most important medical centers and Austria's largest hospital, together with the Medical University of Vienna, one of the continent's most established medical education and research facilities and the largest specialist training institution in the German-speaking region.

This publication, *Architecture for Medicine*, by the art historian Ulrike Matzer and the photographer Stefan Oláh, documents the rich past and important medical-historical role of University Hospital Vienna and MedUni Vienna from the cultural-scientific perspective. Aspects of the development of the city, the history of the institution, and building typologies in the health sector, as well as, not least, the different formal vocabularies that have dominated over the years, have exercised and continue to exercise, to varying degrees, a key influence on the concept of this built ensemble that has such a powerful presence in Vienna's cityscape.

Stefan Oláh's photographic inventory of the striking exteriors and interiors of the complex combines with his close-ups to illustrate the quality of the individual buildings and the medical equipment. At the same time, he also sheds light on the room for maneuver enjoyed by the various architects.

I would like to thank the Rectorate of the Medical University of Vienna for the initiative behind this research and book project and to warmly congratulate Ulrike Matzer and Stefan Oláh for their impressive cultural-scientific and artistic reappraisal of the past and present of Austria's most important medical

medizinischen Kompetenzzentrums Österreichs. Der Publikation
Architektur des medizinischen Wissens, einem künftigen Standardwerk zum
Universitätsklinikum AKH Wien und zur MedUni Wien, wünsche ich
viele interessierte Leser:innen.

Dr. Michael Ludwig
Bürgermeister und Landeshauptmann von Wien

competence center. I trust that the publication *Architecture for Medicine*,
a future standard work on University Hospital Vienna and MedUni Vienna,
will be enjoyed by many interested readers.

Dr. Michael Ludwig
Mayor and Provincial Governor of Vienna

Die Idee, dass die Welt, die wir vorfinden, ein Ergebnis der Gedanken von gestern ist, hat mich immer fasziniert. Ebenso wie der Bau von Kathedralen – Projekte, die eine Generation in dem Wissen begonnen hat, nie das Ende des Vorhabens erleben zu können.

Die Architektur des Neuen Allgemeinen Krankenhauses, die neben historischen Bauten aus der Zeit des Josephinismus und der späten Monarchie meine Generation geprägt hat, ist auch ein schönes Beispiel für Geschichte und generationenübergreifende Ambition. Konzipiert in den 1950er Jahren (das Raum- und Funktionskonzept wurde 1959 auf für heutige Verhältnisse spärlich beschriebenen 578 Seiten Durchschlagpapier erstellt) und 1994 eröffnet, ist das AKH Wien eine Kathedrale der Moderne und heute irgendwie auch schon wieder aus der Zeit gefallen. Das brandneue Gebäude, das der österreichischen Medizin und einer ganzen akademischen Generation am Ende des letzten Jahrhunderts wieder neuen Schwung gegeben hat, und die Hoffnung, auf dem Niveau der Besten der Welt arbeiten und konkurrieren zu können, standen damals in eklatantem Gegensatz zu den Gebäuden der Rokitansky'schen Pathologie, der „Anatomie" in der Währinger Straße oder den Kliniken des Alten AKH, in denen Medizin-Weltgeschichte geschrieben worden ist. Mein Büro stammt bereits aus der Phase der Jugendstil-Erweiterung des Alten AKH ab 1904 unter Kaiser Franz Joseph und war Teil der Schauta'schen Frauenklinik. Viele Wiener:innen wurden hier geboren – manche kommen noch heute auf einen kurzen Besuch zurück zum Ort ihrer Geburt.

Unsere Universität ist ein einzigartiges architektonisches und medizin-historisches Zeugnis, das prägend für viele Generationen von Mediziner:innen und Patient:innen war. Diese Gebäude haben große persönliche Schicksale

---

I have always been fascinated by the notion that the world around us is a product of the ideas of the past. Just as I have always been fascinated by the construction of cathedrals – projects that one generation began in the knowledge that it would never experience the conclusion of the process.

The architecture of University Hospital Vienna, which, together with older buildings from the era of Josephinism and the late Monarchy, shaped my generation, is also an excellent example of historical narrative and multi-generational ambition. Conceived in the 1950s (the spatial and functional concept was set out in 1959 in a 578-page document on carbon paper that is remarkably brief by today's standards) and opened in 1994, University Hospital Vienna is a cathedral of the modern age that already somehow seems to have fallen behind the times. The pristine building that gave new impetus to Austrian medicine and to an entire academic generation at the end of the last century, and the accompanying hope that we would be able to work on the same level as and compete with the best in the world, offered a striking contrast to the buildings of Rokitansky's Pathology Department, the "Anatomie" in Währinger Straße, or the clinics of the Altes AKH, in which global medical history was written. My office dates back to the Jugendstil expansion of the Altes AKH under Emperor Franz Joseph in 1904 and was part of Schauta's Gynecological Clinic. Many Viennese were born here – and many still return today for a brief visit to the place of their birth.

Our university is a unique embodiment of architectural and medical history that has shaped generations of doctors and patients. These buildings have seen dramatic private moments, ideas have been developed here and, from time-to-time, honored by Nobel Prizes, children have been born, lifesaving

gesehen, Ideen wurden entwickelt und teils mit Nobelpreisen gewürdigt, es wurden Kinder geboren, lebensrettende Operationen durchgeführt und Liebesbeziehungen geknüpft. Die derzeit entstehenden Gebäude an unseren großen Baustellen Spitalgasse/Mariannengasse (MedUni Campus Mariannengasse) und Lazarettgasse (MedUni Campus AKH, Eric Kandel Institut – Zentrum für Präzisionsmedizin und Center for Translational Medicine) werden unseren Universitätscampus und neue Generationen von Mediziner:innen in den nächsten Jahrzehnten prägen.

Namens der Medizinischen Universität Wien möchte ich dem Künstler und Fotografen Stefan Oláh, der die aktuelle Architektur unserer Universität und ihrer Kliniken aus Anlass des Jubiläumsjahres 2024 in unnachahmlicher Weise für diesen Band abgelichtet und damit für die Nachwelt festgehalten hat, danken. Mein Dank gebührt ebenfalls Ulrike Matzer für ihre großartige kulturhistorische Einordnung der Architektur unserer Universität.

Univ.-Prof. Dr. Markus Müller
Rektor der Medizinischen Universität Wien

---

operations have been performed, and romances have blossomed. The buildings that are currently being erected on our huge construction sites on Spitalgasse/ Mariannengasse (MedUni Campus Mariannengasse) and Lazarettgasse (MedUni Campus AKH, Eric Kandel Institute – Center for Precision Medicine, and Center for Translational Medicine) will impact upon our university campus and new generations of doctors for decades to come.

In the name of the Medical University of Vienna, I would like to thank the artist and photographer Stefan Oláh, who has photographed the current architecture of our university and its clinics in his own inimitable way, recording these buildings for posterity and enabling us to present this book that marks our anniversary year 2024. And I would also like to thank Ulrike Matzer for her splendid cultural-historical assessment of the architecture of our university.

Univ.-Prof. Dr. Markus Müller
Rector of the Medical University of Vienna

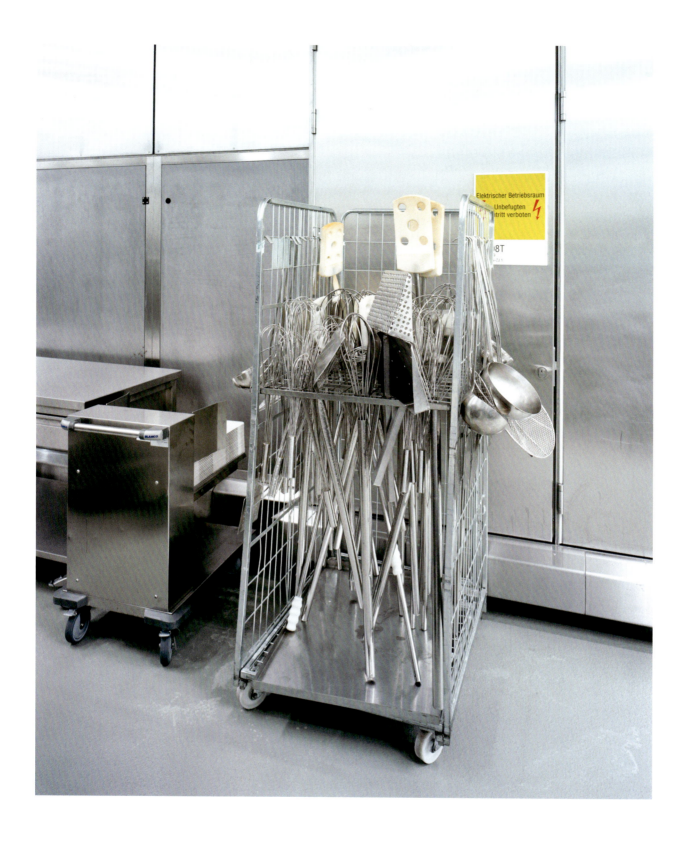

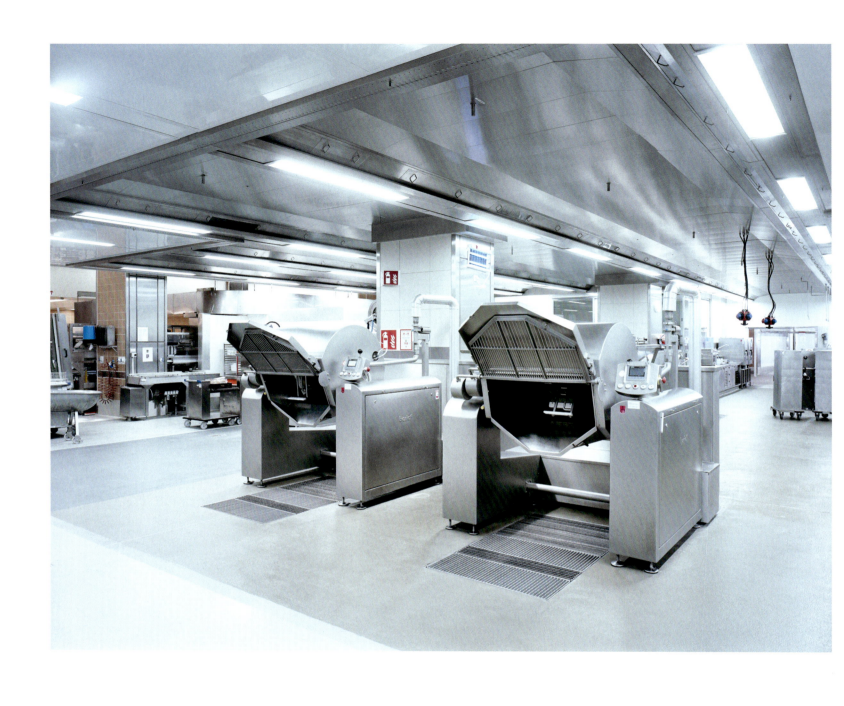

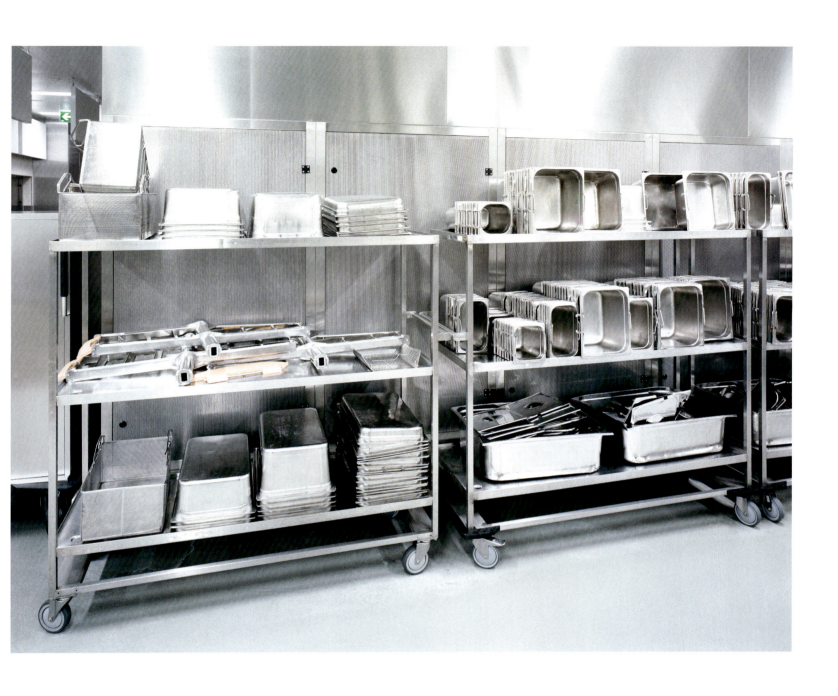

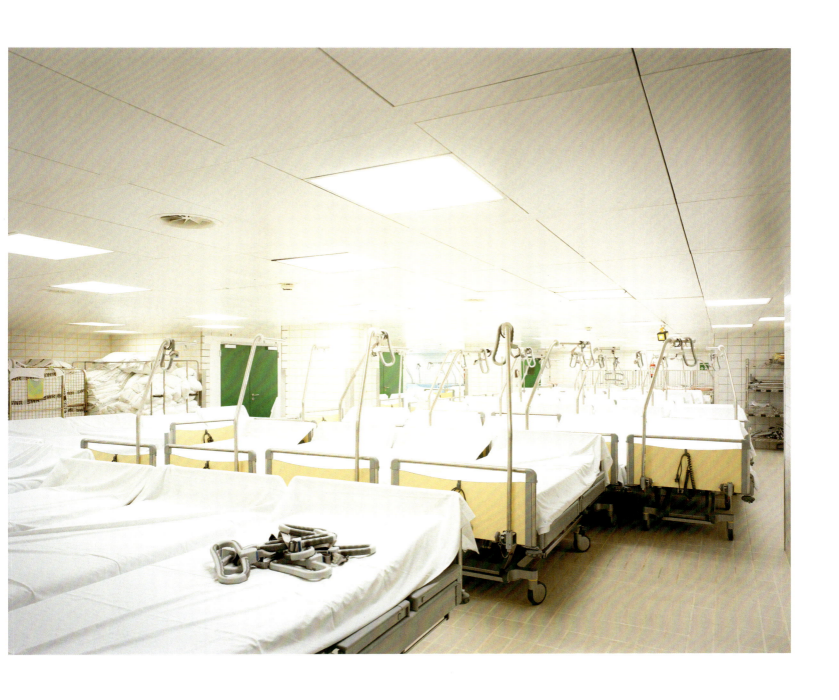

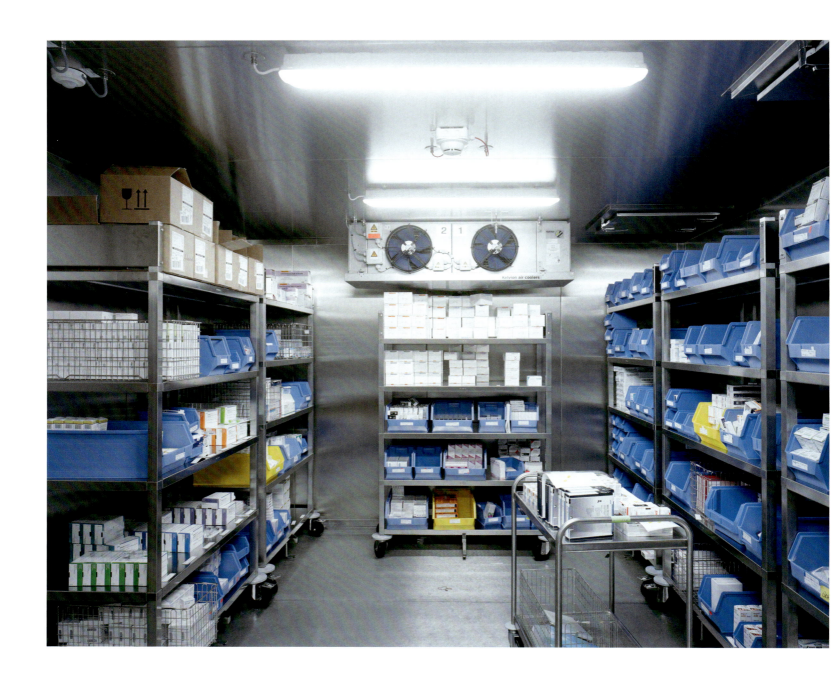

57

64

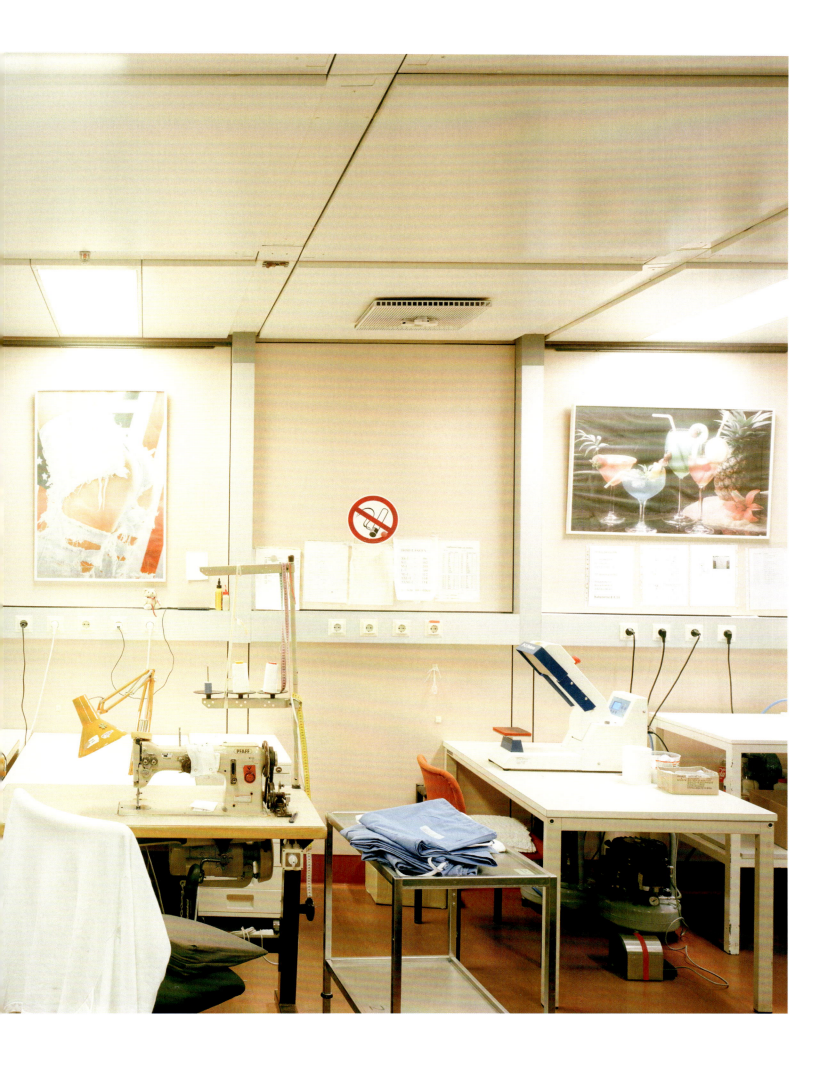

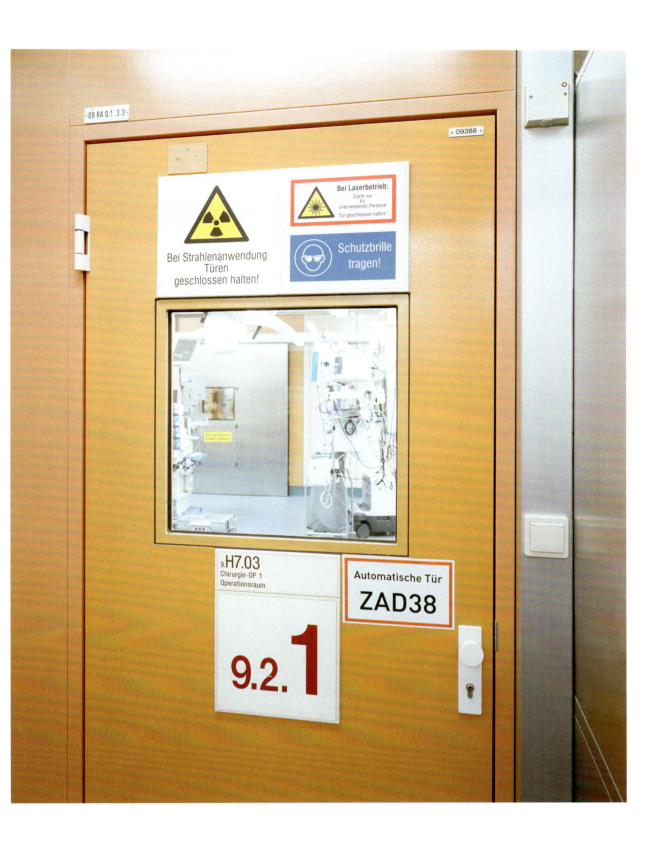

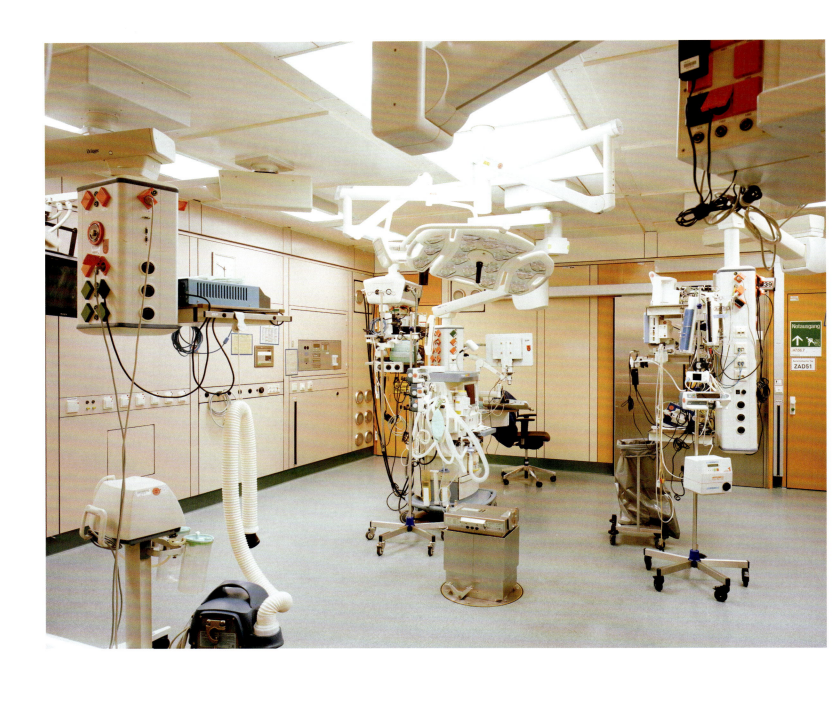

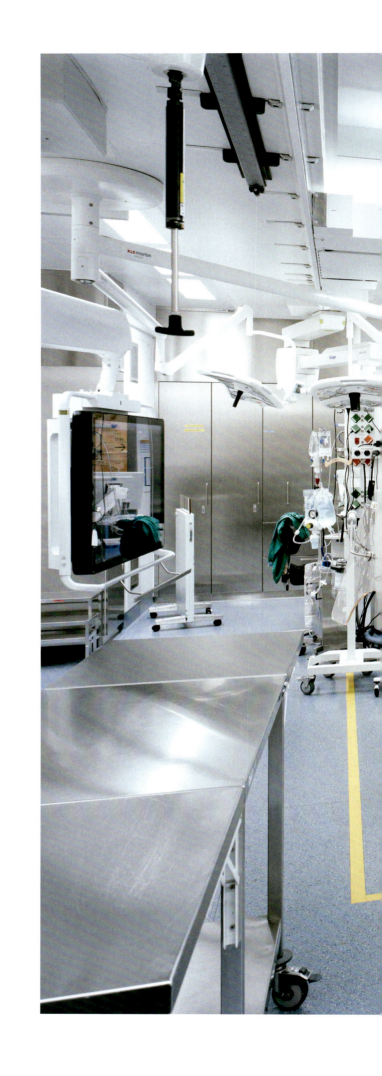

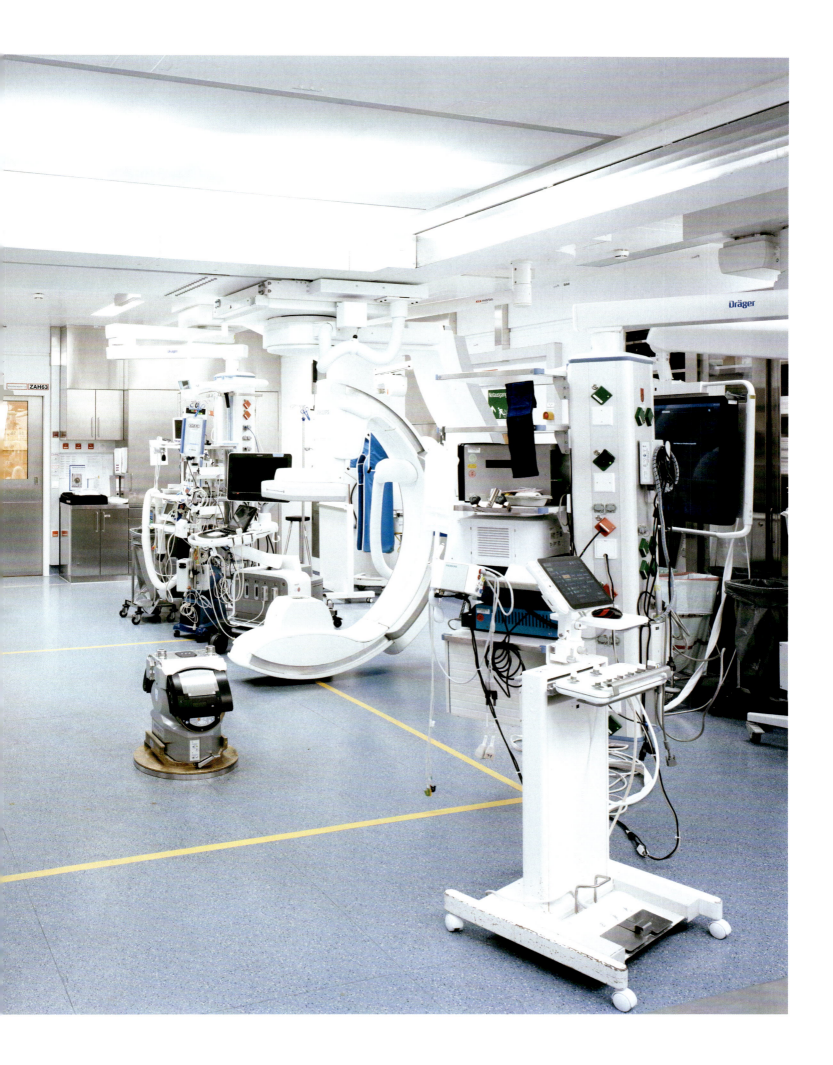

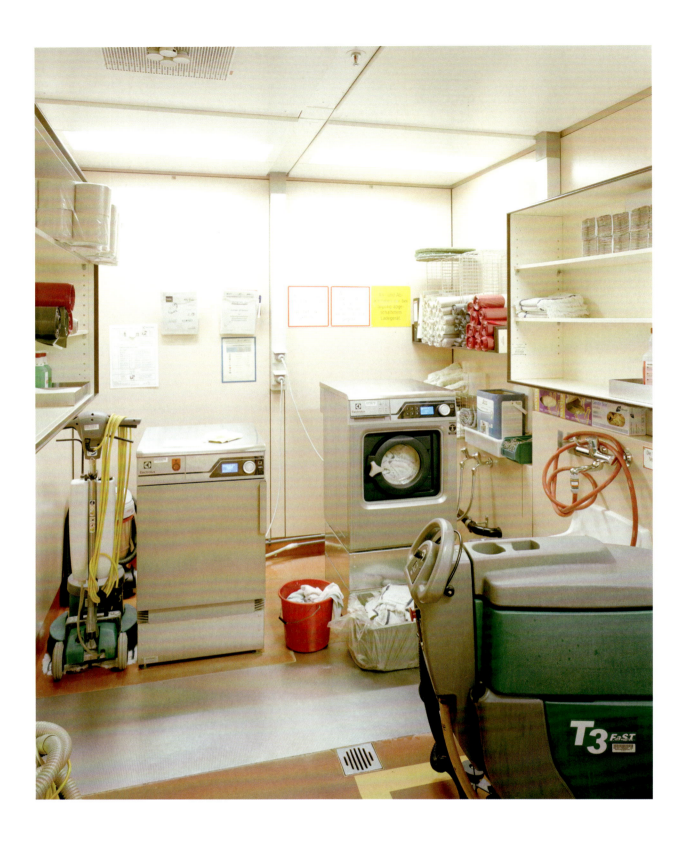

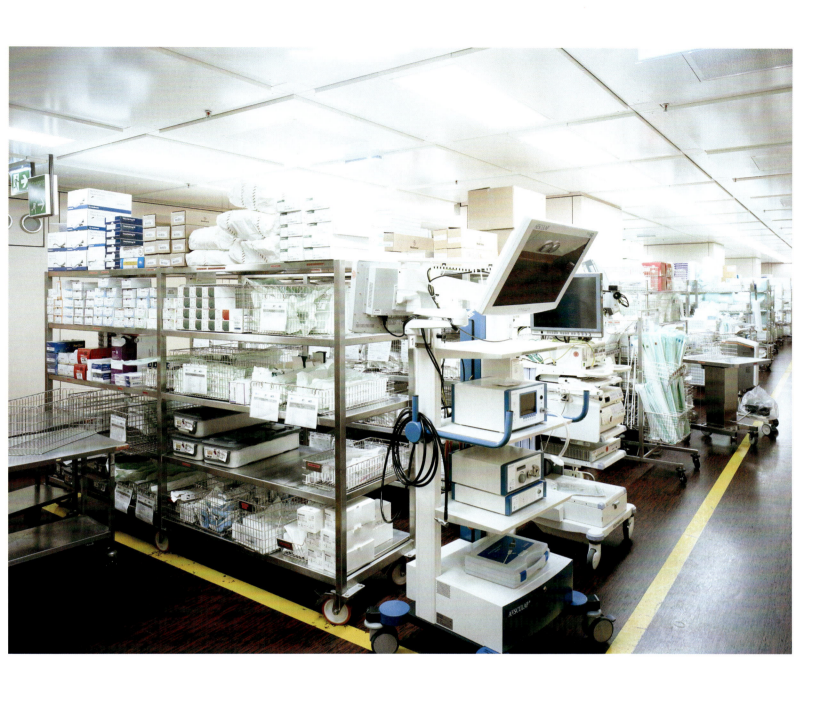

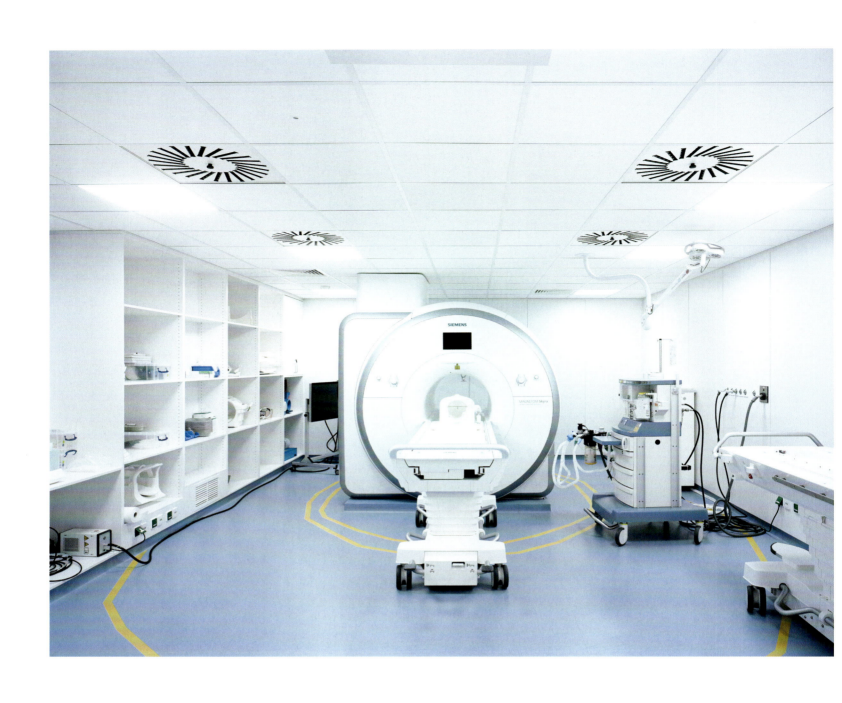

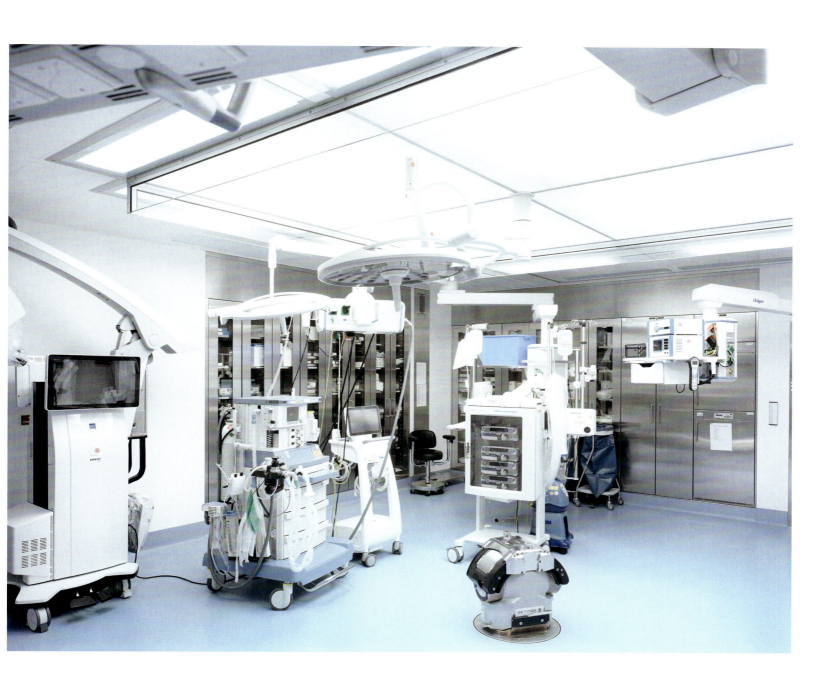

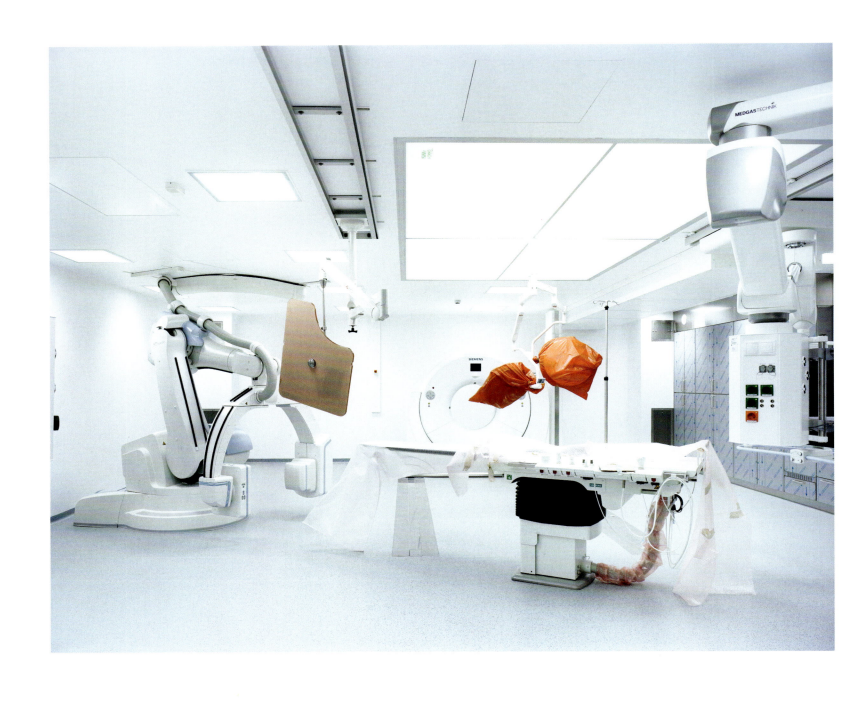

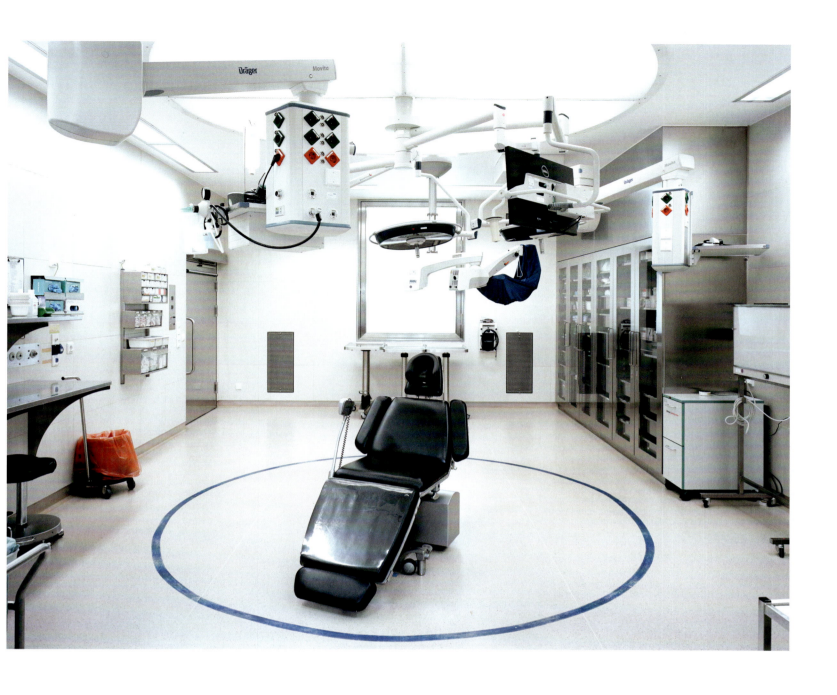

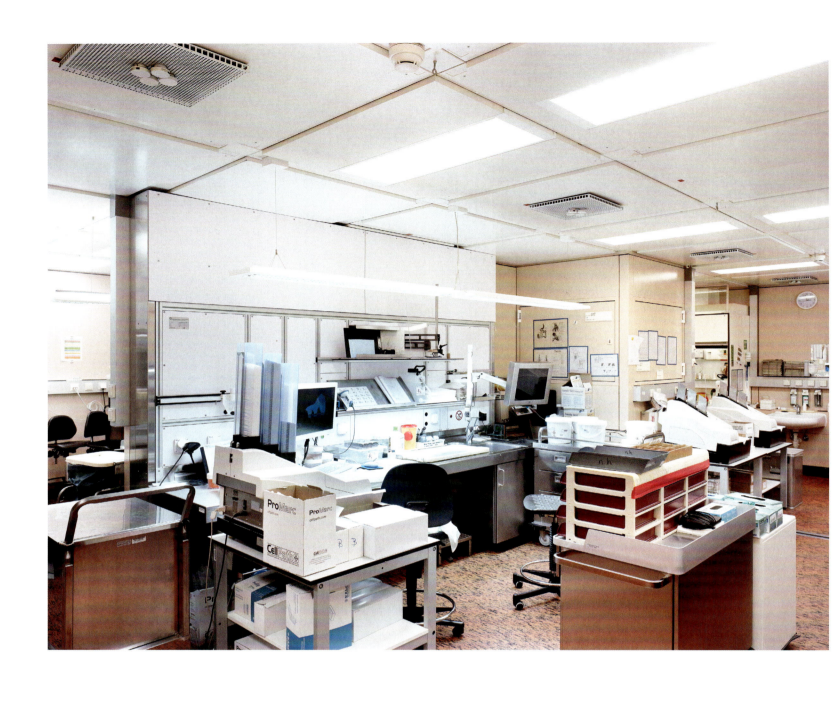

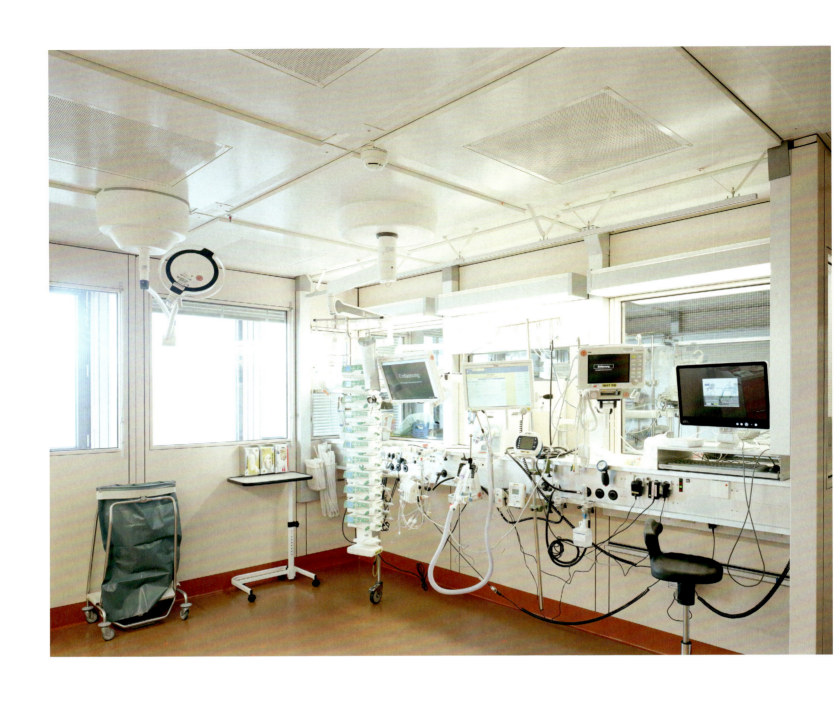

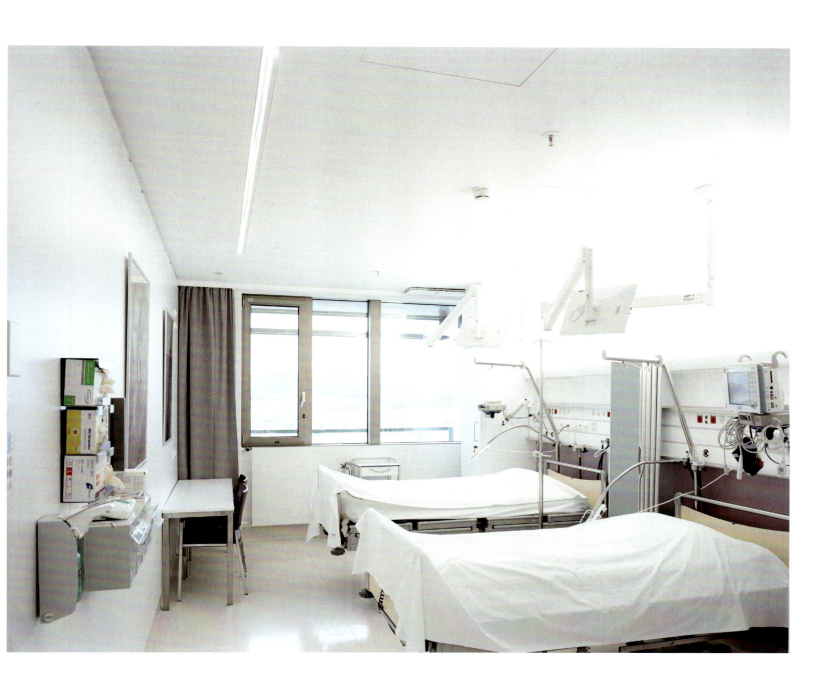

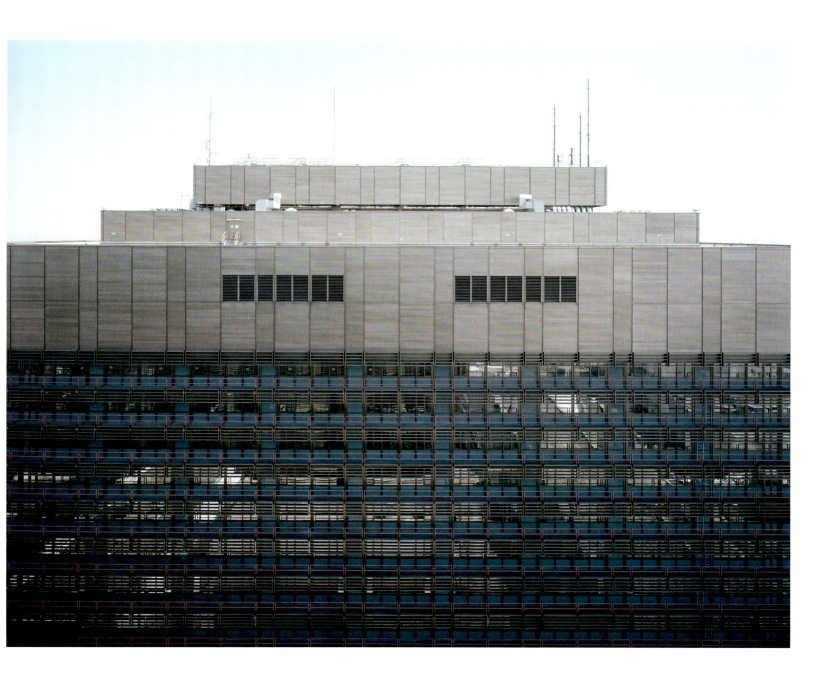

119

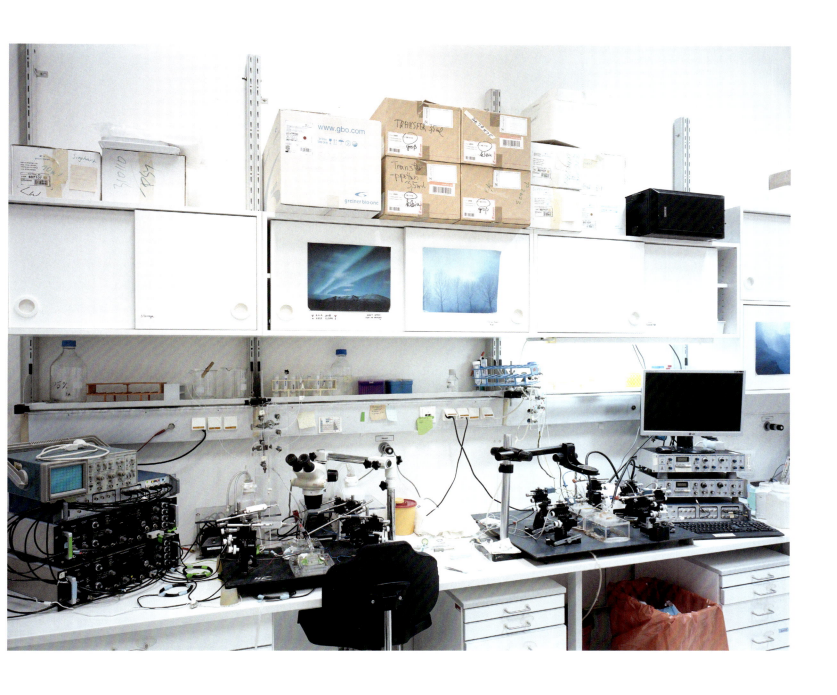

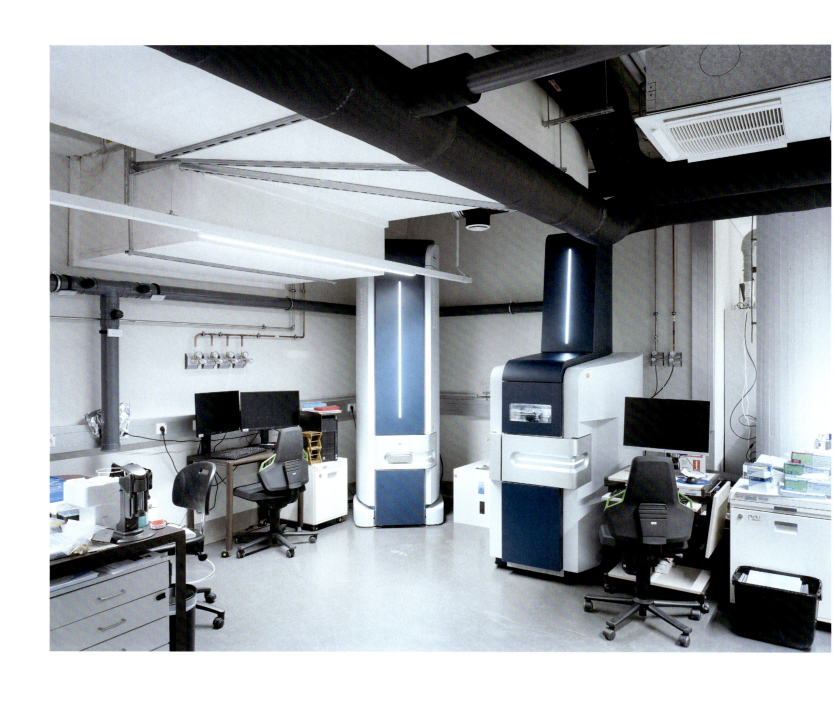

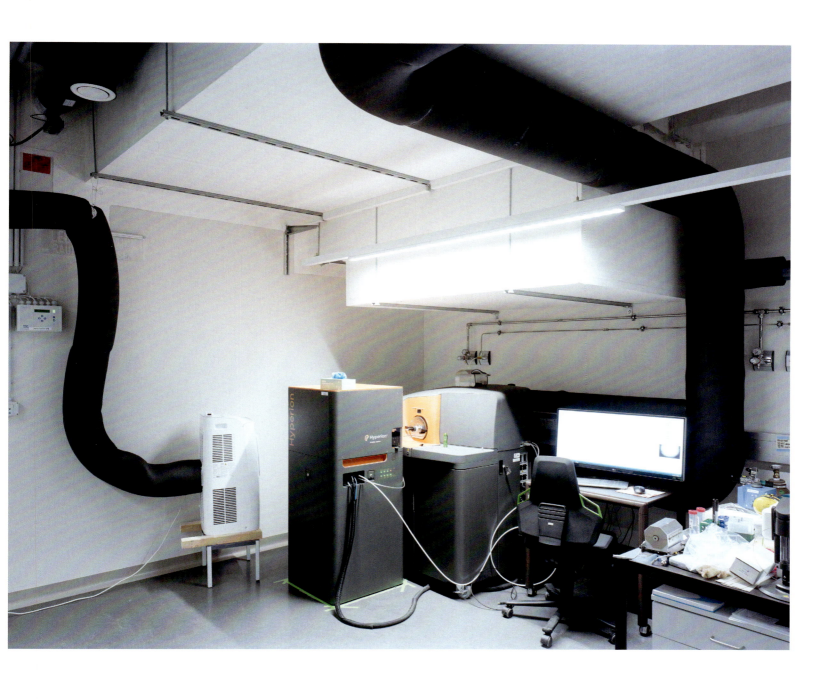

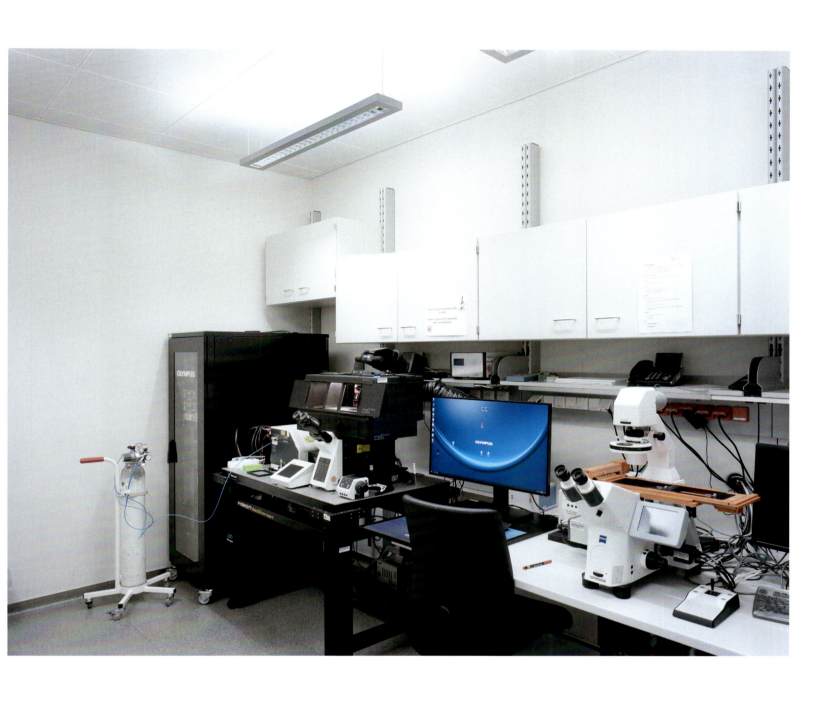

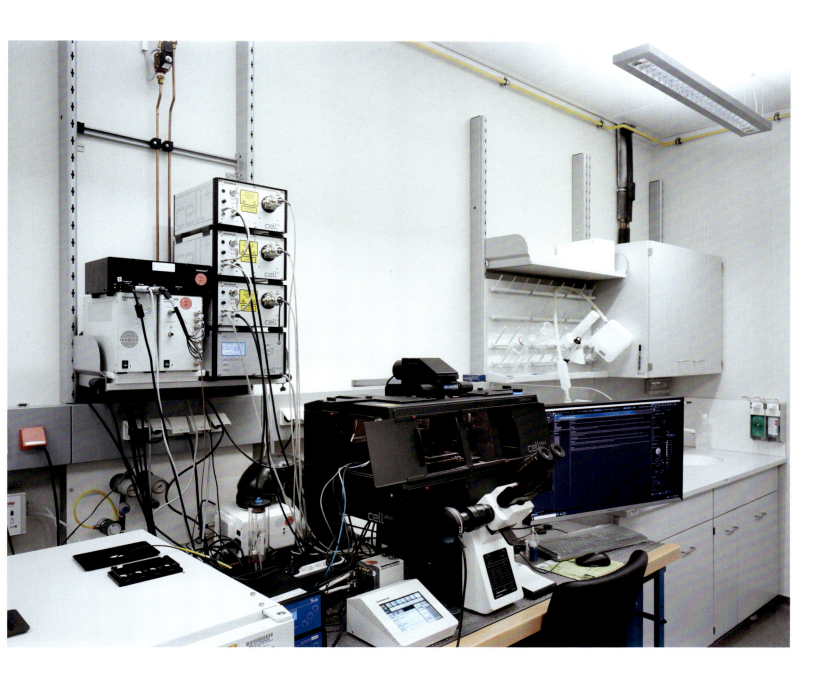

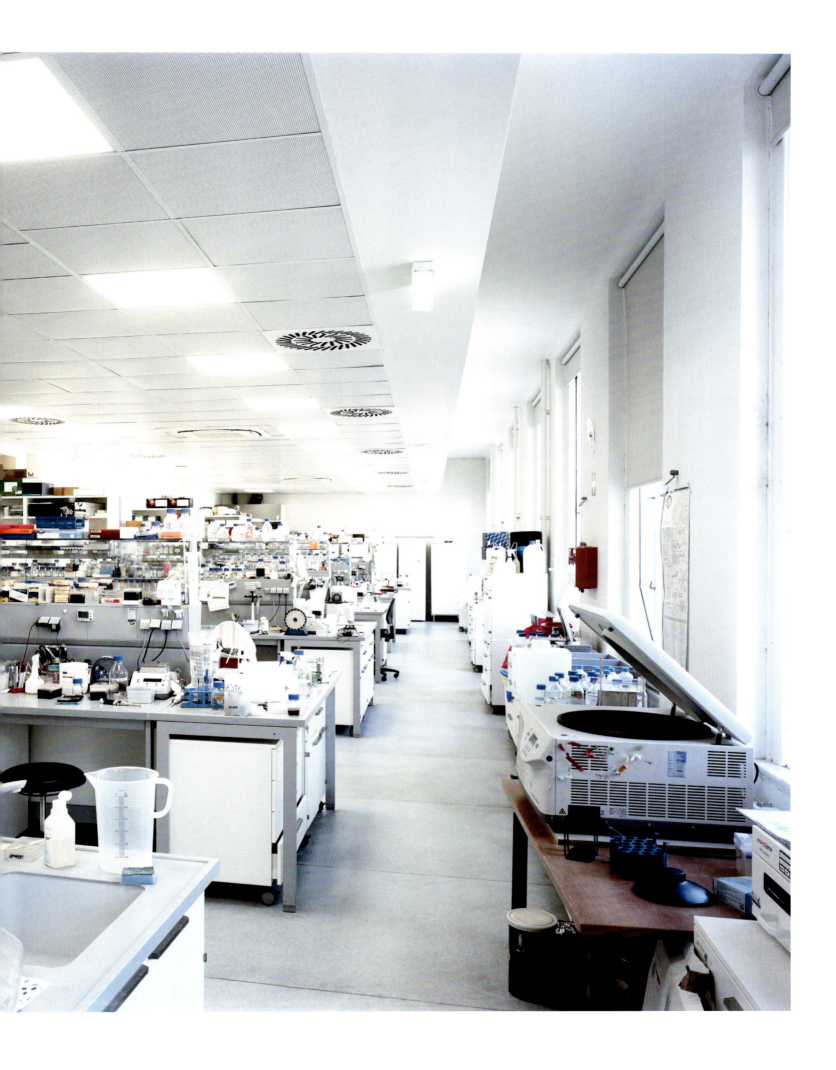

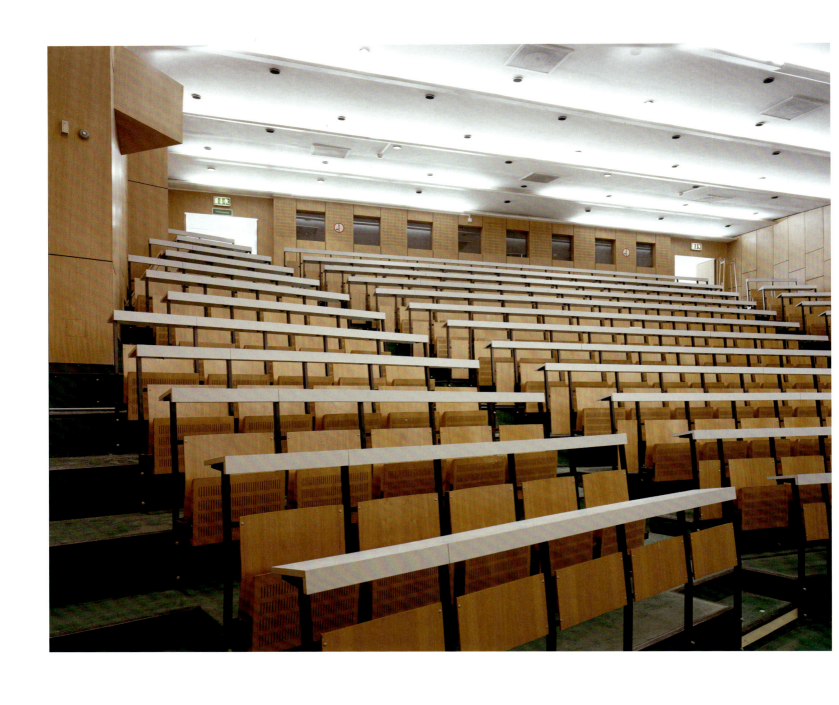

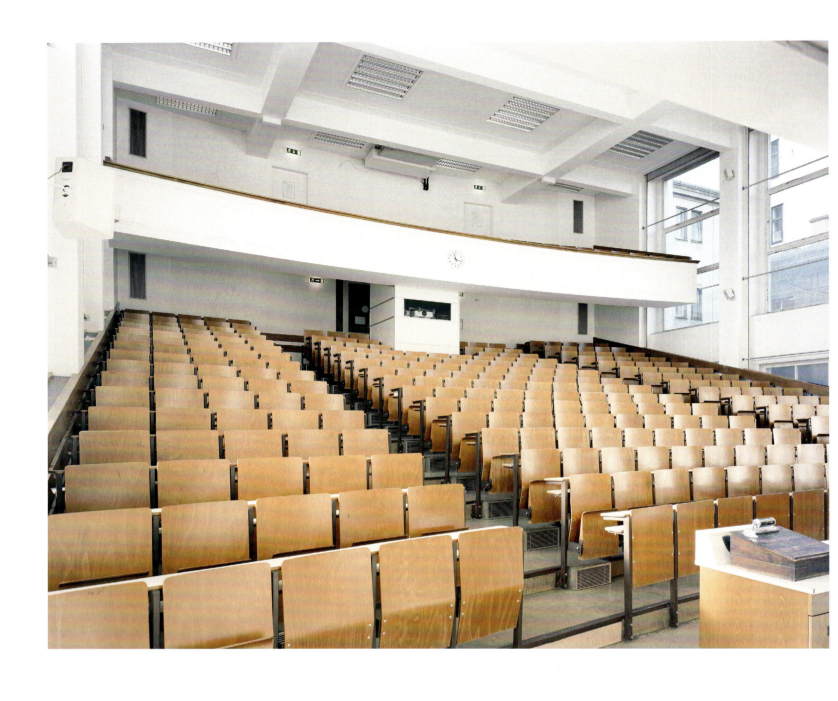

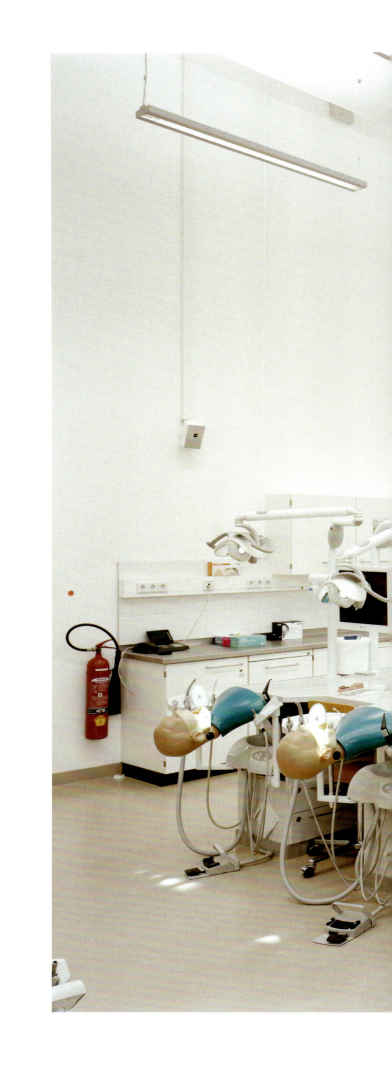

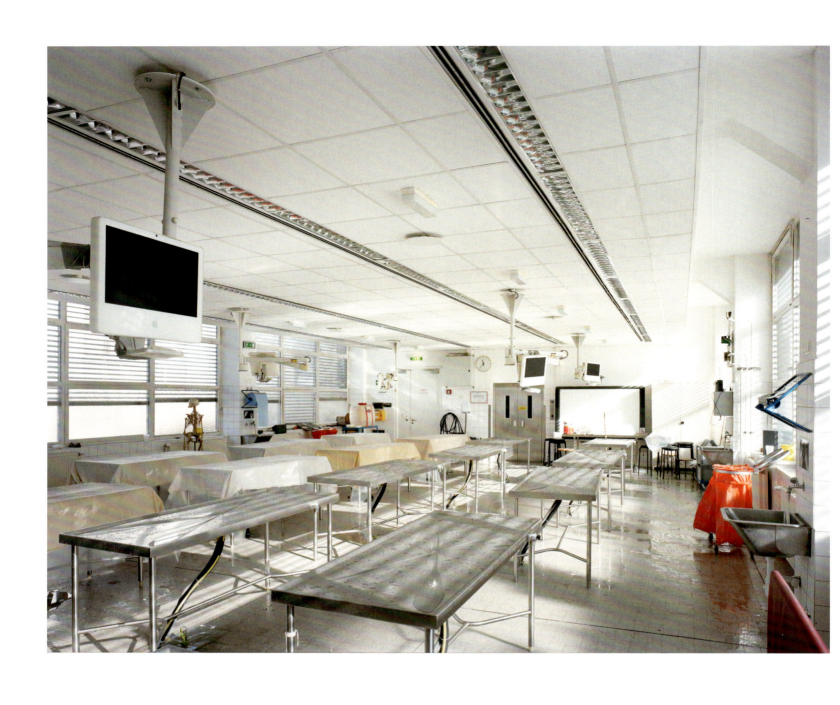

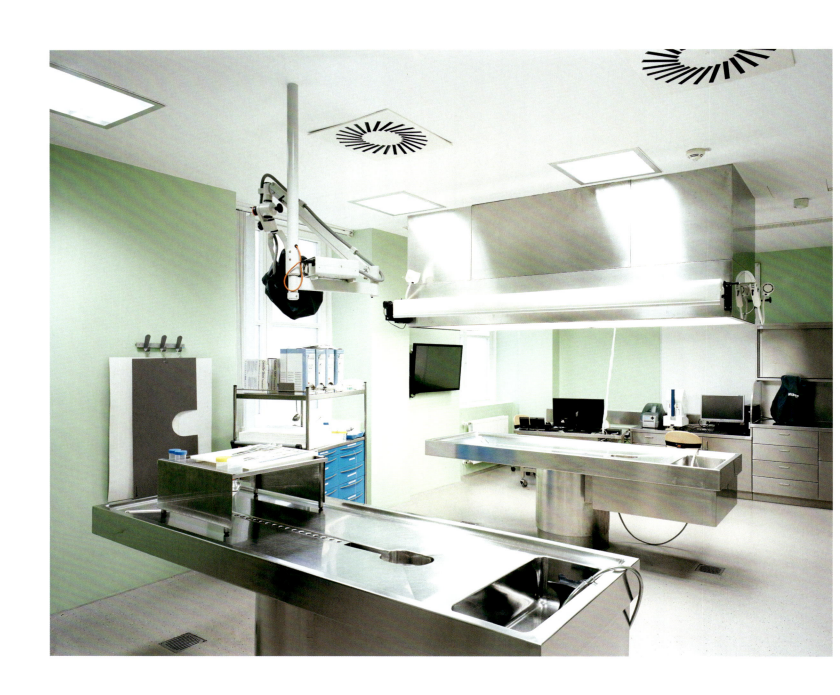

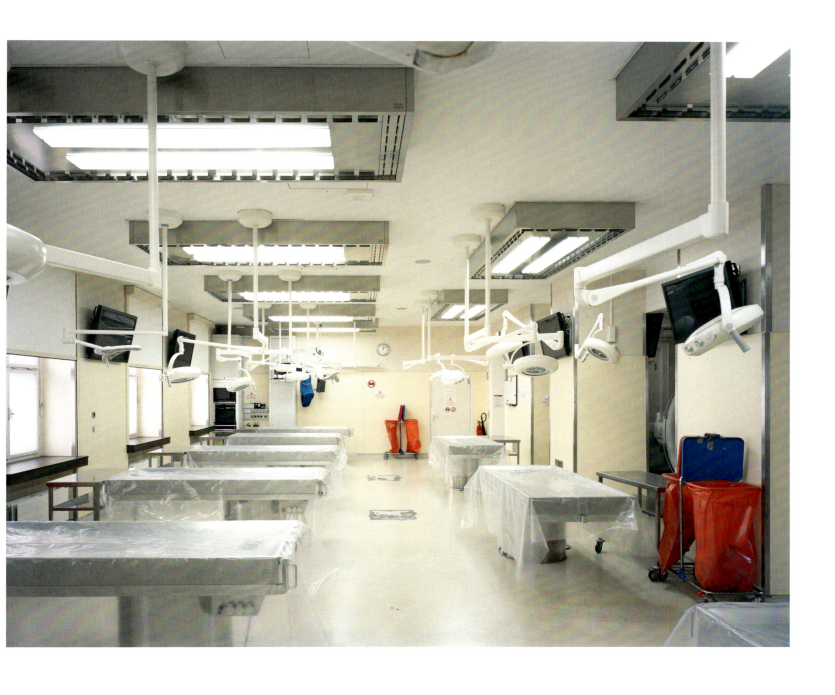

165

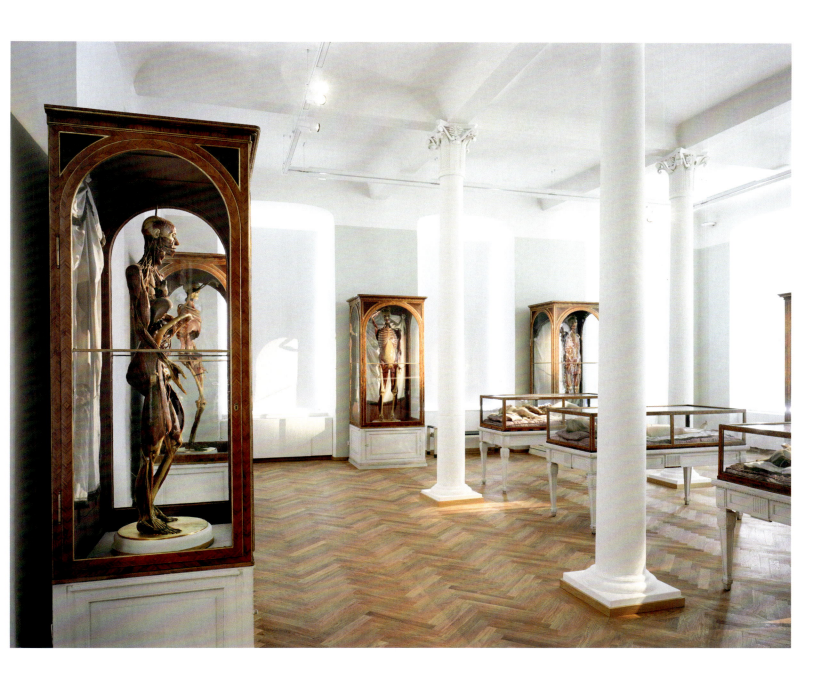

169

179

183

Architektur des medizinischen Wissens
Eine Kulturgeschichte der Medizinischen Universität Wien und des AKH Wien

Ulrike Matzer

Architecture for Medicine
A Cultural History of the Medical University of Vienna and University Hospital Vienna

Ulrike Matzer

Das Universitätsklinikum AKH Wien ist das größte Spital Österreichs und eines der bedeutendsten in Europa, durch den Ruf der Medizinischen Universität gilt es auch international als Instanz. In einschlägigen Rankings nahm es mehrfach eine beachtliche Stellung ein, 2023 wurde es vom US-Nachrichtenmagazin *Newsweek* auf Platz 30 der weltweiten Top-Spitäler gelistet. Zudem verfügt das Wiener Zentralkrankenhaus über eine lange Geschichte: Aus dem einstigen „Großarmenhaus" entwickelte sich ab dem späten 18. Jahrhundert eines der damals modernsten Spitäler. Von Anfang an war dort auch der Klinikunterricht etabliert, der sich zur paradigmatischen Methode medizinischer Ausbildung entwickelte. Im Bett liegende Kranke rückten in das Zentrum der Forschung, die renommierten Vertreter der ersten und zweiten Wiener Schule der Medizin wirkten an dieser Stätte eines praxisorientierten Wissens. Mit dem Ausbau der Grundlagenforschung wurden Spezialisierungen vorangetrieben und die ersten Augen-, Haut- und Hals-Nasen-Ohren-Kliniken der Welt etabliert.

Heute dient das Universitätsklinikum AKH Wien als Lehr- und Forschungsstätte der Medizinischen Universität Wien (MedUni Wien), die auch das gesamte ärztliche Personal des Spitals stellt. Es verfügt nicht nur über die Einrichtungen für die Krankenversorgung, sondern erfüllt auch die Anforderungen des Unterrichts und der medizinisch-klinischen Forschung. Die Patient:innen profitieren unmittelbar von den Innovationen der MedUni Wien. Mit rund 8.000 Studierenden ist sie die derzeit größte medizinische Lehranstalt im deutschsprachigen Raum. Als eine der jüngsten Universitäten kann sie sich zugleich auf eine lange Tradition berufen: Ihre Anfänge als medizinische Fakultät reichen bis zur 1365 erfolgten Gründung der Universität Wien zurück, seit 2004 genießt die MedUni Wien als eigene Hochschule Autonomie. Bereits im Mittelalter eine weithin anerkannte Größe in Fragen des Gesundheitswesens, gilt sie auch heute als Kompetenzzentrum für sämtliche Fächer der Medizin. Mit 30 Universitätskliniken und zwei klinischen Instituten, 13 medizinischen Zentren und zahlreichen hoch spezialisierten Laboren agiert sie europaweit im Spitzenfeld der Biomedizin. Ihre herausragenden wissenschaftlichen Leistungen in diesem Bereich sind spätestens seit der Coronavirus-Pandemie auch der breiten Bevölkerung ein Begriff.

Ebendiese reiche Tradition, die Bedeutung und Strahlkraft des AKH Wien und der Medizinischen Universität Wien waren uns Anlass für den vorliegenden Band. Wir unternehmen hier den Versuch, die Geschichte und Gegenwart dieses „Clusters" medizinischer Exzellenz aus kulturwissenschaftlicher Perspektive darzustellen. Die gebaute Substanz des Wiener Zentralkrankenhauses und seiner Unikliniken rückt hier in den Blick, von den Anfängen bis zur Gegenwart. Die meisten bisherigen Studien über das Wiener Allgemeine Krankenhaus und seine Kliniken sind nämlich als Geschichten bekannter Mediziner angelegt, mehrheitlich wurden sie auch von Ärzt:innen geschrieben.[1] Die Orte ihres Wirkens dagegen sind kaum präsent. Dabei dominieren die Krankenhaus- und Klinikbauten einen beachtlichen Teil des innerstädtischen Gefüges von Wien.

Mit dieser künstlerisch-wissenschaftlichen Publikation wollen wir die reiche Tradition des Wiener Zentralspitals und seiner Unikliniken anhand zeitloser Fotoaufnahmen vor Augen führen. Das Buch bietet einen visuellen Parcours durch die Stätten des medizinischen Wissens und Wirkens. Daneben geben die Motive im Band auch Einblick in kaum bekannte oder nicht allgemein zugängliche Orte des Klinik-, Forschungs- und Lehrbetriebs.

Über drei Jahre hinweg hat Stefan Oláh mit seiner analogen Großbildkamera alle von der MedUni Wien genutzten Bauten dokumentiert. Markante Ansichten wechseln mit Nahaufnahmen von Details, in denen sich die besondere Formensprache eines Gebäudes manifestiert. Charakteristisch für die Haltung Oláhs, für seine Ethik als Fotograf, ist seine Perspektive – ein Zugang, der mit dem Motto des

---

University Hospital Vienna is Austria's largest hospital, one of the most important in Europe, and regarded as an international authority thanks to the reputation of the Medical University of Vienna. It regularly performs impressively in the relevant rankings and occupied 30th place in the list of the world's top hospitals that was published by the US news magazine *Newsweek* in 2023. Vienna's central hospital also has a long history: Starting in the late 18th century, the former "Großarmenhaus" (Large Almshouse) developed into one of the most up-to-date hospitals of the period. From the very beginning, it also offered the clinic-based teaching that evolved into the standard method of medical training. Bedridden patients became the focus of research as well-known representatives of the First and the Second Vienna Schools of Medicine worked at this center of practice-based knowledge. The expansion of basic research drove the growth of specializations and led to the establishment of the world's first ophthalmic, dermatological, and ear, nose, and throat clinics.

Today, University Hospital Vienna is the teaching and research establishment of the Medical University of Vienna (MedUni Vienna), which also supplies the hospital's entire medical personnel. While it houses the facilities for providing patient care, it also meets the demands of teaching and medical-clinical research. The patients benefit directly from the innovations of MedUni Vienna. With around 8,000 students, it is currently the largest medical school in the German-speaking region. And although it is one of the youngest universities, it can also refer to a long history: Its origins as a medical faculty can be traced back to the founding of the University of Vienna in 1365 and MedUni Vienna has enjoyed autonomous university status since 2004. Already widely recognized as an authority in health matters during the Middle Ages, it is now regarded as a competence center for all medical disciplines. With 30 university clinics and two clinical institutes, 13 medical centers, and numerous highly-specialized laboratories, it is a European leader in the field of biomedicine. Its outstanding scientific achievements in this area also became clear to the general public during the coronavirus pandemic.

It is precisely this rich tradition and the importance and reputation of University Hospital Vienna and the Medical University of Vienna that motivated us to produce this publication, which seeks to portray the past and present of this "cluster" of medical excellence from a cultural-scientific perspective. The book focusses on the built substance of Vienna's central hospital and its university clinics from their origins to the present day. Previous studies of University Hospital Vienna and its clinics have predominantly been structured as biographies of medical personalities and most were also written by doctors.[1] In contrast, the places in which they carried out their work are hardly present. And yet the hospital and clinic buildings dominate a considerable part of Vienna's built fabric.

Our aim in producing this artistic and scientific publication is to illustrate the rich tradition of Vienna's central hospital and its university clinics with the help of timeless photographs. The book offers a visual parcours through these places of medical knowledge and activity. And, at the same time, the motifs on these pages provide an insight into little-known clinical, research, and teaching locations that are not accessible to the general public.

During the course of three years, Stefan Oláh documented all the buildings used by MedUni Vienna with his analog large-format camera. Striking general views alternate with close-ups of details that reveal the specific formal vocabulary of a building. One characteristic aspect of Oláh's approach, of his photographic ethic, is his perspective – which echoes University Hospital Vienna's motto of "the human scale": His photographs are always taken from a human standpoint and can be recognized for the way in which they capture the relationship between the body and the space around it. He rigorously renounces the use of

AKH „Die menschliche Größe" korrespondiert: Seine Aufnahmen entstehen immer von einem humanen Standpunkt aus, der eigene Körper in Bezug zum Raum ist das Maß seiner Bilder. Auf Hilfskonstruktionen wie spezielle Gerüste oder auf Luftaufnahmen wird konsequent verzichtet; den Bauten auf Augenhöhe mit wertschätzendem Blick zu begegnen ist seine Maxime. Im Unterschied zu anderen künstlerischen Bildbänden zum Thema Krankenhaus, in denen der Spitalsalltag, die Behandlung und Pflege im Fokus stehen,[2] sind die Aufnahmen von Stefan Oláh stets menschenleer. Als Fotograf konzentriert er sich auf die gebaute Substanz, die Architekturen, die Räume und Interieurs. Zudem ist das thematische Feld hier wesentlich weiter gefasst, neben der Krankenpflege rücken auch die Bereiche der Forschung und Lehre ins Bild. Auch die Größenordnung ist eine gänzlich andere: Mit über 80 einzelnen Gebäudeteilen, die sich vor allem im 9. Wiener Gemeindebezirk (Alsergrund) konzentrieren, sind das Universitätsklinikum AKH Wien und diverse andere Einrichtungen der Medizinischen Universität allein räumlich gesehen ein städtischer Marker. Architekturhistorisch betrachtet finden sich auf diesem Areal verschiedenste Krankenhaus- und Klinikbauten sowie Forschungs- und Lehrinstitute aus knapp 250 Jahren. Mitunter zeigen sich mehrere zeitliche Schichten in einem Motiv: Neu geschaffene Institute sind in historischen Gebäuden untergebracht, alte Hörsäle mit vergleichsweise moderner Technik ausgestattet.

In Summe bieten die Bildmotive eine neue Sicht auf Gewohntes, teils geben sie Einblick in kaum zugängliche oder gänzlich verborgene Bereiche. An diesen Orten, an denen fast rund um die Uhr Hochbetrieb herrscht, stand zum Fotografieren oft nur ein winziges Zeitfenster zur Verfügung; manchmal nutzte Stefan Oláh Pausen, um Innenräume menschenleer abzulichten. Zurechtgerückt wurde dort nichts, die Arbeits- und Studienplätze sind stets so wiedergegeben, wie sie verlassen worden sind. Präsenz wird bei ihm über Abwesenheit

suggeriert; persönliche Gegenstände, Kleidungsstücke oder Geräte fungieren als Platzhalter für die dort tätigen Menschen.[3] Mitunter wirken diese Arbeitsbereiche dadurch etwas unheimlich, etwa im Fall der Universitätszahnklinik, wo sogenannte Phantomköpfe zu Lehrzwecken aufgereiht sind. Die eigentlichen Akteure sind für Stefan Oláh die Architekturen und Räume – und dies korrespondiert mit dem kulturwissenschaftlichen Ansatz, den wir hier verfolgen. Es sind die Orte medizinischen Handelns und Wissens, die aus diesem Blickwinkel ins Zentrum rücken.

Das „Wissen" der Architektur

Den Fokus auf medizinische Handlungsorte zu richten, stellt historisch gesehen einen relativ neuen Zugang dar. Lange wurde Medizingeschichte anhand renommierter Ärzte und ihrer Leistungen geschrieben; die Genese der naturwissenschaftlich fundierten, modernen Medizin fand sich als Ergebnis der erfolgreichen Enträtselung des menschlichen Körpers und seiner Krankheiten dargelegt. Auch wenn sich seit den 1930er Jahren verschiedene Ansätze zu einer Sozialgeschichte der Medizin herausgebildet haben, hielt sich jene fortschrittsbezogene Geschichtsauffassung doch sehr hartnäckig. Erst ab den 1990ern erfuhr dieses Modell zunehmend Kritik durch Medizinhistoriker:innen. Unter einer kulturwissenschaftlichen Perspektive traten sie dem positivistischen Wissenschaftsverständnis der Medizin entgegen. Die naturwissenschaftliche Meistererzählung von einer kontextfreien Medizin, die mit immer besseren Verfahren „objektiv" die „Natur" von Krankheiten erforscht und sie heilt, wurde damit obsolet. Medizinisches Wissen und Handeln ist schließlich niemals außerhalb kultureller und sozialer Dimensionen zu betrachten, sondern als integraler Bestandteil von diesen.[4]

technical aids such as special frameworks and of aerial images; he believes in engaging respectfully with buildings at eyelevel. In contrast with other illustrated books about hospitals that focus on day-to-day hospital life, treatment, and patient care,[2] the photographs of Stefan Oláh never include people. As a photographer, he concentrates on built substance – on architecture, spaces, and interiors. Furthermore, this book addresses a much broader thematic field by shedding light on not just medical care but also the areas of research and teaching. And the scale is also completely different: With over 80 individual building elements, most of which are concentrated in Vienna's 9th District (Alsergrund), University Hospital Vienna and the various other institutions of the Medical University play a key urban role in spatial terms alone. In terms of architectural history, the complex consists of a wide range of hospital and clinic buildings and research and teaching facilities that were built over a period of almost 250 years. A number of historical layers can sometimes appear in the same motif: Newly created institutes are housed in historical buildings and venerable lecture theaters are equipped with contrastingly state-of-the-art technology.

Taken as a whole, these images offer a new perspective on the familiar, while some provide glimpses into scarcely accessible or completely hidden areas. The window of opportunity for taking photographs in such places, which are almost permanently busy, was often very small; Stefan Oláh sometimes used break times to capture deserted interiors. Nothing was adjusted in these spaces; the places of work or study are always reproduced exactly as they were left. Oláh uses absence to suggest presence; personal belongings, items of clothing, or pieces of equipment act as substitutes for the people who occupy a space.[3] This means that some of these workspaces can appear somewhat sinister, as exemplified by the University Clinic of Dentistry, with its rows of so-called phantom heads that are used for teaching

purposes. For Stefan Oláh, the true actors are the architecture and the spaces – and this corresponds with the cultural-scientific approach that we take in this book. This is a perspective that turns the spotlight on the places devoted to medical activity and knowledge.

The "knowledge" of architecture

From a historical standpoint, this focus on places of medical activity is a relatively new approach. The history of medicine has long been told in terms of renowned doctors and their achievements; modern, science-based medicine emerged as a result of the successful demystification of the human body and its illnesses. And even if many serious attempts have been made since the 1930s to address the history of medicine from a social standpoint, the progress-based approach to history has proved highly persistent. This model has only become subject to growing criticism from medical historians since the 1990s. These historians counter the positivistic understanding of medicine as a science by adopting a cultural studies perspective. As a result, the scientific master narrative of a context-free medicine that "objectively" researches into the "nature" of illnesses and heals them with the help of constantly improving methods is becoming obsolete. At the end of the day, medical knowledge and actions can never be considered independently of the cultural and social dimensions of which they are an integral part.[4]

In this sense, *science studies* and *social studies of scientific knowledge* have played a particularly important role in opening up this new understanding of medicine. Illnesses are now understood as historically contingent categories that, rather than just being preexisting biological realities or anthropological constants, are also shaped by a wide range of socio-cultural, political, economic, scientific, and

Vor allem die *science studies* und die *social studies of scientific knowledge* eröffneten in dieser Hinsicht ein neues Verständnis von Medizin. Krankheiten wurden nun als historisch kontingente Kategorien aufgefasst, das heißt nicht mehr als gegebene biologische Realitäten oder anthropologische Konstanten, sondern geprägt von je unterschiedlichen soziokulturellen, politischen, ökonomischen, wissenschaftlichen und technischen Faktoren. Impulsgebend dafür waren soziologische „Laborstudien", die die Produktion wissenschaftlicher Erkenntnisse im Labor zum Gegenstand hatten und vor Augen führten, dass Forschungsergebnisse nicht per se objektiv sind. Medizinisch-technische Objekte und ihre Bedeutung als Erkenntnismedium rückten damit in den Blick. Der Wissenschaftssoziologe Bruno Latour etwa betrachtete Gegenstände nicht als passive Dinge, sondern räumte ihnen eine Rolle als „Aktanten" ein, als soziale Akteure, die im wissenschaftlichen Betrieb Handlungen veranlassen oder erzwingen. Er plädierte dafür, menschliche und nichtmenschliche Akteure auf einer Ebene zu sehen, und schlug ein soziologisches Denken in „Akteur-Netzwerken" vor.[5] Auch Bauten übernehmen in Latours Sicht einen aktiven Part; unter dieser Perspektive lassen sich auch medizinische Handlungsorte neu betrachten.

Architektur spielt generell eine entscheidende Rolle in der sinnlichen Organisation und der Ausgestaltung sozialer Räume. Sie richtet Situationen ein, sie ordnet und steuert Abläufe. Zudem ist Architektur seit jeher ein Feld, das den Umgang mit verschiedensten Wissensformen bedingt.[6] Sie vereint technisches, soziales und künstlerisches Wissen – und im Fall von Krankenhaus- und Klinikbauten insbesondere medizinisches. Von diesem erweiterten Architekturbegriff im Sinne eines „Architekturwissens" gehen wir im Folgenden aus, wenn wir die Geschichte von Krankenhaus- und Klinikbauten am Beispiel des (einstigen) Allgemeinen Krankenhauses und der Medizinischen Universität in Wien betrachten. Denn Architektur wurde

ihrerseits von Krankheiten und dem jeweiligen Stand des Wissens geformt.

Noch weiter gefasst ließe sich auch die Geschichte der Städte unter dem Aspekt der Gesundheit betrachten – schließlich haben die Pandemien des 18. und 19. Jahrhunderts jene Infrastrukturen gebracht, die noch heute unsere Städte bestimmen: Trinkwassersysteme, Kanalisationen, Parks, befestigte Straßen, Schlachthäuser und Friedhöfe außerhalb der bewohnten Gebiete. Davon, wie schmutzig, staubig und stinkend Städte einst waren, mag man sich heute kaum eine Vorstellung machen: Aasgeruch von Fleischmärkten, Pferdemist, Fäkalien und Urin, offene Kloaken, Abwässer von Gewerbebetrieben, Müll, Straßenstaub oder Schlamm, Ruß und Rauch waren allgegenwärtig. In „medizinischen Topografien" wurde Anfang des 19. Jahrhunderts das gesundheitsgefährdende Potenzial einzelner Städte offengelegt; mit einer gezielten Politik der Assanierung suchte man die sanitären Bedingungen zu verbessern und Maßnahmen gegen Krankheitsrisiken zu setzen.[7] Auch das Stadtgebiet von Wien erfuhr im Laufe des 19. Jahrhunderts eine umfassende Neugestaltung unter hygienischen Aspekten: Seit 1826 sind die Straßen mit würfelförmigen Steinen aus Granit befestigt, bald war Wien in ganz Europa für diese Art der Pflasterung berühmt. 1831 begann man mit dem Bau erster Sammelkanäle, nachdem die Donau aus den Ufern getreten war, und auch offene Wasserläufe im Stadtgebiet wurden eingewölbt und als Hauptadern des neuen Kanalnetzes geführt. Diese planmäßige Kanalisierung Wiens und die Versorgung mit Trinkwasser durch den Bau der ersten und zweiten Hochquellenleitung (1873 bzw. 1910 eröffnet) stellen städtebauliche Pionierleistungen dar; Infektionskrankheiten, die durch Keime im Wasser übertragen werden, gingen dadurch entscheidend zurück. Neben solchen stadthygienischen Maßnahmen hatten auch speziell konzipierte Gebäude prophylaktische Funktion im Hinblick auf die mit Krankheit assoziierte „schlechte Luft" und unsichtbare

technical factors. This change of perspective was driven by sociological "laboratory studies," which involved the production of scientific findings in laboratory conditions and demonstrated that research findings are not objective per se. This turned the spotlight onto medical-technical objects and their importance as a medium of perception. For example, the sociologist Bruno Latour, who is particularly known for his work in the scientific field, did not regard objects as passive players but, rather, acknowledged their role as "actants," as social actors that initiate or force things to happen in a scientific context. He argued for considering human and non-human actors on the same level and suggested that we should think sociologically in terms of "actor networks."[5] In Latour's view, buildings also play an active part, and this perspective also offers us a new approach to addressing medical settings.

Architecture generally plays a decisive role in the sensual shaping and configuration of social spaces. It creates situations and organizes and manages processes. Furthermore, architecture has always been a field that requires us to deal with a wide range of forms of knowledge.[6] It unites technical, social, artistic, and – especially in the case of hospital and clinic buildings – medical knowledge. This broader understanding of architecture in the sense of "architectural knowledge" underlies the following investigation of the history of hospital and clinical buildings, which is based on the example of the (former) General Hospital and the Medical University of Vienna. Because their architecture was shaped by illnesses and by the level of knowledge at the time of their creation.

Thinking more widely, the history of cities can also be considered from the health perspective – after all, it was the pandemics of the 18th and 19th centuries that gave rise to the infrastructure that still defines our cities today: drinking water systems, drainage, parks, paved roads, and the moving of abattoirs and cemeteries outside heavily populated

areas. It is now almost impossible to imagine how dirty, dusty, and smelly cities must once have been: the odor of decomposition from meat markets, horse dung, feces and urine, open cesspits, waste water from workshops, the dust or mud of the street, soot, and smoke were ever-present. In the early 19th century, the potential of a city to damage the health of its citizens was revealed in "medical topographies"; targeted strategies for introducing sanitation sought to improve sanitary conditions and address health risks.[7] During the 19th century, Vienna also underwent a comprehensive restructuring that sought to improve public hygiene: From 1826 onwards, the streets were plastered with the small square granite cobblestones for which the city was soon renowned across Europe. In 1831, after the Danube had burst its banks, work began on the construction of the first main sewer and open watercourses in the city were vaulted over to become the principal arteries of its new drainage network. This systematic canalization of Vienna and the supply of drinking water to the city due to the construction of the first and second Spring Water Mains (which started operating in 1873 and 1910, respectively) are pioneering urban planning achievements that led to a decisive reduction in the levels of waterborne infectious diseases. Alongside such urban health measures, specially conceived buildings also acted prophylactically against invisible pathogens and the "bad air" that was associated with illness.[8] The idea of the garden city or the interwar housing program of Vienna City Council, with its focus on air, light, and sunshine, are powerful examples of this trend.

However, considering the urban ensemble as a whole, it is hospital and clinic buildings that most clearly illustrate the technical advances in medicine and medical research since the early 18th century. In such a process, architecture itself becomes a form of medical instrument and there is a close connection between different building types and the latest level of medical knowledge. Hospitals and clinics

Krankheitserreger.[8] Die Idee der Gartenstadt oder das Wohnbauprogramm der Gemeinde Wien während der Zwischenkriegszeit mit seinem Fokus auf Luft, Licht und Sonne stellen diesbezüglich markante Beispiele dar.

Innerhalb des urbanen Ensembles bilden jedoch Krankenhaus- und Klinikbauten am deutlichsten den technischen Fortschritt ab, den Medizin und Krankheitsforschung seit dem frühen 18. Jahrhundert durchlaufen haben. Architektur wird teilweise selbst zum medizinischen Instrument, zwischen den verschiedenen Bautypen und dem jeweiligen Wissensstand der Medizin besteht ein enger Konnex. Die Abhängigkeit von wissenschaftlicher Erkenntnis und neuen Technologien gilt für Krankenhäuser und Kliniken in besonderem Maß.[9] Wie der Wissenschaftshistoriker Peter Galison betont, sind gerade diese Bauten aktive Agenten in der Transformation der wissenschaftlichen Identität und ebenso Evidenz für diese Veränderungen.[10]

Auch wenn uns die Institution Krankenhaus heute selbstverständlich erscheint, stellt sie doch eine vergleichsweise junge Baugattung dar. Diese erst in den vergangenen 300 Jahren gewachsenen Strukturen und ihr Wandel sind gerade am Beispiel des Universitätsklinikums AKH Wien anschaulich nachzuvollziehen. Wie kaum ein anderes Spital in Europa verfügt es über eine sehr reiche Geschichte.

Vom Armenhospital zum Allgemeinkrankenhaus

Der Typus des Krankenhauses hat sich im ausgehenden 18. Jahrhundert aus den damals bestehenden karitativen Institutionen entwickelt, den sogenannten Hospitälern (von lat. *hospitalis* = gastlich bzw. *hospitium* = Herberge, Gastzimmer).[11] Bereits im Frühmittelalter gab es die ersten Wohlfahrtseinrichtungen dieser Art, die als wichtiger Teil der sozialen Organisation fungierten. Hungersnöte, Devastationen durch

Kriege und epidemische Krankheiten ließen eine geschwächte Bevölkerung zurück; Armen und Obdachlosen, aber auch Reisenden und Pilgern boten Hospitäler ein temporäres Asyl. Nicht von ungefähr waren diese Einrichtungen oft an Pilgerrouten gelegen. Im Zuge der Ausbreitung des Christentums bekamen diese „Gasthäuser" zunehmend karitativen Charakter, auch Kranke erhielten nun Fürsorge und Hilfe. Hospitäler wurden so zu einem wichtigen Teil der sozialen Organisation. Architektonisch gesehen waren diese multifunktionalen Einrichtungen als große Hallen angelegt. Nur sehr wenige Bauten dieser Art sind erhalten, das bekannteste und größte Hospital war wohl das im 7. Jahrhundert gegründete Hôtel-Dieu in Paris.

Doch schon damals stand nicht nur der Gedanke der Nächstenliebe dahinter. Hospitäler bildeten auch notwendige hygienische Einrichtungen zur Bekämpfung von Epidemien, denn in diesen abgesonderten und ärztlich überwachten Komplexen konnte man Kranke behandeln oder zumindest isolieren. Somit hatten sie auch bevölkerungspolitisch eine wichtige Funktion. Allerdings waren die alten Hospitäler keine medizinischen Einrichtungen im engeren Sinn; Entwicklungen in der Heilkunde übten daher auch keinen direkten Einfluss auf ihre Anlage aus. Vielmehr zogen damalige Infektionskrankheiten und Seuchen eigene Institutionen nach sich: Früh schon suchte man ansteckende Kranke in gesonderten Anstalten jenseits der Stadtmauern, sogenannten Leprosorien (von griech.-lat. *lépra* = Aussatz), unterzubringen. Im deutschsprachigen Raum wurden diese Einrichtungen später auch „Siechenhäuser" genannt, sie bilden die eigentlichen Vorläufer der modernen Spitäler. Mit der anhebenden Mobilität der Bevölkerung im europäischen Raum breitete sich zur Mitte des 14. Jahrhunderts auch eine dramatische Pestwelle aus, die eine Absonderung der Erkrankten notwendig machte. Seitdem wurden vorsorglich Pesthäuser für den Fall eines neuerlichen Ausbruchs der Seuche errichtet.

are particularly dependent upon scientific evidence and technological innovation.[9] As underlined by the historian of science Peter Galison, it is precisely such buildings that are both active agents in the transformation of scientific identity and concrete proof of this process of change.[10]

But even if we now take the hospital for granted as an institution, it is still a relatively new building type. The forms of and the transformations experienced by such structures as they have evolved over the past 300 years are demonstrated with particular clarity by University Hospital Vienna. There is hardly another hospital in Europe with such a rich history.

From paupers' hospice to general hospital

The first hospitals appeared towards the end of the 18th century as a development of earlier charitable institutions known as hospices (Lat.: *hospitalis* = hospitable and *hospitium* = hostel, guestroom).[11] The earliest such welfare facilities date back to the Early Middle Ages, when they played a key role in the structure of society. While famines, devastation caused by war, and epidemic diseases left behind a weakened population, hospices offered a temporary refuge to the poor and the homeless, but also to travelers and pilgrims. It is no coincidence that they were often located on pilgrimage routes. As Christianity spread, these "guesthouses" became increasingly charitable in nature as they also offered care to the sick and the destitute and, hence, became an important part of the social fabric. In architectural terms, these multifunctional facilities were built as large halls. There are very few remaining examples of such buildings, the best-known and largest of which was probably the Hôtel-Dieu in Paris, which was founded in the 7th century.

But even at that time, these institutions were not only sustained by the notion of loving one's neighbor. As separate and medically supervised complexes, in which the sick could be treated or, at least, isolated, hospices also acted as essential hygienic institutions in the fight against epidemics. Hence, they had a key demographic function. At the same time, however, hospices were not, strictly speaking, medical facilities at all, and developments in medical science had no direct impact upon their design. It was much more common to respond to infectious illnesses and epidemics by building dedicated facilities: Attempts were made from a very early stage to accommodate people suffering from contagious diseases in isolated institutions beyond the city wall – so-called leper houses (Gr./Lat.: *lépra* = leprosy). In the German-speaking region, such institutions were also later known as "Siechenhäuser" (plague houses) and it is these that are the true predecessors of the modern hospital. The increasing mobility of the population in Europe from the mid-14th century also triggered a dramatic plague epidemic, which necessitated the isolation of the sick. From this moment, plague houses were also built in advance in readiness for a repeated outbreak.

From the beginning of the Modern Era, the responsibility for hospitals gradually shifted from religious orders to civic authorities. These urban institutions were often described as "Bürgerspitäler" (public hospitals). But it was only in the 17th century that the idea of offering extra care to needy patients as part of a system of public welfare became more widespread. Plague houses were also often restructured as institutions that offered inpatient care. This was a period in which medical science advanced impressively, theoretical knowledge of anatomy and physiology expanded rapidly, and the discoveries of the circulation of the blood and the medical use of microscopes led to considerable improvements in diagnostic and therapeutic options. Research based on more precise scientific understanding made it easier to differentiate between and to classify

Mit dem Beginn der Neuzeit gingen die Hospitäler allmählich aus den Händen religiöser Ordensgemeinschaften in die Aufsicht der Kommunen über. Diese städtischen Einrichtungen wurden oft als „Bürgerspitäler" bezeichnet. Doch erst im 17. Jahrhundert kristallisierte sich das Bewusstsein heraus, bedürftigen Kranken im Rahmen des öffentlichen Armenwesens mehr Fürsorge angedeihen zu lassen. Auch Pesthäuser wurden häufig zu Institutionen stationärer Krankenpflege reorganisiert. Es war eine Phase, in der die Heilkunde einen beeindruckenden Aufschwung nahm, die theoretischen Kenntnisse der Anatomie und Physiologie erweiterten sich rasch, mit der Entdeckung des Blutkreislaufs und der medizinischen Mikroskopie verbesserten sich die Möglichkeiten der Diagnostik und Therapie beachtlich. Die auf exakten Naturwissenschaften beruhende Forschung erlaubte eine bessere Differenzierung und Klassifizierung von Krankheiten und damit erfolgreiche Methoden der Behandlung. Dass in dieser Phase der medizinische Unterricht am Krankenbett aufgekommen ist, war so gesehen nur folgerichtig: Im frühen 18. Jahrhundert wurde in der niederländischen Universitätsstadt Leiden die „Heilkunst für bettlägerige Kranke" eingeführt. Diese Reform der Ausbildung geht auf die Initiative des niederländischen Arztes und Hochschullehrers Herman Boerhaave zurück, unter ihm avancierte die Leidener Fakultät zum europäischen Zentrum des klinischen Unterrichts.[12] Die klinische Medizin (von griech. *klíne* = Lager, Bett bzw. *klinikós* = bettlägrig) stellt einen Grundzug des modernen Krankenhauswesens dar.

Die Etablierung des Klinikunterrichts
Die Idee, aus dem Hospital eine medizinische Institution werden zu lassen, findet sich im Laufe des 18. Jahrhundert nochmals bestärkt. Das Krankenhaus im eigentlichen Sinn ist als Folge der damaligen wissenschaftlichen Revolution zu sehen: In den Naturwissenschaften jener Zeit (Biologie, Physik und Chemie) wie auch in der Anatomie (als medizinischer Leitwissenschaft) und der Pathologie (Krankheitsforschung) stand die Beobachtung der Natur im Zentrum, und dies wirkte sich auch auf die Heilkunst aus. Hatte man zuvor anhand von Symptomen Krankheiten diagnostiziert, die schon Hippokrates und Galen beschrieben hatten, so stellte man nun vertiefende Beobachtungen an, um daraus eigene Schlüsse zu ziehen. Die vom Wiener Mediziner Leopold Auenbrugger ab 1761 systematisch angewandte Perkussion, das Abklopfen des Körpers der Kranken, ist ein anschauliches Beispiel jener damals entwickelten physikalischen Diagnostik, die auch heute noch als Basismethode der körperlichen Untersuchung gilt. Solche Techniken wie die Perkussion, die Palpation (Tastbefund) oder die Auskultation, das Abhören des Körpers mit dem Stethoskop (eingeführt 1819 vom französischen Arzt René Laennec), konnten im Grunde überall durchgeführt werden. Doch nur an einem Ort, dem Hospital, ließ sich mühelos eine signifikante Anzahl an Beobachtungen kumulieren. Die Symptome an lebenden Kranken (das klinische Erscheinungsbild) wurden dort in Bezug gesetzt zu Läsionen am obduzierten Leichnam (pathologische Anatomie). Diese Vorgehensweise erlaubte es, mehr über eine Krankheit und ihre Entwicklung zu lernen. Ebenjener systematische anatomisch-klinische Zugang konnte nur im (Bürger-)Spital geschehen.

Seit etwa 1700 zeichnete sich in ganz Europa der Wandel vom Hospital als Refugium für Bedürftige zum Krankenhaus für therapierbare Patient:innen ab. Auch die Bezeichnung „Krankenhaus" kommt in jener Phase auf. Diese Einrichtungen boten die Möglichkeit, Krankheitsverläufe über einen längeren Zeitraum hinweg zu studieren, das Krankenhaus begann sich damit auch als Stätte der klinischen Forschung zu entwickeln. Durch die stationäre Krankenpflege bot es sich zur Evaluierung bestimmter Therapien an und wurde zum Ausbildungsort künftiger Mediziner.

Die für die Medizin der Aufklärung zentralen Methoden der

---

illnesses and, hence, led to more successful methods of treatment. It is thus only logical that this period also saw the emergence of medical teaching at the patient's bedside: In the early 18th century, "Medical science for bedridden patients" was introduced in the Dutch university town of Leiden. This reform in training can be traced back to the Dutch doctor and university professor Herman Boerhaave, under whose leadership the faculty in Leiden became the European center of medical teaching.[12] Clinical medicine (Gr.: *klíne* = bed and *klinikós* = bedridden) is a central feature of the modern hospital.

The establishment of clinical teaching
The idea of enabling the hospice to become a medical institution intensified during the course of the 18th century. And the hospital in the true sense can be seen as a consequence of the scientific revolution of that time: The main focus of the natural sciences (biology, physics, and chemistry), anatomy (as the leading branch of medicine), and pathology (the study of illness) was the observation of nature and this also impacted upon medical science. Whereas doctors had previously diagnosed illnesses on the basis of symptoms that had already been described by Hippocrates and Galen, they now made their own in-depth observations in order to draw their own conclusions. Percussion, the tapping of the patient's body, which was systematically employed by the Viennese doctor Leopold Auenbrugger from 1761, is a vivid example of physical diagnosis, which was developed at the time and is still regarded today as one of the basic methods of physical examination. Techniques such as percussion, palpation (examination by touch), or auscultation (listening to the body with a stethoscope as introduced by the French doctor René Laennec in 1819) could essentially be applied anywhere. But there was only one place, the hospital, where a significant number of different observations could be effortlessly gathered together at the same time. Here, the symptoms displayed by living patients (the clinical presentation) could be compared with lesions on corpses that had been examined postmortem (pathological anatomy). This systematic anatomical-clinical method enabled doctors to learn more about a disease and its development. And it could only be applied in a (public) hospital.

In the years following 1700, hospitals across Europe evolved from refuges for the needy into places for treating the sick. This was also the period in which the term "hospital" became firmly established. This focus on healing meant that hospitals offered an opportunity to study the course of a disease over a longer period and, as a result, began to develop into centers of clinical research. The hospital had inpatients, which facilitated the evaluation of specific therapies, and hence became the place in which future doctors were trained.

However, the observational and statistical methods that were central to the medicine of the Enlightenment also shed light on the (then) often fateful consequences of a hospital visit. In wards filled with dozens of beds, cross-contamination was far from uncommon. The health risks associated with hospital visits were ascribed to the circulation of the air. This view of air as a vector that played a central role in the transmission of disease characterized medicine from the antiquity until the late 19th century, not only with regards to *Spitäler*.[13] So-called "miasmas," poor air and putrid vapors, were considered to be responsible for the transmission of illnesses. Scientists regarded the air as a mixture of chemical compounds that could penetrate living organisms via the skin, the breath, or the intake of food. But natural processes of decomposition, vapors rising from the ground, and standing water were also regarded as threats.[14] This suspected correlation between certain levels of temperature and humidity and the occurrence of respiratory diseases, between illness and foul smells, was given a fresh boost towards the end of the 18th century by the rediscovery of the writings of Hippocrates (*Des airs, des lieux et des eaux,*

Beobachtung und der Statistik brachten allerdings auch die (damals) verhängnisvollen Konsequenzen eines Krankenhausaufenthaltes ans Licht. Gegenseitige Ansteckung war in Krankensälen mit Dutzenden Betten keineswegs selten. Man führte die Gesundheitsschädlichkeit des Krankenhauses auf die Luftzirkulation zurück. Die Relevanz, die man der Luft als Vektor der Krankheitsübertragung beimaß, charakterisierte die Medizin von der Antike bis in das späte 19. Jahrhundert, und dies nicht allein im Bereich des Spitals.[13] Sogenannte „Miasmen", schlechte Luft und faulige Dünste, wurden damals für die Übertragung von Krankheiten verantwortlich gemacht. Naturwissenschaftler sahen die Luft als ein Gemisch aus chemischen Verbindungen, das über die Haut, die Atmung oder die Nahrungsaufnahme in lebende Organismen eindringen könne. Aber auch Fäulnisprozesse in der Natur, Ausdünstungen des Bodens oder stehender Gewässer galten als Bedrohung.[14] Diese vermeintliche Korrelation zwischen bestimmten Temperatur- und Luftfeuchtigkeitswerten und dem Auftreten von Atemwegserkrankungen, zwischen Unwohlsein und üblen Gerüchen hatte gegen Ende des 18. Jahrhunderts mit der Wiederentdeckung der Schriften von Hippokrates neuerlich Auftrieb erhalten (*Des airs, des lieux et des eaux*, Paris 1787). Im medizinischen Diskurs wie im sozialen Imaginären war die Miasmentheorie damals omnipräsent.[15] Krankheiten wie die Malaria (von ital. *mal'aria* = schlechte Luft) schienen den Zusammenhang zwischen aus Sümpfen aufsteigenden Miasmen und zeitweisem Fieber zu erhärten. Auch den Ausbruch von Cholera- und Typhusepidemien schrieb man in erster Linie den Dämpfen verseuchter Gewässer zu; Bakterien als Erreger kannte man damals noch nicht. Die Theorie „miasmatischer Infektion" und der Glaube an die Ansteckung durch unspezifische „Kontagien" hielten sich jedenfalls hartnäckig, wiewohl sie zunehmend umstritten waren. Erst die mikrobiologischen Entdeckungen von Louis Pasteur und Robert Koch im späten 19. Jahrhundert widerlegten diese Annahmen definitiv.

Das Augenmerk auf frische, gut zirkulierende Luft spielte daher eine große Rolle für die Architektur der Spitäler, und zwar sehr langfristig. Neben einer topografisch erhöhten Lage der Heilanstalt sollten vereinzelte Pavillons mit quergelüfteten Krankensälen die Übertragung von Infektionen und die Entstehung verbrauchter „Spitalsluft" verhindern. Wobei der Begriff des Pavillonbaus häufig als Synonym für eine offene Bauweise diente. Wesentlich waren jedenfalls voneinander unabhängige Spitalseinheiten und der Luftraum, den jeder Krankensaal enthielt.

Die Herausbildung des Krankenhauses
Der komplexe soziale Wandel vom Hospital zum Krankenhaus findet im Zeitalter des aufgeklärten Absolutismus statt. Die Zeitspanne zwischen 1730 und 1780 lässt sich allgemein als die erste Phase des Krankenhauswesens betrachten. Bürgerspitäler wurden entweder von Grund auf neu errichtet oder man adaptierte bestehende Hospitäler und Seuchenanstalten für die Pflege von Kranken. Eines der ersten staatlichen Krankenhäuser der frühen Aufklärungszeit, die Charité in Berlin, ist ein Beispiel eine solchen Revitalisierung: Der 1710 unter dem preußischen König Friedrich I. präventiv als Pestlazarett errichtete Bau wurde im Jahr 1727 dahingehend umstrukturiert, dass die dortigen Krankenabteilungen als Kliniken angelegt waren. Anstelle der hallenartigen Hospitalsäle hatte man kleinere Zimmereinheiten mit zehn bis zwölf Einzelbetten gebildet. Die dadurch mögliche stationäre Behandlung und die Unterweisung angehender Ärzte am Krankenbett wirkten sich äußerst positiv auf die Reform des Medizinalwesens aus.

Als eigentliche „Geburtsstunde" des europäischen Krankenhauses gilt allgemein jedoch jene Zäsur, die der Brand des Pariser Hôtel-Dieu Ende 1772 markiert: Das auf der Île de la Cité gelegene Hospital war das größte im Königreich Frankreich; seine disparate Architektur, die sich bis zu beiden Ufern der Seine ausdehnte, wurde ein Raub der Flammen,

Paris, 1787). The theory of miasmas was omnipresent at the time in both the medical debate and the collective imagination.[15] Diseases such as malaria (Ital.: *mal'aria* = bad air) appeared to confirm the link between miasmas coming from marshland and occasional fevers. Even outbreaks of cholera and typhus were principally ascribed to the vapors given off by contaminated bodies of water; the pathogenic role of bacteria was then still unknown. The theory of "miasmatic infection" and the belief in contamination by unspecified "contagions" persisted stubbornly, despite increasing skepticism. Only the microbiological discoveries made by Louis Pasteur and Robert Koch towards the end of the 19th century definitively refuted these assumptions.

The importance of fresh, well-circulating air thus played a major role in the architecture of hospitals, and continued to do so for many decades. Besides an elevated location, a sanatorium should consist of isolated pavilions with cross-ventilated wards that prevented the transmission of infections and the creation of stale "hospital air." Indeed, the term pavilion came to be widely used as a synonym for detached buildings. And the key parameters were the creation of separate hospital units and the volume of air enclosed in each ward.

The emergence of the hospital
The complex social transformation represented by the emergence of the modern hospital took place during the age of enlightened absolutism. The years between 1730 and 1780 can generally be regarded as the first phase of the hospital era. Either public hospitals were newly built from scratch, or existing hospices or plague houses were adapted so that they could care for the sick. One of the first public hospitals of the early Enlightenment, the Charité in Berlin, is an example of such a revitalization project: Originally built preventively as a plague house in 1710 under the Prussian King Frederick I, the building was restructured in 1727 with the aim of arranging the patient areas in the form of clinics.

The cavernous wards were replaced by smaller units with ten to twelve beds. This new structure, which facilitated the treatment of inpatients and the training of the aspiring doctors who gathered around these inpatients' beds, had an extremely positive impact on the reform of medicine.

However, it is the fire that broke out in the Hôtel-Dieu in Paris at the end of 1772 that is regarded as the turning point, the hour of birth of the European hospital: The complex on the Île de la Cité was the largest hospital in the Kingdom of France; its disparate range of buildings, which spilled over onto both banks of the River Seine, went up in flames, and several wings were completely destroyed. The huge fire triggered a fundamental debate that was decisive for the history of hospitals. The discussion about the possible reconstruction was seen, in Paris, as an opportunity to develop a radically new hospital concept; a commission of the Académie des Sciences was appointed in 1785 to develop proposals for hospital reform. Two of its members, the surgeon Jacques-René Tenon and the physicist Charles-Augustin Coulomb, travelled to England to study buildings in the country. Tenon published their findings in 1788 in his renowned paper *Mémoire sur les hôpitaux de Paris*. The doctors of the period also investigated the problems and possibilities of the hospital in detail and recorded their conclusions in a series of important publications on the subject. These works also included some newly defined architectural typologies. The turmoil of the French Revolution of 1789 ensured that many of these ambitious projects remained on paper. But even if the recommendations for a reform of Paris's hospitals failed to lead to concrete decisions, they were intensely discussed in the German-speaking region.

Hospitals as "machines for healing"
The basic theory behind these French projects of the 1780s involves the transformation of the hospital building from a neutral, functional

mehrere Gebäudeflügel wurden komplett zerstört. Dieser Großbrand löste eine Grundsatzdebatte aus, die für die Spitalsgeschichte entscheidend war. Im Zuge der Diskussion über einen möglichen Wiederaufbau arbeitete man in Paris an einem grundlegend neuen Spitalskonzept; eine im Jahr 1785 einberufene Kommission der Académie des sciences sollte Reformvorschläge für das Krankenhauswesen vorlegen. Zwei ihrer Mitglieder, der Chirurg Jacques-René Tenon und der Physiker Charles-Augustin Coulomb, unternahmen Studienreisen nach England, um dortige Bauten zu besichtigen. Die Schlussfolgerungen veröffentlichte Tenon 1788 in seiner bekannten Schrift *Mémoire sur les hôpitaux de Paris*. Auch die Ärzteschaft setzte sich damals eingehend mit den Problemen und Möglichkeiten des Krankenhauses auseinander, was eine Reihe bedeutsamer Publikationen zum Spitalswesen zur Folge hatte. Auch neue architektonische Typen sind darin bereits definiert. Viele der ambitionierten Projekte blieben angesichts der Wirren der Französischen Revolution 1789 jedoch Manuskripte. Wenngleich die Empfehlungen für eine Reform des Pariser Kranken-hauswesens damals keine konkreten Entscheidungen zeitigten, wurden sie im deutschsprachigen Raum intensiv diskutiert.

Krankenhäuser als „Heilmaschinen"
Was sich theoretisch fundiert in den französischen Spitalsentwürfen der 1780er Jahre vollzieht, ist der Wandel der Krankenhausarchitektur von einer neutralen, zweckmäßigen Hülle zu einer „Heilmaschine". Dieser auf Jacques-René Tenon zurückgehende Begriff einer *machine à guérir* steht vor allem für die Entwicklung der Krankensäle zu „Luftsystemen". Hygienische Imperative begannen nun stärker Beachtung zu finden, die öffentliche Gesundheit avancierte in jener Zeit zum großen politischen Sujet. In Sachen Spitalsarchitektur war eines der damaligen Grundprinzipien das Pavillonsystem mit voneinander unabhängigen Gebäudeeinheiten. Die spezielle Raumstruktur der

Pavillons sollte durch gründliche Belüftung die Entstehung von Krankheiten durch „Luftinfektionen" verhindern. Diese Bedeutung, die frischer Luft und dem Licht für das Wohlbefinden und die Heilung von Kranken seitdem zugesprochen wird, hat die Gestalt der Krankensäle und der Spitalsbauten insgesamt entscheidend geprägt.

Doch erst ab der Mitte des 19. Jahrhunderts wird in der Krankenhausplanung der Pavillontypus ernsthaft aufgegriffen. Als konsequente Umsetzung jener Empfehlungen, die die französische Kommission Ende der 1780er Jahre vorgelegt hatte, gilt das 1854 eröffnete Hôpital Lariboisière im Norden von Paris. Dieses in Reaktion auf die schwere Choleraepidemie des Jahres 1832 konzipierte Spital sollte international als Modell für ähnliche Anlagen dienen. Die auf einem weitläufigen Grundstück situierte Anlage ist symmetrisch konzipiert (mit Trakten für Männer und Frauen), die zweistöckigen Pavillons stehen beidseitig orthogonal als Flügel von der zentralen Struktur ab – was auf dem Grundriss wie ein doppelter Kamm aussieht. Durch verglaste Gänge sind diese Pavillons miteinander verbunden. Die Struktur dieses ersten modernen Pavillonspitals wurde typisch für das 19. Jahrhundert. In solchen ein- bis dreigeschoßigen Bauten waren Krankensäle mit bis zu 30 Betten untergebracht.

Zeitgleich zum Aufkommen des Pavillonkrankenhauses hatte auch Florence Nightingale ihre *Notes on Hospitals* (1859) verfasst – eine Schrift, die bald als essenziell für Architekten galt. Die britische Krankenschwester und Sozialreformerin war während ihres Einsatzes im Krimkrieg 1854/55 mit katastrophalen Zuständen in den Lazaretten konfrontiert. Dieser erste Stellungskrieg der Moderne forderte zahlreiche Opfer, die Verwundeten und Kranken lagen in ungeheizten, muffigen Stationen. Nightingale war daher vor allem mit der Organisation eines grundlegenden Krankenhausbetriebes befasst. Als maßgebliche Autorität in Sachen des Gesundheitswesens empfahl sie die Anlage von Spitälern im Pavillonstil, wie er im Hôpital Lariboisière

envelope into a "machine for healing." This notion of the *machine à guérir*, which can be traced back to Jacques-René Tenon, primarily stands for the development of wards into "airing systems." During this period, greater attention was paid to hygienic requirements and public health became a major political issue. One of the basic principles of the hospital architecture of the time was the pavilion system, with its independent building units. The special spatial structure and thorough ventilation of these pavilions should prevent the spread of illness by "airborne infection." The significance subsequently attributed to fresh air and light for the welfare and healing of patients went on to decisively influence the design of wards and of hospital buildings in general.

But it was only in the mid-19th century that hospital designs began to widely adopt the typology of the pavilion. The Hôpital Lariboisière in the north of Paris, which opened in 1854, is seen as a rigorous realization of the recommendations presented by the French commission at the end of the 1780s. The hospital, which was conceived in reaction to the serious cholera epidemic of 1832, was also intended to serve as an international model for similar facilities. Set in spacious grounds, the complex has a symmetrical layout (with blocks for male and female patients) and two-story pavilions that are placed as orthogonal wings on both sides of the central structure – resulting in a site plan that resembles two combs placed back-to-back. The pavilions are connected by glazed walkways. The structure of this first modern pavilion hospital was typical for the 19th century. Each of these single- to three-story buildings contained wards with up to 30 beds.

At the same time as the pavilion hospital was emerging, Florence Nightingale was writing her *Notes on Hospitals* (1859) – a book that soon came to be regarded as essential reading for architects. The British nurse and social reformer was confronted with catastrophic conditions in the field hospitals during her service in the Crimean War in 1854/55.

This first modern war of attrition claimed countless victims who, injured or struck down by disease, lay in unheated, unventilated nursing stations. As a result, Nightingale's primary concern was the basic organization of the hospital. An important authority in healthcare issues, she recommended the layout of hospitals in the pavilion style as realized at the Hôpital Lariboisière. Her ward plan envisaged large, open spaces that were illuminated by windows on both sides and occupied by 24 to 30 beds arranged in two rows. Many of the building standards established at the time were retained until the 20th century – and most of the hospitals that were built in Vienna around 1900 and still exist today were also realized in line with the pavilion system.

The discussions following the fire at the Hôtel-Dieu resulted in a veritable explosion in hospital building. This fact was analyzed from the scientific-historical perspective by Michel Foucault in the 1970s in the study *Les machines à guérir*.[16] And even if this overview largely fails to address these developments from the standpoint of architectural history, it comprehensively portrays the then "medicalization" of the hospital. At the very end of the 18th century, the hospital truly became a medical facility. The doctors and surgeons who were committed to this reform also insisted upon the integration of medical teaching into the hospital. Lessons at the patient's bedside should enable medicine to become more effective as a means of healing.

The clinic – as defined by Foucault – is an organized and monitored environment, a place of controlled knowledge.[17] Whereas illnesses had previously been defined independently from the patient's body, the individual now became the focus of the doctor's attention. In contrast to the hospital, where the poor, the wretched, and the sick were admitted, the clinic was a place of research, where patients were treated systematically. In other words, clinical practice is empirical. In clinics, postmortems are performed, the doctor sees deep into the body, and diseases can be localized. This new medical understanding, which

umgesetzt worden war. Ihr Abteilungsplan sah große, offene, beidseitig mit Fenstern belichtete Räume für 24 bis 30 Betten vor, die in zwei Reihen aufgestellt waren. Die baulichen Standards aus jener Zeit sollten sich zum Teil bis in das beginnende 20. Jahrhundert halten – auch die meisten noch bestehenden Krankenanstalten in Wien wurden um 1900 im Pavillonsystem errichtet.

Jedenfalls hatten die Diskussionen nach dem Brand des Hôtel-Dieu eine veritable Akkumulation von Krankenhausbauten zur Folge. Diese Tatsache analysierte Michel Foucault in den 1970er Jahren in der von ihm verantworteten Studie *Les machines à guérir* aus wissenschaftshistorischer Sicht.[16] Auch wenn die architekturgeschichtliche Seite in dieser Zusammenschau eher vernachlässigt wird, findet sich die damalige „Medikalisierung" des Spitals darin umfassend geschildert. Im ausgehenden 18. Jahrhundert avancierte das Krankenhaus zu einer medizinischen Einrichtung im engeren Sinn. Die Mediziner und Chirurgen, die sich für diese Reform engagierten, insistierten auch darauf, den Klinikunterricht in das Spital zu integrieren. Durch Lektionen am Krankenbett sollte die Medizin eine effizientere Heiltechnik werden.

Bei der Klinik handelt es sich – mit Foucault gesprochen – um ein organisiertes und überwachtes Milieu, um einen Bereich kontrollierten Wissens.[17] Wurden Krankheiten zuvor unabhängig vom Körper definiert, so rückt nun das Individuum in das Zentrum des ärztlichen Blicks. Im Unterschied zum Hospital, in dem Arme, Elende und Kranke Aufnahme fanden, wird in der Klinik geforscht, Kranke werden systematisch behandelt. Klinische Praxis ist dadurch empirisch. Die Obduktion wird in die Klinik eingeführt, der ärztliche Blick dringt in den Körper, Krankheiten lassen sich lokalisieren. Diese neue medizinische Wahrnehmung, die sich zum Ende des 18. Jahrhunderts etabliert, bildet den Kern der klinischen Erfahrung. Das Wissen über einzelne Krankheiten verändert sich grundlegend in dieser Phase, auch die ärztliche Ausbildungs- und Zulassungspraxis wird dadurch problematisiert.

Der josephinische Gebäudekomplex:
Allgemeines Krankenhaus, Garnisonsspital, Narrenturm und Josephinum

In der Zeit des aufgeklärten Absolutismus erlangten die Verwaltung des Gesundheitswesens und eine systematische medizinische Ausbildung wesentliche Bedeutung für den Staat.[18] Hatte die private Sphäre der Bürger:innen die Politik bis dahin nicht gekümmert, begann sich im 18. Jahrhundert der Staat für das Leben seiner Untergebenen zu interessieren. Dieses Faktum, dass menschliches Leben mit seinen biologischen Funktionen zum Politikum wird, fasste Michel Foucault mit dem Begriff der Biomacht (frz. *biopouvoir*).[19] Nun sah der Staat die Bevölkerung von biologischen Prozessen beherrscht. In neuen Disziplinen wie der Statistik, der Demografie oder der Epidemiologie wurden diesbezügliche Daten analysiert, die Geburten- und Sterberate der Population, die Alterskurve und der Gesundheitszustand gerieten in den Blick. Aus demografischer Sicht wurde das Leben als solches als Ressource betrachtet – schließlich hingen die Effizienz der nationalen Verteidigung und der industrielle Aufschwung davon ab. Politiker und Analysten suchten daher nach Mitteln, die Bevölkerung zu vergrößern und ihren Gesundheitszustand zu heben. Die damaligen sozialpolitischen Maßnahmen sind in diesem Kontext zu sehen. Gerade in Zeiten von Kriegen, Epidemien und Hungersnöten war eine wachsende und gesunde Population essenziell, Gesundheitspolitik war nicht zuletzt ökonomisches Kalkül. Die individuelle und die kollektive Gesundheit, die Disziplinierung einzelner Körper und die Regulierung der Gesamtbevölkerung lassen sich mit Foucault gesprochen als Biopolitik betrachten. Dem Wortsinn nach meint dies eine Politik, die sich mit dem Leben (griech. *bíos*) befasst.[20]

took root towards the end of the 18th century, forms the core of the clinical experience. This was a period in which levels of knowledge about individual diseases changed fundamentally – and this raised questions about the training and certification of doctors.

The Josephine building complex:
The General Hospital, Garrison Hospital, Narrenturm, and Josephinum

During the age of enlightened absolutism, the administration of the healthcare system and systematic medical training became important issues for the state.[18] Whereas politicians had previously failed to feel any responsibility for the private concerns of the public, 18th-century governments became increasingly interested in the lives of their citizens. This phenomenon, in which human life and all its biological functions becomes a political issue, is captured by Michel Foucault in the term biopower (Fr.: *biopouvoir*).[19] The state now saw the population as being subject to biological processes. New disciplines such as statistics, demography, and epidemiology analyzed the relevant data and focused attention on, for example, birth rates and death rates, the age curve, and the state of health of the population. From the demographic point of view, life as such was regarded as a resource – after all, it determined the efficiency of both the defense of the nation and industrial growth. Hence, politicians and analysts sought ways of increasing the population and improving its state of health. This is the context in which we should examine the socio-political measures of the day. In a time of wars, epidemics, and famines it was essential that the population should grow and remain healthy and health policy was, not least, based on economic calculation. Individual and collective good health, the disciplining of the body, and the regulation of the

population as a whole can be regarded, to borrow Foucault's definition, as biopolitics or, literally, politics that addresses life (Gr.: *bíos*).[20]

Vienna's Medical Faculty and its responsibility for the healthcare system

During the Habsburg monarchy, the era of Maria Theresa and Joseph II saw significant reform in the healthcare system. While Empress Maria Theresa had been striving since 1740 to systematically improve the welfare of the entire population, her son and successor Joseph II began his period of absolute government in 1780 by tackling the reorganization of the hospital system. Before the introduction of these major reforms towards the end of the 18th century, the Medical Faculty of the University of Vienna, which dated back to 1365, had held the principle responsibility for healthcare. In the Late Middle Ages, learned doctors had successfully defended their position against representatives of other healing professions.[21] In cities with universities (such as Bologna, Padua, Paris, or Vienna), graduate doctors who had received a theoretical education came together under the auspices of a medical faculty. This closed organizational form guaranteed a certain prestige and tactical political advantage. The sitting of examinations and awarding of titles not only safeguarded a specific standard of training, but also clearly distinguished those who had undergone this training from those on the outside. Only individuals who were successful in an examination held by the faculty could continue to practice. All other healers were thus disadvantaged from the start, with women and Jews in particular being treated like heretics.[22] The surgeons and apothecaries who were organized in guilds and had only enjoyed an artisanal training were regarded as competitors by the Medical Faculty, which successfully defended its position as the sole official representative of the medical profession. Non-academic healers such as barber-surgeons or midwives were at least permitted to undergo a

*Die Wiener medizinische Fakultät als Trägerin
des Gesundheitswesens*

In der Habsburgermonarchie fanden in der Ära Maria Theresias und Josephs II. maßgebliche Reformen des Gesundheitswesens statt. War Kaiserin Maria Theresia ab 1740 bereits um einen systematischen Ausbau der Wohlfahrt für die gesamte Bevölkerung bemüht, so nahm sich ihr Sohn und Nachfolger Joseph II. mit Beginn seiner Alleinherrschaft im Jahr 1780 der Reorganisation des Spitalswesens an. Bis zu diesen großen gesundheitspolitischen Reformen gegen Ende des 18. Jahrhunderts hatte vorwiegend die medizinische Fakultät der 1365 gegründeten Universität Wien als Trägerin des Gesundheitswesens fungiert. Im späten Mittelalter war es den gelehrten Medizinern gelungen, sich gegenüber Vertreter:innen anderer Heilberufe durchzusetzen.[21] In Städten, in denen eine Universität bestand (wie in Bologna, Padua, Paris oder Wien), wurden die theoretisch gebildeten, promovierten Ärzte durch eine medizinische Fakultät zusammengefasst. Diese geschlossene Organisationsform garantierte ein gewisses Prestige und politisch-taktische Überlegenheit. Durch die Abnahme von Prüfungen und die Verleihung von Titeln wurde ein bestimmter Ausbildungsstandard gesichert, aber auch eine Abgrenzung nach außen erzielt. Nur wer sich erfolgreich einer Prüfung durch die Fakultät unterzog, durfte weiter praktizieren. Dadurch erfuhren alle anderen Heiler:innen von vornherein eine Diskriminierung; insbesondere Frauen und jüdische Personen wurden wie Ketzer:innen behandelt.[22] Die lediglich handwerklich ausgebildeten Chirurgen und Apotheker, die ihrerseits in Zünften organisiert waren, sah man an der medizinischen Fakultät als Konkurrenz, doch konnte man sich ihnen gegenüber den Alleinvertretungsanspruch sichern. Nichtakademische Heilkundige wie Bader, Wundärzte und Hebammen durften an der Fakultät zumindest eine Lehrzeit absolvieren. Auch die Apotheken wurden von den *medici* der Universität kontrolliert. Die Fakultät übte somit die Funktion einer Lehr- und Standesorganisation aus. Ihre Ärzte wirkten als beratendes Sanitätsorgan der Regierung wie als Gerichtsgutachter, auch Maßnahmen zur Seuchenprävention arbeiteten sie aus.[23] Diese enorm breit gefasste Agenda zeitigte naturgemäß eher durchwachsene Resultate.

Die Neuordnung der medizinischen Fakultät
Einen ersten wesentlichen Lösungsversuch unternahm Maria Theresias Leibarzt Gerard van Swieten, den sie 1745 aus dem niederländischen Leiden als „Protomedicus" an den Wiener Hof berufen hatte: Er reformierte das Medizinstudium und fügte der theoretischen Lehre an der Universität die empirische Schulung hinzu.[24] Zu diesem Zweck ließ er an der Universität ein chemisches Laboratorium einrichten. Dieses Learning by Doing, wie man es heute nennen würde, war an der damaligen Medizinfakultät völlig neu. Van Swieten war es auch, der in Wien den klinischen Unterricht mit Demonstrationen am Krankenbett eingeführt hat. Die mit seinem einstigen Studienkollegen Anton de Haen im Bürgerspital installierte stationäre Klinik gilt als die erste im mitteleuropäischen Raum. Mit dieser zwölf Betten umfassenden Einrichtung avancierte Wien (nach dem Vorbild Leidens) zum Zentrum klinischer Ausbildung. „Weg vom Lehrbuch, hin zum Patienten" lautete de Haens Devise. Auch die pathologische Obduktion und die Chirurgie (als bisher verachtetes handwerkliches Fach) bildeten nun konstitutive Elemente des Klinikunterrichts.

Maria Theresia ernannte van Swieten 1749 zum Direktor und Präses der medizinischen Fakultät. In dieser Funktion baute er die mittelalterliche Korporation zu einer staatlich reglementierten Lehrinstitution um und unterteilte die Medizin in einzelne Disziplinen. Unter seiner Ägide blühte die Fakultät regelrecht auf und gewann beträchtlich an Attraktivität.[25] Van Swietens Neuordnung der medizinischen Fakultät und seine Umgestaltung des österreichischen Gesund-

period of training at the faculty. And even the apothecaries were subject to the control of the *medici* of the university. Thus, the faculty functioned as an educational and professional body. Its doctors advised the government in medical matters, acted as court experts, and also developed measures for preventing epidemics.[23] This extremely broad agenda naturally led to somewhat mixed results.

The reorganization of the Medical Faculty
A first significant attempt to improve this situation was made by Maria Theresa's personal physician, Gerard van Swieten, whom the Empress had summoned from Leiden in the Netherlands in 1745 to take up the position of "Protomedicus" at the Vienna court. Van Swieten reformed the study of medicine by adding empirical training to the university-based teaching of theory.[24] To this end, he commissioned the construction of a chemistry laboratory at the university. This "learning by doing" method, as we would call it today, was completely new for the Medical Faculty. Van Swieten also introduced bedside demonstrations to Vienna's clinical teaching curriculum. The inpatient clinic that he opened in the public hospital together with his former fellow student Anton de Haen is regarded as the first in Central Europe. With its twelve beds, the facility enabled Vienna to emulate Leiden as a center of clinical training. "Away from the textbook and towards the patients," was de Haen's slogan. The pathological postmortem and surgery (which had previously been despised as an artisanal activity) were now integral elements of clinical teaching.

In 1749, Maria Theresa appointed van Swieten as Director and President of the Medical Faculty. In this function, he developed the medieval fraternity into a publicly regulated teaching institution and subdivided medicine into a series of individual disciplines. The faculty flourished under his leadership and significantly expanded its appeal.[25] Van Swieten's reorganization of the Medical Faculty and reshaping of the Austrian healthcare system should be seen in the context of Maria Theresa's major administrative reform of 1748/49. The construction of the university's new main building, the Neue Aula in Vienna's 1st District (1753–55), was also initiated by this tireless scientific organizer. The monumental classical baroque building embodied the renewal of the university as an institution and the renunciation of the Jesuit dominance of higher education.

Van Swieten's aspiration to improve the welfare of the population appeared to anticipate the later reforms of Emperor Joseph II. His Sanitary and Quarantine Regulation of 1770 was the first attempt to standardize the healthcare system of the entire Monarchy, and he also initiated the concept of prophylactic medicine. The new statutory authority that was established under his leadership, the Imperial Sanitary Commission, also began to collect and evaluate data about the health of the population. In addition to this, van Swieten is also regarded as the founder of the First Vienna School of Medicine. The high educational standards that he had known in the Netherlands slowly established themselves in the metropolis on the Danube. It was to such preeminent foreign figures as Anton de Haen and Gerard van Swieten that Viennese medicine owed its ascendency.

A central hospital for Vienna
The General Hospital, which opened in 1784, was intended to provide the Vienna School with a new domain. Joseph II had taken the decisive step towards reforming the hospital system in the Habsburg monarchy shortly after ascending the throne in 1780 and his initiative went on to have an impact across Central Europe. While his desire to push through radical reforms had met with little success as long as he was Maria Theresa's "junior partner," he was now able to implement these decisively in just a few years. The Emperor turned, in particular, to the ideas of the Enlightenment thinker and political theorist Joseph von

heitswesens sind im Kontext der großen theresianischen Verwaltungs-reform von 1748/49 zu sehen. Auch die Errichtung des neuen Uni-versitätshauptgebäudes (1753–55), der Neuen Aula, im 1. Wiener Gemeindebezirk geht auf die Initiative dieses umtriebigen Wissen-schaftsorganisators zurück. Dieser barockklassizistische Monumental-bau stand für die Erneuerung der Institution Universität und die Abkehr von der Dominanz der Jesuiten über das höhere Bildungswesen.

In seinem Wunsch, die öffentliche Wohlfahrt zu heben, schien van Swieten die späteren Reformen Kaiser Josephs II. zu antizipieren. Seine im Jahr 1770 erlassene Sanitäts- und Kontumazordnung (Quaran-täneregelung) bildete die erste Vereinheitlichung des Gesundheits-wesens in der gesamten Monarchie, auch das Konzept einer prophylak-tischen Medizin geht auf ihn zurück. Die unter seiner Ägide neu geschaffene Behörde, die Sanitätshofkommission, begann nun auch, Gesundheitsdaten der Bevölkerung zu sammeln und auszuwerten. Darüber hinaus gilt van Swieten als Begründer der ersten Wiener Schule der Medizin. Das hohe Niveau der Ausbildung, das er aus den Niederlanden kannte, stellte sich nun langsam auch in der Donau-metropole ein. Ihren Aufstieg verdankte die Wiener Medizin so überragenden ausländischen Persönlichkeiten wie Anton de Haen und Gerard van Swieten.

Ein Zentralkrankenhaus für Wien
Mit dem 1784 eröffneten Allgemeinen Krankenhaus sollte die Wiener Schule eine neue Wirkungsstätte erhalten. Den entscheidenden Schritt zu einer Reform des Hospitalwesens in der Habsburgermonarchie hatte Joseph II. kurz nach seiner Thronbesteigung im Jahr 1780 getan, und seine Initiative sollte sich auf ganz Mitteleuropa auswirken. Hatte er als „Juniorpartner" Maria Theresias seinen Willen zu umwälzenden Reformen kaum durchsetzen können, so führte er diese nun konse-quent in wenigen Jahren durch. Vor allem die Gedanken des Aufklärers

und Staatstheoretikers Joseph von Sonnenfels, der eine gute Gesund-heitsversorgung als bürgerliches Recht ansah, griff Joseph II. auf: „Allgemeine Krankenhäuser" mit kostenloser medizinischer Betreuung sollten nicht nur Stätten der Heilung sein, sondern auch Orte zur Ausbildung künftiger Mediziner.[26]

Schon im ersten Jahr seiner Alleinregentschaft erließ Kaiser Joseph II. per Hofdekret die völlige Umgestaltung des Sanitätswesens. Ziel dieser 1781 verfügten „Direktiv-Regeln" war eine Zentralisierung aller damaligen Krankenanstalten Wiens.[27] Die Realisierung eines neuen Großkrankenhauses hatte für Joseph II. Priorität, bereits als Mitregent hatte er eine Reform des Spitalswesens angestrebt und war 1777 nach Paris gereist, um dort vorbildliche Einrichtungen in Augen-schein zu nehmen. Allen voran interessierte ihn das Zentralspital Hôtel-Dieu, das seit dem Brand im Jahr 1772 nur zum Teil wieder aufgebaut worden war. Nicht alle der gut 3.000 dort Untergebrachten waren krank; viele hatte man präventiv von der Straße geholt, damit sie aus Not keine Unruhe stiften. Paris war damals ein großer Moloch mit enormen Verkehrs- und Hygieneproblemen – diese Zustände sind vor dem Hintergrund des raschen Wachstums der Städte zu sehen, was auch Armut und katastrophale Sanitärverhältnisse mit sich brachte. Die im Hôtel-Dieu herrschenden Bedingungen wirkten auf Joseph II. und seinen mitreisenden Leibchirurgen Giovanni Alessandro Brambilla jedenfalls desaströs, bis zu 40 Elende waren in den Sälen, vier oder fünf notdürftig versorgte Personen teilten sich jeweils ein großes Bett. Die Sterberate im Haus lag damals bei 25 Prozent.[28]

Parallel zu seiner eigenen „Fact-Finding-Mission" hatte Joseph II. den Militärchirurgen Johann Hunczovsky auf Studienreise nach England, Italien und Frankreich geschickt. Den Bericht darüber legte der Arzt dem Kaiser vor und veröffentlichte ihn auch kurz danach.[29] 1783 gab Joseph II. seine Absicht bekannt, das bestehende Wiener Großarmenhaus (Invalidenhaus) in der Alservorstadt zum modernsten

Sonnenfels, who regarded healthcare as a civil right: "General hospitals" with free medical care should be places for not only healing the sick but also training future doctors.[26]

In his first year of absolute government, Emperor Joseph II issued a court decree that sought to completely restructure the healthcare system. The objective of these "Directive Rules," which were enacted in 1781, was to centralize all of Vienna's medical facilities.[27] The erection of a major new hospital was a priority for Joseph II, who had already sought to reform the hospital system when he was co-regent and had travelled to Paris in 1777 in order to visit model establishments in the city. He had been particularly fascinated by the central hospital, the Hôtel-Dieu, which had only been partly rebuilt following the fire of 1772. Not all of its more than 3,000 occupants were ill; many had been preventively removed from the streets for fear that their poverty would trigger unrest. At the time, Paris was a monster of a city with enormous traffic and hygiene problems – which had been caused by the same rapid urban growth that had also led to the widespread destitution and catastrophic sanitary situation. In any event, the appalling conditions in the Hôtel-Dieu had a profound effect on Joseph II and his travelling companion, his personal physician Giovanni Alessandro Brambilla. Every room was occupied by up to 40 wretched and minimally treated patients, four or five in each large bed. The death rate in the hospital was around 25 percent.[28]

In parallel with his own "fact-finding mission," Joseph II had sent the military surgeon Johann Hunczovsky on a study tour of England, Italy, and France. The doctor presented the report of his journey to the Emperor and published it shortly afterwards.[29] In 1783, Joseph II announced his intention to oversee the conversion of Vienna's existing large almshouse (the Invalidenhaus) in Alservorstadt into Europe's largest and most modern hospital. On August 16, 1784, he was able to open the hospital and oversee the admission of the first patient, shortly

after having presented a "message to the public" to this effect.[30] The conversion was preceded by a competition, in which plans for the central hospital were presented by a number of prominent doctors including Maximilian Stoll, the Director of the Medical Clinic, and Joseph von Quarin, the Emperor's personal physician. Quarin emerged as the winner of the competition and was designated as the director of the hospital in 1783. The competition process had also addressed a series of fundamental questions, including the pros and contras of a large hospital and the advantages of a new building over a conversion. In any event, Quarin was now responsible for the expansion of the huge complex, which was exclusively designated for the treatment of Vienna's civilian population. The architectural implementation was the responsibility of the builder Josef Gerl, who was familiar with major projects. With the exception of the ambitious central avant-corps on the Alser Straße facade, which is based on designs by Isidor Canevale, the transformation of the building substance was generally sober and solid. Above the main entrance, we can still see the dedication to Joseph II, which communicates both the purpose of the complex and the self-image of the monarch: "SALUTI ET SOLATIO AEGRORUM" (for the healing and the comfort of the sick).

The founding of the General Hospital in 1784 did not only mark the beginning of modern healthcare in the Habsburg monarchy; the opening of this large clinic for 2,000 patients also had an impact on hospital reform across Central Europe. The realization of the idea of a central hospital for Vienna in such a short time was a true feat of strength. If almost 90 percent of the built substance had not already existed, it would certainly not have been possible to create the huge complex. The Large Almshouse, which dated back to 1693 and had offered refuge to the sick, the homeless, and invalids from the Turkish Wars of the 1680s, had a traditional hospital form: three wings arranged around courtyards, in the first of which there was a smaller, free-

und größten Krankenhaus von Europa umbauen zu lassen. Schon am 16. August 1784 konnte er das Spital eröffnen und die ersten Kranken einweisen, kurz zuvor hatte er eine diesbezügliche „Nachricht an das Publikum" adressiert.[30] Dem Umbau war ein Wettbewerb namhafter Ärzte vorausgegangen, die Pläne für das Zentralkrankenhaus vorlegen sollten; unter ihnen auch der Vorstand der Medizinischen Klinik, Maximilian Stoll, und der Leibarzt des Kaisers, Joseph von Quarin. Letzterer ging als Sieger dieser Konkurrenz hervor und wurde 1783 designierter Spitalsdirektor. Im Zuge des Wettbewerbs hatte man auch grundsätzliche Fragen diskutiert, das Pro und Contra eines Großspitals, die Vorteile eines Neubaus gegenüber jenen einer Adaptierung. Quarin jedenfalls war fortan für die Erweiterung der enormen Anlage verantwortlich, die ausschließlich für die medizinische Versorgung der Wiener Zivilbevölkerung gedacht war. Die architektonische Umsetzung oblag dem mit Großprojekten vertrauten Baumeister Josef Gerl. Abgesehen vom ambitionierter gestalteten Mittelrisalit an der Fassade zur Alser Straße, der auf Entwürfe von Isidor Canevale zurückgeht, fiel die Überformung der Substanz schlicht und solide aus. Über dem Haupteingang ist auch die Widmungstafel Josephs II. angebracht, die den Zweck der Anlage und das Selbstverständnis des Monarchen kommuniziert: „SALUTI ET SOLATIO AEGRORUM" (Zum Heil und Trost der Kranken).

Die Gründung des Allgemeinen Krankenhauses im Jahr 1784 markiert nicht nur den Beginn des modernen Gesundheitswesens in der Habsburgermonarchie; die Eröffnung dieses Großklinikums für 2.000 Kranke wirkte sich auch auf die Reform des Spitalswesens in ganz Mitteleuropa aus. In derart kurzer Zeit die Idee eines Zentralspitals für Wien umzusetzen, kam einem veritablen Kraftakt gleich. Hätte die bauliche Substanz nicht bereits zu knapp 90 Prozent bestanden, wäre dieser gewaltige Komplex gewiss nicht realisierbar gewesen. Das 1693 erbaute Großarmenhaus, ein weitläufiges Geviert, das bereits drei

Trakte und ein kleineres freistehendes Gebäude im ersten Hof umfasste, war noch ein Hospital nach altem Muster: Invalide infolge der Türkenkriege der 1680er Jahre fanden dort ebenso ein Refugium wie Obdachlose und Kranke. Über Jahrzehnte hatte man das Armenhaus für diverse soziale Zwecke genutzt. Auf diesem Areal im Bereich des Alserbachs hatten bereits früh mehrere kleine Bauten bestanden, die der Krankenpflege dienten. 1657 wurde dort der städtische Kontumazhof errichtet, um von der Pest Genesene und deren pflegende Angehörige vorsichtshalber in Quarantäne (ital. *contumacia*) zu halten. Wenig später, 1686, widmete der kaiserliche Rat Johann Theobald Franck testamentarisch eine große Parzelle als Baugrund für ein Soldatenspital (dieses Grundstück entspricht etwa dem heutigen Hof 1 des Alten AKH). 1693 begann man mit dem Bau der vier Trakte um den Hof, und bald diente die Anlage als Hospital für dienstunfähige Soldaten, aber auch zur Unterbringung zahlreicher Armer. Um 1700 wurden dort bereits über 1.000 Personen versorgt, und gegen das Jahr 1715 war die Zahl auf 2.500 gestiegen, da kontinuierlich weitergebaut wurde. Die bedeutende Erweiterung ab 1726 verdankte sich neuerlich einer privaten Stiftung: Hofkammerrat Freiherr Ignaz von Thavonat hatte seinen gesamten Besitz dem Armen- bzw. Invalidenhaus hinterlassen. In der Legende des Kupferstichs von Salomon Kleiner wird diese zweifache Funktion der Anlage benannt, die Trakte im Hintergrund sind als „Tavornatische Stifftung" ausgewiesen. (A) Dieser von Franz Anton Pilgram, einem Schüler von Lucas von Hildebrandt, ausgeführte Baukomplex wirkt auf dem Stich allerdings wesentlich symmetrischer und aufwändiger gestaltet, als dies um 1730 tatsächlich der Fall gewesen sein kann. Auch die vier Fensterreihen übereinander an der Eingangsfront scheinen fraglich. Jedenfalls waren nach damaligen Angaben an die 3.500 Personen dort einquartiert. Doch auch diese Thavonat'schen Höfe reichten bald nicht mehr für die vielen Bedürftigen, weshalb ab 1752 wiederum nach Plänen von Franz Anton Pilgram

standing building. The almshouse had served various social purposes over the decades. The site close to the Alserbach stream had long been occupied by small buildings in which care was provided to the sick. The city's quarantine station was built there in 1657 so that both those who were recovering from the plague and the relatives who were looking after them could be kept in quarantine as a precautionary measure. A little later, in 1686, the Imperial Councilor Johann Theobald Franck bequeathed a large building plot (that roughly corresponds with the first courtyard of today's Altes AKH) for the construction of a military hospital. Work on the first phase – the four wings around the courtyard – began in 1693 and the complex was soon being used as a hospital for disabled soldiers, as well as for the accommodation of many of the city's poor. In 1700, the establishment was already caring for 1,000 people and continuous expansion work meant that this number had risen to 2,500 by around 1715. The major enlargement that began in 1726 was made possible by another private donation: The Court Chamberlain Freiherr Ignaz von Thavonat had left his entire estate to the Almshouse and Invalidenhaus. The label on the copperplate print by Salomon Kleiner describes these twin functions of the complex (Almshouse and Military Hospital) and identifies the blocks in the background as the "Tavornatische Stiftung" (Thavonat Foundation). (A) However, this print portrays the complex, which was realized by Franz Anton Pilgram, a pupil of Lucas von Hildebrandt, as being far more symmetrical and elaborately detailed than can have been the case around 1730. And the four rows of windows on the entrance facade, each aligned above the other, also appear questionable. In any event, contemporary records tell us that around 3,500 people were accommodated in the complex. But even the courtyards of the Thavonat Foundation soon became too small for the many needy, as a result of which three further courtyards designed by Franz Anton Pilgram (now courtyards 3, 5, and 6) were added to the grid from 1752.

With a capacity of around 6,000, the complex was now a city within the city. From the functional perspective, the architectural designs of the military hospital and the almshouse were virtually identical, and these enabled them to be swiftly repurposed. This flexibility proved extremely helpful some years later when these same wings were rapidly transformed into the Josephine central hospital.

The directives for the reorganization of the healthcare system that were issued by Joseph II in 1781 could be described as a demand for the disentanglement and functional separation of individual areas: Regardless of the form of previous welfare institutions, foundling hospitals and orphanages should be built for abandoned and destitute children, and "birthing houses" for needy expectant mothers; "mental patients" were to be accommodated in "madhouses," and, not least, treatable patients were to be cared for in their own hospital. In contrast, the chronically sick and (according to the language of the day) "the nauseating and those who awaken a sense of disgust" were to be accommodated in plague houses. In this catalog of measures, Joseph II determined that the building complex of the Large Almshouse should be the main hospital and, as such, exclusively reserved for "real patients." Its previous inhabitants were moved out and partly accommodated in secularized monasteries.

The new General Hospital was seen as a means of centralizing and rationalizing healthcare in Vienna and the surrounding region – the population of the imperial capital and royal seat had already reached 250,000. The conversion of the Large Almshouse was completed within just two years. From today's perspective, the approach that was taken to the restoration and partial expansion appears remarkably modern and the result is aptly summed up by the contemporary term *refurbished*. With its large courtyards and many wings, the building was more suitable than any other in Vienna for use as a large hospital. It offered the opportunity to concentrate a wide

Prospectus Domus pauperum et Hospitalis militum una cum a. Ædificiū Funda. Prospect des Armen Haußes und Soldaten Spitahl mit der a. Tavornatischen Stiff.
tionis Tavornatianæ in platea Alsensi. b. Xenodochium Hispanicum. c. Templum tung ut der Alser-Gaßen. b. Das Spanische Spitahl. c. Die Kirchen S. Mariæ von
Mariæ de Monte Serrato Ref. Ord. S. Benedicti. Perg Serrato reform. Benedictiner-Ordens.

Sal. Kleiner I. E. M. del.   Cum Priv. Sac. Cæs. Maj.   I. A. Corvinus sculp.

A   Salomon Kleiner, „Prospect des Armen Hausses und Soldaten
         Spitahl mit der a. Tavornatischen Stifftung [...]", 1733, Kupferstich
Salomon Kleiner, "View of the Almshouse and Military Hospital with
the Thavonat Foundation [...]," 1733, copperplate

197

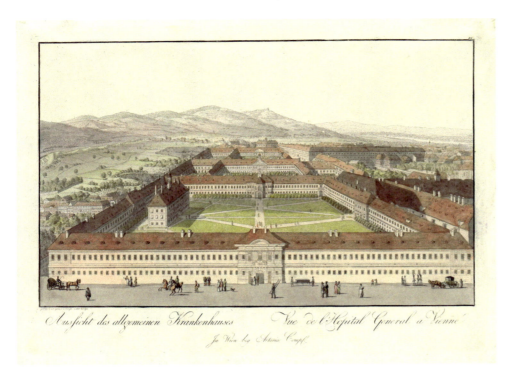

Aussicht des allgemeinen Krankenhauses   Vue de l'Hôpital Général à Vienne
Zu Wien bei Artaria Comp.

B   Joseph und Peter Schaffer, Allgemeines Krankenhaus, um 1795,
     Radierung, koloriert, aus: *Sammlung von ... Aussichten der
     Residenzstadt Wien von ihren Vorstädten und einigen umliegenden
     Oertern (Ansichten der Residenzstadt Wien)*, Wien 1798
Joseph and Peter Schaffer, General Hospital, around 1795, etching,
colored, from: *Collection of ... views of the royal seat of Vienna from its
suburbs and several surrounding locations*
(Views of the royal seat of Vienna), Vienna, 1798

Allgemeines Krankenhaus.

C   Tranquillo Mollo, Allgemeines Krankenhaus, 1822, Kupferstich,
     koloriert, aus: *Wien's vorzüglichste Gebäude und Monumente /
     Les principaux batiments et monuments de Vienne*, Wien 1823
Tranquillo Mollo, General Hospital, 1822, copperplate, colored, from:
*Vienna's principle buildings and monuments / Les principaux batiments
et monuments de Vienne*, Vienna, 1823

drei weitere Höfe (heute die Höfe Nr. 3, 5, 6) im Rastersystem angebaut wurden. Mit einer Aufnahmekapazität von ca. 6.000 Personen bildete dieser Komplex bereits damals eine Stadt in der Stadt. Die architektonische Gestaltung des Soldatenspitals und die des Armenhauses wiesen funktionell betrachtet kaum Unterschiede auf, weshalb sich Umwidmungen zügig vornehmen ließen. Ebendies kam später der schnellen Einrichtung des josephinischen Zentralspitals in diesen Trakten entgegen.

Die von Joseph II. 1781 erlassenen Direktiven zur Reorganisation des Gesundheitswesens könnte man als Entflechtung und funktionelle Trennung einzelner Bereiche bezeichnen: Unabhängig von den bisherigen Wohlfahrtsanstalten sollten Findel- und Waisenhäuser für ausgesetzte oder Not leidende Kinder errichtet werden, desgleichen „Gebärhäuser" für hilfsbedürftige Schwangere; „Geisteskranke" seien in „Tollhäusern" unterzubringen, und nicht zuletzt war die Pflege heilbarer Kranker in einem eigenen Spital vorgesehen. Chronisch Kranke sowie „Ekelhafte und Abscheuerweckende" (laut damaliger Diktion) sollten dagegen in Siechenhäusern Unterkunft finden. In diesem Maßnahmenkatalog legte Joseph II. fest, dass der Gebäudekomplex des Großarmenhauses als Hauptspital ausschließlich den „wirklich Kranken" vorbehalten sein sollte. Die bislang dort Versorgten wurden abgesiedelt und zum Teil in säkularisierten Klöstern untergebracht.

Mit der Inbetriebnahme des neuen Generalspitals sollte die Krankenpflege im Großraum Wien eine Zentralisierung und Rationalisierung erfahren – die Reichshaupt- und Residenzstadt zählte damals bereits 250.000 Einwohner:innen. Innerhalb von nur zwei Jahren hatte man den Umbau des großen Armenhauses durchgeführt. Die behutsame Sanierung und partielle Erweiterung stellt aus heutiger Sicht eine sehr zeitgemäße Herangehensweise dar, das Ergebnis ließe sich mit dem neudeutschen Attribut *refurbished* gut fassen. Dieser Komplex mit seinen großen Höfen und zahlreichen Flügeln bot sich jedenfalls wie

kein anderes Objekt in Wien als Großkrankenhaus an. Hier konnte man verschiedenste Abteilungen auf einem Areal konzentrieren, ohne auf eine strikte bauliche Trennung zu verzichten. Die Dimension der Anlage wird in der Vogelschau von Joseph und Peter Schaffer ersichtlich, schon damals hat dieses enorme Ensemble das Stadtbild bestimmt. (B) Als prominentes Motiv wurde diese kolorierte Radierung damals in Mappenwerken mit repräsentativen Ansichten von Wien vertrieben. Auch im gut 25 Jahre später aufgelegten Werk von Tranquillo Mollo figuriert das Allgemeine Krankenhaus unter den wichtigsten Bauten Wiens. (C)

Das Garnisonsspital
Während Joseph II. eine Reorganisation der Krankenpflege für die Zivilbevölkerung Wiens vornahm, stellte er von Anfang an auch Überlegungen zur besseren Versorgung des Militärs an. Damit einhergehend wollte er das System der chirurgischen Ausbildung reformieren. In diesem Bereich war der aus Pavia stammende Leibchirurg des Kaisers, Giovanni Alessandro Brambilla, dessen engster Berater. Zeitgleich mit dem Zentralspital entstand in unmittelbarer Nachbarschaft ein gänzlich neu errichteter Gebäudekomplex für das Militär. Für dieses 1787 eröffnete Garnisonsspital hatte man den Bereich des alten Kontumazhofs gewählt, der in den Phasen zwischen den Pestepidemien als Armenhaus genutzt worden war und nun abgetragen werden konnte. Mit ihren großzügigen Dimensionen greift die Anlage das Hof-Trakt-System des Allgemeinen Krankenhauses auf; zwecks besserer Belüftung hatte man die Räume äußerst hoch dimensioniert. Diese räumlichen Qualitäten kamen im Zuge der denkmalgerechten Wiederherstellung in jüngster Zeit wieder zur Geltung (2008–13), als das ehemalige Garnisonsspital als Zahnklinikum der MedUni Wien adaptiert wurde (seit 1927 war das Zahnärztliche Institut der medizinischen Fakultät hier untergebracht).

range of departments on one site, while still allowing these to be accommodated in separate structures. The scale of the enormous complex and the way it already dominated the cityscape become apparent in the bird's-eye view by Joseph and Peter Schaffer. (B) This colored engraving was frequently used at the time as a motif in portfolios of representative views of Vienna. And the General Hospital was still featured as one of Vienna's most important buildings in a work published by Tranquillo Mollo a good 25 years later. (C)

The Garrison Hospital
While Joseph II's reorganization of healthcare was undertaken in the name of the civilian population, he was also considering, from the very start, how better care could be provided to soldiers. In parallel with this, he also wanted to reform the system of surgical training. His closest advisor in this area was his Pavia-born personal physician, Giovanni Alessandro Brambilla. While the central hospital was being realized, a completely new complex was being built on an adjacent site for the use of the military. This Garrison Hospital, which was opened in 1787, was erected on the site of the former quarantine station, which had been used as an almshouse between the plague epidemics and could now be demolished. The generously dimensioned design adopted the wing-and-courtyard system of the General Hospital and the interiors were also very lofty in order to improve ventilation. These spatial qualities were rediscovered during the recent, historically accurate restoration (2008–13), which accompanied the remodeling of the former Garrison Hospital as the Clinic of Dentistry of MedUni Vienna (the Dental Institute of the Medical Faculty had been housed here since 1927).

The Narrenturm
The Court Architect Isidor Canevale became involved in the design of the hospital campus in 1783, but the only building that can definitely be ascribed to him is the Narrenturm ("Tower of Fools"), which Joseph II commissioned in 1784 as the first specialist psychiatric department in a hospital. Built by Canevale on a small plot between the civilian and military parts of the hospital complex that was far away from the main entrance, the Narrenturm is one of the most idiosyncratic buildings of early Classicism: The bulky, completely unadorned tower has the geometrical form of a cylinder. (D) This reduction to a clear form recalls the tendencies of so-called Revolutionary Classicism, with which the architect, who had come to Vienna from Paris, must have been familiar. The building was intended for the housing of the "insane" (as people suffering from mental and psychological illnesses were once known) and the patients included both soldiers and members of the civilian population. The building is a manifestation of the acceptance that such conditions are medical in nature – even if it resembles, from today's perspective, a prison. The circular, five-story structure is adorned with mighty rustication and the narrow windows, which resemble arrow slits, further emphasize the forbidding, fortress-like appearance of a building that consciously wants to be understood as *architecture parlante* or speaking architecture. The Narrenturm was constructed rapidly and started operating several months before the main hospital. For their own safety, the psychologically ill patients committed to the facility were confined in individual cells – from the medical perspective this represented a huge improvement on the previous shared rooms. However, the building only fulfilled its intended purpose for a few years before coming to be regarded as obsolete. While the "raving mad" of Enlightenment Vienna were still likened to dangerous animals that had to be imprisoned behind fortress-like walls and kept calm in dark cells, the increasingly therapy-oriented psychiatry that emerged after 1800 sought to improve the symptoms of some patients, or even heal them completely. With the introduction in the 1830s of the "no-restraint" system, an approach to psychiatric treatment that had emerged in

Der Narrenturm

Der als Hofarchitekt wirkende Isidor Canevale war ab dem Jahr 1783 auch in Planungen am Krankenhausareal involviert; gesichert ist seine Urheberschaft jedoch nur am Narrenturm, den Joseph II. 1784 als erste dezidiert psychiatrische Abteilung eines Krankenhauses errichten ließ. Auf einer kleinen Parzelle zwischen dem Zivil- und dem Militärbereich der Spitalsanlage, fern vom Haupteingang, entwarf Canevale einen der eigenwilligsten Bauten des Frühklassizismus: Der völlig schmucklose, wuchtige Turm hat die geometrische Form eines Zylinders. (D) Die Reduktion auf eine klare Form erinnert an Strömungen des sogenannten Revolutionsklassizismus, mit denen der aus Paris nach Wien gekommene Architekt wohl vertraut gewesen sein dürfte. Gedacht war dieser Bau für die Unterbringung der „Wahnwitzigen" (wie man Personen mit seelisch-geistiger Erkrankung einst nannte), und zwar sowohl aus dem zivilen wie aus dem militärischen Bereich. In diesem Bau manifestiert sich somit die Anerkennung eines medizinisch relevanten Leidens – auch wenn er aus heutiger Sicht einem Kerker ähnelt. Der fünfgeschoßige Rundbau ist von einer kräftigen Rustizierung umzogen; die an Schießscharten gemahnenden Fensterschlitze betonen das abweisende, festungsartige Erscheinungsbild noch zusätzlich, das sich bewusst als *architecture parlante*, als sprechende Architektur, verstanden wissen will. Nach kurzer Bauzeit konnte der Narrenturm bereits einige Monate vor dem Hauptspital in Betrieb genommen werden. Die hier eingewiesenen psychisch Kranken waren zu ihrem eigenen Schutz in Einzelzellen untergebracht – aus medizinischer Sicht ein wesentlicher Fortschritt gegenüber den bis dahin mehrfach belegten Sälen.

Bald nach seiner Errichtung war der Bau allerdings obsolet, den ihm zugedachten Zweck erfüllte er nur wenige Jahre. Sah man „Tobsüchtige" im Wien der Aufklärung noch wie gefährliche Tiere an, die hinter festungsartigen Mauern einzuschließen und in Dunkelzellen ruhigzustellen waren, so trachtete ab 1800 eine zunehmend

therapeutisch orientierte Psychiatrie danach, zumindest bei einem Teil der Kranken eine Besserung der Symptomatik oder gar eine Heilung zu erlangen. Als in den 1830er Jahren von England ausgehend das „No-Restraint"-System aufkam, ein von Zwangsmitteln absehendes psychiatrisches Behandlungskonzept, war die Anlage des Turms im Prinzip überholt.[31] Bereits 1822 hatte man als Ersatz für den Narrenturm eine den damaligen Erkenntnissen entsprechende Einrichtung für psychisch Kranke geplant, doch aus Geldmangel wurde erst 1848 mit dem Bau dieser „k.k. Irrenanstalt" auf dem sogenannten Brünnlfeld, einem Grünland in der Nähe des Allgemeinen Krankenhauses (heute: Michelbeuern), begonnen. Nach der 1853 erfolgten Fertigstellung der großzügigen Anlage konnte man die Patient:innen dorthin übersiedeln; bis 1869 wurde jedoch ein Teil der Kranken weiterhin im Narrenturm untergebracht. Mittlerweile ist der Rundbau denkmalgeschützt und generalsaniert, seit 2012 fungiert er als Außenstelle des Naturhistorischen Museums und beherbergt die ab dem Jahr 1796 angelegte pathologisch-anatomische Sammlung des Allgemeinen Krankenhauses der Stadt Wien.[32] In den 1970er Jahren kamen weitere Kollektionen aus dem deutschsprachigen Raum zu den Tausenden Wachs- und Feuchtpräparaten hinzu.

War der Narrenturm funktional gesehen eine relativ kurzlebige Institution, so hat die Anlage des Allgemeinen Krankenhauses ihre historische Wandlungsfähigkeit ohne wesentliche Umgestaltung mehrfach unter Beweis gestellt. Sie gilt als Musterbeispiel eines „Neubaus von innen", der unter Erhaltung der Fassade aus dem einstigen Großarmenhaus hervorgegangen ist. Als eines von wenigen Krankenhäusern vermochte es auch in späterer Zeit ohne wesentliche Veränderungen des Innenraums zu bestehen.[33] Über die gesamte Tiefe der Trakte wurden damals Krankensäle geschaffen, was eine Querlüftung durch die Fenster an den Längsseiten erlaubte. Bei der Adaptierung ging man auf die Forderung guter Durchlüftung ein, ohne

England and renounced the use of coercive methods, the layout of the tower had essentially become outdated.[31] The first plans for a replacement for the Narrenturm that corresponded with the latest ideas about the treatment of the mentally ill were drawn up in 1822, but a lack of funds meant that the construction of this "Imperial and Royal Mental Asylum" on the so-called Brünnlfeld (now Michelbeuern), a green space close to the General Hospital, only began in 1848. Patients could be transferred to the spacious new facility as soon as it was completed in 1853, but some remained in the Narrenturm until 1869. The listed and fully refurbished circular building became a satellite of the Natural History Museum in 2012 and is now home to the pathological anatomical collection of University Hospital Vienna, whose oldest items date back to 1796.[32] During the 1970s, the thousands of wax models and humidified specimens were joined by further collections from the German-speaking region.

While the Narrenturm had a relatively short life as a functioning facility, the design of the General Hospital has demonstrated its ability to adapt to a new use while undergoing minimal modification on a number of occasions. It is regarded as a model of a "new building on the inside," which was created within the Large Almshouse while the facade was retained. It is one of few hospitals that have been able to remain functioning over a very long period without significantly altering their interior spaces.[33] The original wards occupied the entire depth of the building, which permitted them to be cross-ventilated through the windows on the longitudinal facades. Hence, these spaces could be adapted to meet later ventilation requirements without having to rigorously implement the pavilion system.

This adaptation of the complex marked the functional transformation between the old and the new types of hospital, a process that continued later with the incorporation of laboratories, x-ray rooms, and other medical-technical facilities. The strongly articulated layout of the

original building permitted continuous adaptation and, in particular, created space for emerging medical specialties. This architectural complex of the old General Hospital (or Altes AKH, as it has been called since the construction of the Neues AKH – the new General Hospital or University Hospital Vienna) became the foundation upon which Vienna built its reputation as the "global metropolis of medicine" in the 19th century.

This Josephine foundation exemplifies the way in which the adaptability of a hospital is optimized by built forms that are as unspecific and functionally flexible as possible. As a general hospital with 2,000 beds, the Altes AKH was already a magnificent creation. But it became truly exceptional through the integration of the clinical school, which was installed in the so-called "Stöckl" or courtyard pavilion, the small free-standing building in the first courtyard. It was in this clinic with a dozen beds – for six women and six men – that Maximilian Stoll, Anton de Haen's successor as director of the clinic, instructed his pupils. This facility can be regarded as the forerunner of later university clinics. And for Joseph II, the "birthing house," with its low threshold requirements for admission, was also a significant institution: unmarried expectant mothers were able to enter the building anonymously and wearing a veil and an average of 100 births were registered every month. These measures, which were intended to prevent life-threatening abortions and infanticide, represent a striking example of authoritarian biopolitics. In return, the women were required to make themselves available to the doctors as "demonstration material."

The Josephinum

By establishing the "Josephine Academy" for the training of military physicians and, in particular, surgeons, Joseph II had established a further institution – alongside the General Hospital – that can be seen

D   Joseph Schaffer, Der Narrenturm, 1787, Radierung, teilweise
     koloriert, aus: *Vue de différens Bourgs Villages et Villes de Autriche
     sup. et inf., de Stirie, de Carintie*, Wien um 1810
Joseph Schaffer, The Narrenturm, 1787, etching, partly colored, from:
*Vue de différens Bourgs Villages et Villes de Autriche sup. et inf., de Stirie,
de Carintie*, Vienna, around 1810

E   Ferdinand Landerer, Academia Medico-Chirurgica Viennensis,
     1785, Kupferstich
Ferdinand Landerer, Academia Medico-Chirurgica Viennensis, 1785,
copperplate

201

F Carl Schütz, „Josephinische Medico Chirurgische Militair
    Academie und Gewehr Fabrik in der Waringer Gasse"
    (Josephinum), 1787, Kupferstich und Radierung, koloriert
Carl Schütz, "Josephinum," 1787, copperplate and etching, colored

G Johann Hieronymus Löschenkohl, „Einweihung der
    Josephinischen Militärakademie der Chirurgie, Wien, am
    7. November 1785", 1786, Kupferstich, koloriert
Johann Hieronymus Löschenkohl, "Inauguration of the Josephinum,
Vienna, November 7, 1785," 1786, copperplate, colored

das Pavillonsystem im strengen Sinne auszuführen.

Mit der Adaptierung dieses Komplexes fand der Funktionswandel vom alten Hospital zum neuen Typus des Krankenhauses statt, der sich später durch den Einbau von Laboratorien, Röntgenzimmern und anderen medizinisch-technischen Anlagen fortsetzen sollte. Eine von Anfang an stark gegliederte Aufteilung des Baus ermöglichte kontinuierliche Anpassungen und schuf insbesondere Raum für die sich herausbildenden Spezialfächer der Medizin. In diesem architektonischen Komplex des Alten AKH (wie man es seit der Errichtung des Neuen AKH nennt) konnte sich der Ruf der Stadt Wien als „Weltmetropole der Medizin" des 19. Jahrhunderts etablieren.

Die josephinische Gründung steht beispielhaft dafür, dass ein Krankenhaus umso wandlungsfähiger ist, je unspezifischer die Bauformen und je vielseitiger sie für unterschiedliche Funktionen nutzbar sind. Als ein Allgemeinkrankenhaus mit 2.000 Betten war das Spital bereits damals eine großartige Schöpfung. Außerordentlichen Charakter erhielt es jedoch durch die Einbeziehung der klinischen Lehrschule, die im freistehenden kleinen Gebäude des ersten Hofes, dem sogenannten „Stöckl", eingerichtet war. In dieser Klinik mit einem Dutzend Betten – jeweils sechs für Frauen und Männer – unterwies Maximilian Stoll seine Schüler; als Nachfolger Anton de Haens wirkte er in diesen Jahren als Klinikvorstand. Diese Einrichtung kann man als Vorläuferin der späteren Universitätskliniken sehen. Auch das „Gebärhaus" mit seinen niederschwelligen Aufnahmebedingungen war eine für Joseph II. signifikante Institution: Anonym und verschleiert konnten ledige Schwangere das Haus betreten, im Schnitt 100 Geburten monatlich wurden dort registriert. Diese Maßnahme, die lebensgefährlichen Abtreibungen und Kindstötungen vorbeugen sollte, stellt ein markantes Beispiel obrigkeitsstaatlicher Biopolitik dar. Als Gegenleistung mussten sich die Frauen den Medizinern als „Anschauungsmaterial" zur Verfügung stellen.

Das Josephinum

Mit der „Josephinischen Akademie" zur Ausbildung von Militärchirurgen und Wundärzten hatte Joseph II. parallel zum Allgemeinen Krankenhaus eine weitere Institution etabliert, die als Manifest seiner medizinischen Reformen schlechthin betrachtet werden kann.[34] Dieser 1785 fertiggestellte Bau zählt zu den bedeutendsten Beispielen des Klassizismus in Wien und gilt als Hauptwerk des Hofarchitekten Isidor Canevale. Wesentlich stärker als die zuvor genannten Gebäude ist die militärchirurgische Akademie von traditionellen Würdeformeln geprägt. Dies zeigt die Tendenz zur repräsentativen Gestaltung der für die Lehre vorgesehenen Bauten. Die nach französischem Vorbild konzipierte Anlage mit einem Ehrenhof (cour d'honneur) und räumlich gestaffelter Fassade ließe eher ein elegantes Stadtschloss vermuten denn eine wissenschaftliche Institution. (E) Ein direkter formaler Bezug besteht auch zu dem Platz vor der Hofbibliothek im Bereich der kaiserlichen Hofburg (heute: Josefsplatz), der kurz zuvor angelegt worden war. Bewusst hatten sich der Kaiser und sein Architekt dazu entschieden, die „Academia Medico-Chirurgica Viennensis" zum Glanzstück des großen neuen Medizin-Distrikts zu erheben. Die Gestaltung des Baus lässt sich als höchste Wertschätzung der akademischen Lehre verstehen. (F)

Es nimmt nicht wunder, dass der Bereich des Militärsanitätswesens im Fokus der josephinischen Gesundheitspolitik stand – war doch die Außenpolitik der Monarchie von Expansion und damit von Kriegen bestimmt. Ein schlagkräftiges Heer bedurfte gesunder Soldaten, eine gute medizinische Versorgung im Feld war essenziell. Da Joseph II. auch als Oberbefehlshaber des Heeres fungierte, fanden seine Direktiven sofort Gehör. Mit der 1784 gegründeten „k. k. medizinisch-chirurgischen Josephs-Academie" schuf er sich seine eigene, der Militärverwaltung unterstehende Institution – neben der medizinischen Fakultät die zweite fachliche Ausbildungsstätte in Wien. Beraten wurde

as a perfect manifestation of his medical reforms.[34] Completed in 1785, the building is one of Vienna's most important examples of Classicism and regarded as one of the principal works of the Court Architect Isidor Canevale. The academy of military surgery has a far stronger air of dignity and tradition than the buildings described above. This demonstrates the trend towards the elegant design of educational buildings. With its cour d'honneur and layered facade, both created in line with French models, the complex is more suggestive of an elegant city palace than a scientific institution. (E) There is also a direct formal relationship with the square in front of the Imperial Library in the Hofburg (now Josefsplatz), which had recently been laid out. The Emperor and his architect had consciously decided to establish the "Academia Medico-Chirurgica Viennensis" as the showpiece of the large new medical district. The design of the building can be seen as symbolizing the high esteem in which academic teaching was held. (F) Given that the foreign policy of the Monarchy was defined by expansion and, hence, war, it is no surprise that military medicine was the focus of Josephine healthcare policy. A strong army required healthy soldiers, and good medical care on the battlefield was essential. As Joseph II was also the supreme commander of the army, his directives were always listened to. By founding his "Imperial and Royal Medical Surgical Joseph's Academy" in 1784, he created his very own institution, which was under the control of the military authorities and, alongside the Medical Faculty, the second specialist training facility in Vienna. Joseph II was advised by Giovanni Alessandro Brambilla, who, as First Field Surgeon, had been responsible for all military medicine since 1783. During his visit to his sister Marie Antoinette in Versailles in 1777, the Emperor had inspected Paris's hospitals and military facilities. He had been particularly impressed by the Académie royale de chirurgie, which he used as a model when creating his military surgical academy a few years later. The instruction provided in this institution,

which was soon known as the "Josephinum," was very different to that offered in medical faculties: While universities first taught the scientific basics, before adding anatomy, physiology, pathology, pharmacology, and the clinical subjects, the Josephinum accompanied the teaching of theory with medical practice in the hospital. The reputation of this novel teaching concept spread rapidly and it was soon being "copied," sometimes with expert support from Vienna, with the result that a number of comparable institutions emerged across Europe. The granting of the title of doctor to the surgeons who completed their studies at the Josephinum was the basis of them being awarded the same status as doctors of medicine. The practice-oriented study of surgery and the theoretical study of medicine were finally unified in 1872, since when graduates have been awarded the professional title of "Dr. med. univ." (Lat.: doctor medicinae universae) or "doctor of all medical sciences."[35]

The buildings of the Josephine Academy were deliberately located close to the Garrison Hospital in order to safeguard the intended close relationship between theory and practice. In 1783/84, work was being carried out on all the buildings in the complex at the same time: on the General Hospital, the Narrenturm (which had been executed in line with a design from the Emperor himself), the military hospital, and the Josephinum. The opening ceremony for the latter was held on November 7, 1785, after just two years on site, and documented in a series of variously colored engravings by Johann Hieronymus Löschenkohl. (G) The central lecture theater, with its rising rows of seating, is impressively light and airy – a special atmosphere, which resulted from contemporary ideas about "healthy building" and can be enjoyed again today, following the latest restoration. Regarded as highly innovative when it opened, the training facility was also notable for its extensive collection of special teaching aids: Alongside the latest surgical instruments, these included the around 1,200 anatomical and

Joseph II. von Giovanni Alessandro Brambilla, dem als Oberfeld-chirurgen seit 1783 das gesamte Militärgesundheitswesen oblag. Im Zuge des Besuchs seiner Schwester Marie Antoinette in Versailles im Jahr 1777 hatte der Kaiser die Spitäler und Militäreinrichtungen von Paris inspiziert. Besonders angetan war er von der Académie royale de chirurgie, an deren Vorbild er seine wenige Jahre später gegründete militärchirurgische Akademie orientierte. Diese bald „Josephinum" genannte Institution unterschied sich in ihrer Lehre wesentlich von jener der medizinischen Fakultäten: Wurden an Universitäten erst naturwissenschaftliche Grundkenntnisse vermittelt, bevor Anatomie, Physiologie, Pathologie, Arzneimittelkunde und die klinischen Fächer hinzukamen, so erfolgte am Josephinum parallel zum Theorieunterricht die medizinische Praxis im Spital. Dieses neuartige Lehrkonzept wurde bald in ganz Europa berühmt und teils unter fachkundiger Beratung aus Wien „kopiert", mehrere vergleichbare Institute entstan-den. Die Promotion der Chirurgen mit Abschluss ihres Studiums am Josephinum war die Grundlage ihrer Gleichstellung mit den Doktoren der Medizin. Im Jahr 1872 schließlich erfolgte die Vereinigung des praxisnahen chirurgischen und des theoretischen medizinischen Studiums, seitdem wird in Österreich ein sogenanntes Berufsdoktorat als „Dr. med. univ." (lat. *doctor medicinae universae*), also als „Doktor der gesamten Heilkunde", verliehen.[35]

Das Gebäude der Josephinischen Akademie wurde bewusst in Nähe zum Garnisonsspital situiert, um den angestrebten Praxisbezug zu garantieren. In den Jahren 1783/84 ging die Arbeit an allen Bauten auf diesem Areal zugleich voran: am Allgemeinen Krankenhaus, am Narrenturm (der nach Entwürfen des Kaisers selbst entstanden war), am Militärspital und am Josephinum. Nach kaum zwei Jahren Bauzeit wurde Letzteres am 7. November 1785 eröffnet, diese Zeremonie ist in mehreren unterschiedlich kolorierten Stichen von Johann Hieronymus Löschenkohl dokumentiert. (G) Der zentrale Hörsaal mit seinen

ansteigenden Sitzreihen beeindruckt durch seine helle, luftige Wirkung – diese besondere, den damaligen Überlegungen zum „gesunden Bauen" geschuldete Atmosphäre ist nach der jüngsten Restaurierung heute wieder zu spüren. Die einst so innovative Ausbildungsstätte zeichnete sich nicht zuletzt durch eine umfassende Sammlung spezieller Lehrbehelfe aus: Neben modernsten chirur-gischen Instrumenten sind dies die rund 1.200 anatomischen und geburtshilflichen Wachs-modelle des menschlichen Körpers, die der Kaiser beim Direktor des naturgeschichtlichen Museums La Specola in Florenz geordert hatte. 1784 wurden bereits die ersten, zum Teil lebensgroßen Wachspräparate auf Maultieren über die Alpen bis Linz und dann am Schiffsweg nach Wien transportiert. Schon damals standen die Modelle nicht nur den Studenten am Josephinum als An-schauungsmaterial zur Verfügung, sondern – ganz im Sinne der Aufklärung – auch allen anderen Interessierten. Nach der in den Jahren 2019–22 erfolgten Generalsanierung des Baus wurde der einstige Zustand der Räumlichkeiten aus dem 18. Jahrhundert teilweise wiederhergestellt, nach wie vor sind dort die Wachspräparate in den originalen Rosenholz- und Palisandervitrinen mit venezianischem Glas zu sehen.

In diesem frühklassizistischen Bau wurde im Jahr 1920 auch das auf Betreiben des Medizinhistorikers Max Neuburger 1914 gegründete Institut für Geschichte der Medizin eingerichtet.[36] Heute sind zudem große Teile der historischen Sammlungen der MedUni Wien hier untergebracht. Dieser medizinhistorische Bestand, der so unterschied-liche Objekte wie Lehrmittel, Instrumente, Archivalien und Bildwerke umfasst, gilt als einer der größten der Welt; die berühmten anato-mischen Wachsmodelle machen ihn europaweit einzigartig. Mit den wertvollen Bänden der historischen Bibliothek repräsentieren die Sammlungen im Josephinum das reiche kulturelle Erbe der heutigen Medizinischen Universität.[37]

---

obstetric wax models of the human body that the Emperor had ordered from the Director of La Specola, the natural history museum in Florence. The first load of partly life-size wax specimens was transported over the Alps to Linz and then by ship to Vienna in 1784. Even back then the models were available as illustrative material not only to the students of the Josephinum but also – in keeping with the spirit of the Enlighten-ment – to anyone else who was interested. Due to the restoration of some of the rooms to their original 18th-century condition during the general refurbishment of the building between 2019 and 2022, these wax specimens can now once again be seen in the original rosewood and palisade display cabinets with Venetian glass doors.

In 1920, this early classicist building became home to the Institute for the History of Medicine, which had been founded in 1914 on the initiative of the medical historian Max Neuburger.[36] Today, it also accommodates large parts of the historical collections of MedUni Vienna. This medical-historical material, which contains such disparate objects as teaching aids, instruments, archive material, and paintings, is regarded as one of the largest in the world and is unique in Europe on account of the famous anatomical wax models. And the rich historical heritage of the Medical University of Vienna is also represented by the valuable volumes in the Josephinum's historic library.[37]

The reorganization of the General Hospital
By opening Vienna's new central hospital, Emperor Joseph II had established the benchmark for large hospitals in Central Europe. The institution was regarded internationally as a model, the approximately 100 wards, each accommodating an average of 20 patients, were spacious and, unlike in the Hôtel-Dieu in Paris, everyone here had their own bed. It is significant that the demolition of the old building of the Charité in Berlin and the construction of a spacious new complex began almost immediately, in 1785.[38] Nevertheless, the death of

Joseph II in 1790 was soon followed in Vienna by serious discussion of the idea of abandoning the General Hospital and setting up a number of smaller hospitals as a replacement. Emperor Leopold II, Joseph's successor to the throne, had little time for his brother's Enlightenment ambitions. Justifications included such problems as the lack of running water or the impractical design of the Narrenturm. However, the huge cost of such a restructuring put an end to these plans and the Josephine hospital complex remained. In 1795, Johann Peter Frank from the University of Pavia (in the then Habsburg Lombardy) was appointed as the new director of the General Hospital in Vienna, where he also succeeded Maximilian Stoll at the Medical Clinic. In this function, he carried out a fundamental modernization: He doubled the number of clinic beds, paid particular attention to cleanliness and the satisfactory ventilation of the wards, and also oversaw the construction of a separate morgue with a dissecting room. Frank is regarded as a public health pioneer and was responsible for the introduction of hygiene as a university subject. His six-volume handbook *System einer vollständigen medicinischen Polizey* (1779–1819) is considered to be a basic work of social medicine.[39] Frank's reorganization opened up new perspectives for medical research. During the following decades, the General Hospital and its clinics developed into the most important research center in the city and became the workplace of numerous doctors who established the global reputation of the Second Vienna School of Medicine in the 19th century: Carl von Rokitansky, Josef Škoda, Ferdinand von Hebra, Ignaz Philipp Semmelweis, Ludwig Türck, Franz Schuh, and Theodor Billroth, to name just a few.

The development of specialties and special clinics
While the needs of the medical fields of the 18th century would have been met by an internal clinic and a clinic for obstetrical surgery, the 19th century brought a growing trend towards specialization: In 1812,

Die Reorganisation des Allgemeinen Krankenhauses

Mit der Eröffnung des neuen Zentralspitals in Wien hatte Kaiser Joseph II. in Mitteleuropa den Maßstab für Großkrankenhäuser gesetzt. Die Einrichtung wurde international als ein Vorbild gesehen, die gut 100 Krankenzimmer für durchschnittlich 20 Patient:innen waren geräumig, und im Unterschied zum Pariser Hôtel-Dieu hatten hier alle ihr eigenes Bett. Bezeichnenderweise begann man in Berlin 1785 sofort damit, den alten Bau der Charité abzureißen und durch eine großzügige Gebäudeanlage zu ersetzen.[38] Nichtsdestotrotz hatte man in Wien kurz nach dem Tod Josephs II. im Jahr 1790 ernsthaft erwogen, das Allgemeine Krankenhaus aufzulassen und stattdessen mehrere kleine Spitäler einzurichten. Kaiser Leopold II., Josephs Bruder und Nachfolger auf dem Thron, konnte dessen aufklärerischen Ambitionen nur wenig abgewinnen. Diverse Mängel wie das Fehlen von fließendem Wasser oder die unzweckmäßige Bauart des Narrenturms wurden als Gründe ins Treffen geführt. Die großen Unkosten, die eine Umgruppierung mit sich gebracht hätte, verhinderten jedoch diese Pläne. Der josephinische Spitalskomplex blieb somit weiter bestehen. 1795 berief man Johann Peter Frank von der Universität Pavia (in der damals habsburgischen Lombardei) zum neuen Direktor des Allgemeinen Krankenhauses in Wien, wo er auch die Nachfolge Maximilian Stolls an der Medizinischen Klinik antrat. In dieser Funktion setzte er eine grundlegende Modernisierung ins Werk: Er verdoppelte die Anzahl der Klinikbetten und legte besonderen Wert auf Sauberkeit und gute Belüftung der Krankenzimmer; auch ein eigenes Leichenhaus mit einem Seziersaal ließ er einrichten. Frank gilt als Pionier des öffentlichen Gesundheitswesens, die Einführung der Hygiene als universitäres Fach geht auf ihn zurück. Sein sechsbändiges Handbuch *System einer vollständigen medicinischen Polizey* (1779–1819) wird als grundlegendes Werk der Sozialmedizin angesehen.[39] Mit seiner Reorganisation eröffnete Frank der medizinischen Forschung neue

Perspektiven. Das Allgemeine Krankenhaus mit seinen Kliniken entwickelte sich in den Folgejahrzehnten zum wichtigsten medizinischen Forschungszentrum der Stadt, hier wirkten zahlreiche Ärzte, die den Weltruf der zweiten Wiener Medizinischen Schule im 19. Jahrhundert begründeten: Carl von Rokitansky, Josef Škoda, Ferdinand von Hebra, Ignaz Philipp Semmelweis, Ludwig Türck, Franz Schuh oder Theodor Billroth, um nur einige zu nennen.

Die Herausbildung von Spezialfächern und -kliniken

Hatten im späten 18. Jahrhundert die medizinischen Fächer aus einer internen und einer geburtshilflich-chirurgischen Klinik bestanden, so setzte im 19. Jahrhundert bald eine Tendenz zu Spezialisierungen ein: Im Jahr 1812 wurde an der Wiener medizinischen Fakultät die erste ophthalmologische Klinik der Welt gegründet; diese Loslösung der Augenheilkunde von der Chirurgie bildete den Auftakt zu jener Ausdifferenzierung der Medizin in einzelne Fachdisziplinen, die um die Mitte des 19. Jahrhunderts gerade vom Allgemeinen Krankenhaus ausging und der Wiener Schule ihr charakteristisches Gepräge verlieh.[40] 1849 erfolgte die Gründung der Klinik für Haut- und Geschlechtskrankheiten sowie des Physiologischen Instituts, 1850 kamen die II. Medizinische Klinik und die Kinderklinik (St. Anna Kinderspital) hinzu, 1854 das Histologisch-Embryologische Institut. Die II. Augenklinik wurde 1858 eröffnet, im Jahr 1870 etablierte man die erste laryngologische Klinik der Welt. Auch die 1872 in diesem Komplex eingerichtete Ohrenklinik war weltweit die erste. 1870 wurde an der „Irrenanstalt" am Brünnlfeld (die den Narrenturm abgelöst hatte) die I. Psychiatrische Klinik implementiert. (H) 1781 rief man das Institut für Medizinische Chemie ins Leben und 1875 schließlich die II. Hals-Nasen-Ohren-Klinik. Die Zahnheilkunde hatte lange Zeit einen schlechten Ruf, zu groß war die Angst der Leute vor „Zahnbrechern", die ihr Handwerk auf Jahrmärkten ausgeübt hatten. Erst mit dem

---

Vienna's Medical Faculty became home to the world's first ophthalmic clinic and this dissociation of ophthalmology from general surgery was the prelude to a differentiation of medicine into individual specialties that emanated from the General Hospital in the middle of the 19th century and lent the Vienna School its distinctive character.[40] The Clinic for Skin and Venereal Diseases and the Physiological Institute were founded in 1849, the Second Medical Clinic and the Children's Clinic (St. Anna's Children's Hospital) in 1850, and the Histological-Embryological Institute in 1854. The Second Ophthalmic Clinic was opened in 1858 and 1870 saw the establishment of the world's first laryngological clinic. The Otolaryngologic Clinic that was opened in the complex in 1872 was also the first worldwide. In 1870, the First Psychiatric Clinic was opened at the "Lunatic Asylum" on the Brünnlfeld (which had replaced the Narrenturm). (H) The Institute for Medical Chemistry was established in 1871 and, finally, the Second Ear, Nose, and Throat Clinic in 1875. Dentistry had long enjoyed a poor reputation due to the widespread public fear of "tooth breakers," who had plied their trade at fairgrounds. Training facilities in this field were only established following the emergence of new methods that sought to preserve the patient's teeth. The Vienna Dental Ambulatory was opened in 1890 and renamed the Dental Institute in 1894.[41] The abovementioned double clinics, which are a particular Viennese phenomenon, were created due to the huge number of students coming to Vienna, which was regarded as the mecca of medicine. These various institutes and clinics naturally required suitable spaces.[42] In 1832–34, 50 years after its establishment, the General Hospital had already been extended in the form of a further, three-story wing that was realized under Emperor Francis I; this block, which encloses today's courtyards 8 and 9, had replaced the local cemetery.

The development of the clinic was accompanied by the emergence of pathological anatomy (the investigation of abnormal

changes to the body), which would go on to hugely accelerate the formation of theories. Thousands of postmortem examinations were carried out every year in the Department of Pathology of the Altes AKH and the results of these could be compared with the associated clinical symptoms. This was also the central facility for the carrying out of all judicial postmortems. It is thus no surprise that the first Institute for Forensic Medicine was created in the Vienna Medical Faculty in 1804.[43] On the initiative of Carl von Rokitansky, a separate Pathological Anatomical Institute was erected in front of one of the side facades of the General Hospital in 1859–62 as a replacement for the former Department of Pathology. (I) Contemporaries saw the building designed by Ludwig Zettl as a "Palace of Science."[44] The parapet of the symmetrical historicist structure is crowned with sculptures and the purpose of the building is referred to in the Latin dedication: "To the investigation of the location and cause of illnesses." Several generations of pathologists worked in the institute; the listed building is now home to the Center for Brain Research of MedUni Vienna.

The "Doctors' Quarter" as a city within the city

By the end of the 19th century, the General Hospital and its various extensions and the institutes of the Medical Faculty already formed an impressive ensemble of buildings that have dominated the urban district between Währinger Straße, Alser Straße, and Spitalgasse ever since. Not far from the Ringstraße, the elegant boulevard whose construction dates back to those same decades, this district became home to an extremely dense network of scientific institutions. Heinrich von Ferstel, the architect who had been entrusted with the design of the new building for the university on the Ring (1868–84), planned to create a true "university quarter" – an accumulation of research

H Psychiatrisch-Neurologische Klinik des Allgemeinen
Krankenhauses, Lazarettgasse 14, um 1930, Ansichtskarte
Psychiatric and Neurological Clinic of the General Hospital,
Lazarettgasse 14, around 1930, postcard

I Pathologisch-Anatomisches Institut, Alser Straße / Spitalgasse,
um 1865, Fotografie (anonym)
Pathological Anatomical Institute, Alser Straße / Spitalgasse,
around 1865, photograph (anonymous)

facilities that could be reached on foot and also included the (old) General Hospital and the Josephinum. The abovementioned emergence of new specialties and clinics in the second half of the 19th century had created a strong medical community of doctors, professors, and private tutors. Their dominance of the area soon led to it being renamed the "Doctors' Quarter."[45]

The reform of teaching after 1848
The new status achieved by research due to the creation of the appropriate facilities can be attributed to the reform of teaching that followed the quashing of the revolution of 1848.[46] Up to this point, students had been taught in ways that differed fundamentally from the approach taken by today's universities. The Theresian-Josephine reforms had placed the universities under the strict control of the state through the creation of the Imperial Commission on Education in 1760. The university teaching of the time was based on the primacy of utility; the Enlightenment state was interested less in scholars than in serviceable doctors. The fact that medical research was able to develop at all is largely down to the abovementioned protagonists of the First Vienna School. In other respects, however, the unimpeded development of the sciences was prevented by restrictions and censorship. Ultimately, the March Revolution triggered major improvements in the operation of the university: The demands of students for academic freedom were rapidly accepted and the Imperial Commission on Education was replaced by the newly created Ministry for Public Education.[47] But it would still take some time before the new university, whose organization was modeled on that of Germany's flourishing universities, would also find its rightful place in the built fabric of the city. Practical medical teaching had already transferred to the abovementioned clinics at the General Hospital and the theoretical courses largely took place in the Neue Aula (which was handed over to

the Academy of Sciences in 1857). In the second half of the 19th century, the development of scientific institutions was finally promoted with great enthusiasm. The laboratories and institutes that had been created in the wake of the neo-absolutist reforms were extremely beneficial for the development of innovative, research-led teaching. This was a period in which the prestige of science had never been greater.

Despite its impressive size, the representative new main building of the University of Vienna only offered space for the university administration and for theoretical teaching. This meant that the other university institutions that were relocating as part of the reshaping of the city had to be accommodated in separate buildings. Priority was given to the Chemistry Laboratory, which was located some distance away in the Theresian Academy. The functional expansion from inorganic to organic chemistry that continued throughout the 19th century opened up new opportunities for experimental research but also drove the need for more laboratory space. Given that chemistry teaching was largely aimed at medical students, there were loud demands for the erection of an up-to-date building in the Doctors' Quarter. Heinrich von Ferstel's neo-renaissance Chemistry Institute in Währinger Straße opened in 1872. The composition of the building is closely based on the prestigious Chemistry Institute in Gießen (1828): In addition to lecture theaters and research laboratories, the home of the head of the institute was also located in the complex so that he could maintain control of his domain. In contrast with the richly ornamented teaching block, the lower residential wing is set back and very simple. A strikingly designed brick building, the Chemistry Institute played an important role and, as the first new building of the University of Vienna to be completed after 1848, was regarded as the embodiment of progress in the debate about the creation of a new center for the Alma Mater Rudolphina.[48] The spatial proximity to the

Aufkommen neuer, erhaltender Methoden wurden entsprechende Ausbildungsstätten eingerichtet. Das Wiener Zahnambulatorium wurde 1890 eröffnet und 1894 in Zahnärztliches Universitätsinstitut umbenannt.[41] Die erwähnten Doppelkliniken stellen ein Wiener Spezifikum dar, ihre Einrichtung erfolgte aufgrund der großen Zahl an Studenten, die Stadt Wien galt damals als Mekka der Medizin. Die diversen Institute und Kliniken erforderten freilich adäquate Räume.[42] Bereits 50 Jahre nach seiner Gründung, 1832–34, war das Allgemeine Krankenhaus unter Kaiser Franz I. um weitere, jeweils drei Stockwerke hohe Neubauflügel erweitert worden; diese Gebäudetrakte um die heutigen Höfe 8 und 9 legte man anstelle des dortigen Friedhofs an.

Im Rahmen der Klinik war auch die pathologische Anatomie (Untersuchung krankhafter Veränderungen des Körpers) entstanden, die die Theoriebildung enorm beschleunigen sollte. In der Prosektur des Alten AKH wurden jährlich Tausende Sektionen durchgeführt, und diese Befunde ließen sich mit den klinischen Krankheitsbildern vergleichen. Auch alle gerichtlichen Obduktionen wurden hier zentral vorgenommen. Es überrascht daher nicht, dass das erste Institut für Gerichtsmedizin im Jahr 1804 an der Wiener medizinischen Fakultät entstanden war.[43] Auf Betreiben Carl von Rokitanskys wurde in den Jahren 1859–62 ein eigenes Pathologisch-Anatomisches Institut einer Seitenfront des Allgemeinen Krankenhauses vorgebaut, das die einstige Prosektur ersetzte. (I) Zeitgenossen erschien das von Ludwig Zettl konzipierte Gebäude als ein „Palast der Wissenschaft".[44] Die Attika des symmetrisch angelegten historistischen Baus ist mit Skulpturen bekrönt, auf den Zweck des Hauses verweist die lateinische Widmungsinschrift: „Der Erforschung des Sitzes und der Ursache der Krankheiten". An diesem Institut wirkten mehrere Generationen von Pathologen; heute ist in diesem denkmalgeschützten Bau das Institut für Hirnforschung der MedUni Wien untergebracht.

Das „Medizinerviertel" als Stadt in der Stadt

Mit diesen Erweiterungen des Allgemeinen Krankenhauses und den Institutsgebäuden der medizinischen Fakultät war bis zum Ende des 19. Jahrhunderts ein beeindruckendes Ensemble an Bauten entstanden, welches seither den Stadtteil zwischen Währinger Straße, Alser Straße und Spitalgasse prägt. Unweit der Ringstraße gelegen, des Prachtboulevards, dessen Bebauung aus jenen Jahrzehnten datiert, bildete sich in diesem Distrikt ein äußerst dichtes Netz an wissenschaftlichen Einrichtungen heraus. Heinrich von Ferstel, der als Architekt mit der Planung des neuen Gebäudes für die Universität am Ring (1868–84) betraut worden war, hatte die Anlage eines regelrechten „Universitätsviertels" im Sinn – eine Kumulation verschiedenster Forschungsstätten in fußläufiger Distanz, die auch das (Alte) Allgemeine Krankenhaus und das Josephinum einbeziehen sollte. Durch die erwähnte Herausbildung neuer Spezialfächer und Kliniken in der zweiten Hälfte des 19. Jahrhunderts hatte sich eine starke medizinische Community aus Ärzten, Professoren und Privatdozenten gebildet. Ihre Dominanz in diesem Quartier führte bald zu dessen Umbenennung in „Medizinerviertel".[45]

Die Reform des Unterrichtswesens nach 1848
Dass der Forschung durch entsprechende Stätten ein eigener Stellenwert zukam, ist der Reform des Unterrichtswesens nach der Niederschlagung der Revolution von 1848 zu verdanken.[46] Davor unterschied sich der Studienbetrieb grundlegend von jenem der heutigen Universitäten. Die theresianisch-josephinischen Reformen hatten die Hochschulen unter strenge staatliche Aufsicht gestellt, 1760 wurde hierfür die Studienhofkommission eingerichtet. Die universitäre Lehre war damals vom Primat der Nützlichkeit getragen; dem aufgeklärten Staat war nicht an Gelehrten gelegen, sondern an brauchbaren Ärzten. Dass

other teaching and research buildings was not only welcomed by the students. This well-situated institute was also very conducive to interdisciplinary exchange: It was a meeting point for pharmaceutical, medical, and chemical expertise that demonstrated the relevance of chemistry for many fields. Today, the building with the elegant glazed terracotta facade is occupied by the Center for Pathobiochemistry and Genetics of the Medical University.

In 1886, an imposing new building at the nearby junction between Schwarzspanierstraße and Währinger Straße became the home of the Anatomical Institute. During the preceding decades, the former weapons factory that occupied the site had accommodated a number of the Medical Faculty's theoretical institutes. One of those who had worked here was the renowned anatomy professor Joseph Hyrtl. The new building of the "Anatomie" was not only a point of reference for generations of doctors in the areas of histology, physiology, and pharmacology; the institute led by the social democratic politician and health specialist Julius Tandler was also the main setting of the anti-Semitic riots that took place at the University of Vienna between the wars.[49] Largely destroyed by bombs in 1945, the building was re-erected during the postwar period and only the retained central section of the former historicist structure reminds us of the original substance. It now houses the Center for Anatomy and Cell Biology of MedUni Vienna.

Heinrich von Ferstel's labors ensured that the triangular section of Vienna-Alsergrund that spreads outwards from the main building of the University of Vienna developed into a veritable "science district." The close proximity of a variety of medical institutes not only meant that distances were short, but also encouraged close and productive networking. For example, Vienna's doctors were some of the first to recognize the potential of x-rays. Having been discovered in 1895, these were soon being used in the x-ray department of the General Hospital,

which was established in 1898. In 1910, the Imperial Academy of Sciences opened the Radium Institute, the world's first facility devoted to the investigation of radioactivity, in what is now Boltzmanngasse. This concentration of a range of specialties in the Doctors' Quarter contributed to the recognition of Vienna, around 1900, as one of the world's leading scientific metropolises, especially in the areas of medicine and physics.[50] Taken as a whole, the numerous institutes, laboratories, and clinics in Vienna's 9th District exemplify what cultural historians call *entangled spaces of knowledge*.[51] This recognition of the enormous cultural significance of such physical places is a consequence of the *spatial turn* in the cultural sciences that took place towards the end of the 1980s. This paradigm change turned the spotlight onto the spatial and (socio-)geographical dimension.[52]

In any event, there is a close correlation between the history of science in the late 19th and early 20th centuries and the remodeling of Vienna that was taking place at the same time. The impressive concentration of clinics, institutes, and research laboratories clearly stimulated scientific activity. In this sense, the medical district exemplifies the dialectic relationship between science and cities: they create and depend upon each other.[53] The metropolis of Vienna benefitted from this interaction just as much as the above-listed disciplines.

The "New Clinics" of the General Hospital

As the 19th century drew to a close, the steady increase in the number of clinics meant that the lack of space in the existing General Hospital was becoming critical. Of the 2,000 beds in the Altes AKH before the fin de siècle, half were already being used for clinical purposes and the number of students was also constantly rising. Discussions about erecting a new building that could remedy the "oppressive confinement

sich die medizinische Forschung trotzdem entwickeln konnte, ist den erwähnten Protagonisten der ersten Wiener Schule zu verdanken. Ansonsten waren der freien Entfaltung der Wissenschaften durch Gängelung und Zensur jedoch Schranken gesetzt. Die Märzrevolution brachte schließlich große Errungenschaften für den Universitätsbetrieb: Der studentischen Forderung nach Lehr- und Lernfreiheit wurde sofort stattgegeben, und das neu geschaffene Ministerium für öffentlichen Unterricht löste die Studienhofkommission ab.[47] Doch es sollte eine Weile dauern, bis die neue, am Vorbild der prosperierenden Hochschulen Deutschlands ausgerichtete Universität auch baulich im Stadtbild den ihr gebührenden Platz erhielt. Der praktische medizinische Lehrbetrieb war damals ohnehin bereits in den erwähnten Kliniken am Allgemeinen Krankenhaus angesiedelt, die theoretischen Kurse fanden vornehmlich in der Neuen Aula statt (1857 wurde diese an die Akademie der Wissenschaften übergeben). In der zweiten Hälfte des 19. Jahrhunderts schließlich trieb man den Ausbau wissenschaftlicher Institutionen mit großem Elan voran. Die im Zuge der neoabsolutistischen Reform geschaffenen Laboratorien und Institute waren der Entwicklung innovativer, forschungsgeleiteter Lehre äußerst förderlich, das Prestige der Wissenschaft war in dieser Zeit hoch wie nie.

Da das neue repräsentative Hauptgebäude der Universität Wien bei aller Größe bloß Raum für die Administration und die theoretische Lehre bot, waren andere universitäre Einrichtungen wie Laboratorien im Zuge der urbanen Neugestaltung in separaten Häusern unterzubringen. Priorität hatte hierbei das chemische Labor, das damals weit entfernt in der Theresianischen Akademie untergebracht war. Die sich im 19. Jahrhundert vollziehende fachliche Ausweitung von der anorganischen zur organischen Chemie eröffnete neue Möglichkeiten experimenteller Forschung, brachte aber auch einen erhöhten Bedarf an Laborräumlichkeiten mit sich. Da der Chemieunterricht vor allem auf Medizinstudenten ausgerichtet war, wurde die Forderung nach

einem zeitgemäßen Gebäude im Medizinerviertel laut. Bereits 1872 wurde der von Heinrich von Ferstel entworfene Neorenaissance-Bau des Chemischen Instituts in der Währinger Straße eröffnet. In seiner Struktur ist das Haus eng an das renommierte Gießener Chemie-Institut (1828) angelehnt: Neben Hörsälen und Forschungslaboratorien war hier auch die Wohnung des Institutsleiters untergebracht, um diesem die Kontrolle über seinen Bereich zu gewähren. Im Gegensatz zum reich ornamentierten Lehrtrakt ist der niedrige Wohnbau schlicht gehalten und zurückversetzt. In seiner markanten Gestaltung als Ziegelbau nahm das Chemische Institut eine herausragende Rolle ein, als erster Neubau der Universität Wien nach 1848 galt es als Inbild von Fortschritt in der Debatte um ein neues architektonisches Zentrum der Alma Mater Rudolphina.[48] Die räumliche Nähe zu anderen Lehr- und Forschungsgebäuden kam nicht nur den Studenten zupass. Auch dem interdisziplinären Austausch war dieses gut gelegene Institut sehr dienlich: Pharmazeutische, medizinische und chemische Expertise kamen hier zusammen, die Querschnittsmaterie Chemie hatte für viele Bereiche Relevanz. Mittlerweile beherbergt der mit glasierten Terrakotten verzierte Bau das Zentrum für Pathobiochemie und Genetik der Medizinischen Universität.

Unweit davon wurde 1886 an der Ecke Schwarzspanierstraße und Währinger Straße ein imposanter Neubau errichtet, in den das Anatomische Institut einzog. Schon in den Jahrzehnten zuvor waren an dieser Stelle (der damaligen alten Gewehrfabrik) einige theoretische Institute der medizinischen Fakultät untergebracht gewesen, der renommierte Anatomieprofessor Joseph Hyrtl hatte dort gewirkt. Das neue Gebäude der „Anatomie" bildete nicht nur einen wichtigen Identifikationsort für Generationen von Mediziner:innen in den Bereichen Histologie, Physiologie und Pharmakologie; in der Zwischenkriegszeit war das vom sozialdemokratischen Gesundheitspolitiker Julius Tandler geleitete Institut auch Hauptschauplatz der antisemitischen Ausschreitungen an

of these inadequate spaces,"[54] had been going on since the 1870s. By the end of the century, these discussions had become a debate about erecting a veritable "hospital city" with 40 separate pavilions.

As one of the largest planned complexes of the period, these so-called "New Clinics" were a prototype for the architecture of healthcare buildings at the beginning of the 20th century.[55] Characteristically for the period, they embody the transition from smaller volumes to a denser concept featuring buildings that may still have been referred to as "pavilions" but were more substantial in scale. The New Clinics of the General Hospital that were built between 1904 and 1923 are only a fragment of the original huge project but they still represent one of the highpoints of the development of hospital building in Vienna. Their design initially embodied the latest standards in both medicine and construction. However, the planning process dragged on for years, during which not only ideas about hospital building but also the formal language of architecture underwent fundamental change. Almost 30 years passed between the initial concept and the launch of the first phase.

The enormous growth in the population of Vienna during the 19th century and epidemic infectious diseases such as cholera and tuberculosis led to chronic overcrowding in the city's hospitals. At the same time, there was a rapidly growing need for special facilities such as operating rooms, laboratories, clinical lecture theaters, and spaces for diagnosis, therapy, and outpatient visits. From the 1880s onwards, this led to a surge in the construction of hospital buildings in Vienna. The years immediately before the First World War were particularly notable for the realization of a number of important large-scale facilities.

During the discussion about a suitable location for the New Clinics, attention turned to the western edge of the city. Affordable sites in green surroundings seemed ideal for the construction of large

complexes – as exemplified by the psychiatric sanatorium and care home Am Steinhof (1905–07), which was designed by Otto Wagner and whose 60 pavilions were laid out like a functionally arranged city. The fear of contagion and the need to isolate the sick also meant that institutions had been erected outside the city boundary for centuries, from the plague houses of the Middle Ages to later infection hospitals. But there was still a very strong argument for locating the New Clinics close to the existing "welfare cluster" in Alsergrund. During the course of the 19th century, the General Hospital and its university clinics had become a globally recognized center of medical research and teaching. Pressure from the clinic professors finally ensured that the New Clinics were also built on this site and that this concentration of healthcare facilities continued.

After a planning phase lasting over two decades, the first elements of the new complex were constructed between 1904 and 1908. The university's two Gynecological Clinics, which were built during this phase, date back to the general plan by Franz Berger, who was regarded as a specialist for sanatorium design. The new buildings for the First and Second Gynecological Clinics were constructed on Spitalgasse, while Berger laid out the rest of the buildings on the Brünnlfeld, which he accessed from Lazarettgasse. The divergent characteristics of these two sites meant that they were laid out very differently: While the Gynecological Clinics were symmetrically arranged on both sides of the central element of the former almshouse, which consisted of the administration building and the church, Berger was able to plan the ensemble on the Brünnlfeld with much more freedom, due to the fact that the psychiatric hospital occupying the site was already earmarked for demolition (although this eventually only happened in 1974). Friedrich Schauta and Rudolf Chrobak, the gynecologists who accompanied the construction of the Gynecological Clinics from the medical perspective, weighed up the relative advantages of a horizontal

der Universität Wien.[49] 1945 durch Bomben weitgehend zerstört, wurde das Gebäude in der Nachkriegszeit neu errichtet; lediglich der erhalten gebliebene Mittelteil des ehemals historischen Baus erinnert noch an die originale Substanz. Heute hat dort das Zentrum für Anatomie und Zellbiologie der MedUni Wien seinen Sitz.

Das sich vom Hauptgebäude der Universität Wien aufspannende Dreieck in Wien-Alsergrund avancierte jedenfalls durch den Einsatz Heinrich von Ferstels zu einem veritablen „Wissenschaftsgrätzel". Diverse medizinische Institute in unmittelbarer Umgebung bedeuteten nicht nur kurze Wege; sie förderten auch eine enge und produktive Vernetzung. So waren die Mediziner in Wien etwa unter den ersten, die das Potenzial der 1895 entdeckten Röntgenstrahlen erkannten und für sich nutzbar machten; 1898 wurde die Röntgenzentrale des Allgemeinen Krankenhauses etabliert. 1910 eröffnete die kaiserliche Akademie der Wissenschaften in der heutigen Boltzmanngasse das Radium-Institut als weltweit erste Einrichtung zur Erforschung der Radioaktivität. Diese Konzentration unterschiedlicher Fachrichtungen im Medizinerviertel trug mit dazu bei, dass Wien um 1900 zu den weltweit führenden Wissenschaftsmetropolen zählte, insbesondere in den Bereichen Medizin und Physik.[50] Die zahlreichen Institute, Laboratorien und Kliniken im 9. Wiener Gemeindebezirk bildeten in ihrer Gesamtheit das, was man kulturhistorisch gesprochen *entangled spaces of knowledge*[51] nennt, miteinander verwobene Räume des Wissens. Ebenjene physischen Stätten als kulturelle Größe zu sehen, ist eine Folge des *spatial turn* in den Kulturwissenschaften gegen Ende der 1980er Jahre. Mit diesem Paradigmenwechsel rückte die räumliche und (sozio-)geografische Dimension in den Blick.[52]

Die Wissenschaftsgeschichte des späten 19. und frühen 20. Jahrhunderts ist jedenfalls eng mit der urbanen Umgestaltung Wiens in jener Phase verknüpft. Die beeindruckende Ballung von Kliniken, Instituten und Forschungslaboren stimulierte ganz offensichtlich die

wissenschaftliche Aktivität. Der medizinische Distrikt steht somit beispielhaft für das dialektische Verhältnis von Wissenschaft und Stadt: Beide bringen einander hervor, und zugleich bedingen sie einander.[53] Die Metropole Wien profitierte ebenso von dieser Interaktion wie die genannten Disziplinen.

Die „Neuen Kliniken" des Allgemeinen Krankenhauses

Die Raumnot im bestehenden Allgemeinen Krankenhaus hatte sich im ausgehenden 19. Jahrhundert allerdings zugespitzt, forderten die sich mehrenden Kliniken doch zunehmend Platz. Von den 2.000 Spitalsbetten des Alten AKH waren vor der Jahrhundertwende bereits die Hälfte klinischen Zwecken gewidmet, und auch die Zahl der Studenten war beständig gestiegen. Um dieser „drückenden Enge unzureichender Räumlichkeiten"[54] Abhilfe zu schaffen, stellte man ab den 1870er Jahren Überlegungen zu einem Neubau an. Von einer regelrechten „Spitalstadt" aus 40 einzelnen Pavillons war zur Jahrhundertwende die Rede.

Als eine der größten geplanten Anlagen der Zeit stehen diese sogenannten „Neuen Kliniken" prototypisch für die Architektur von Gesundheitsbauten zu Beginn des 20. Jahrhunderts.[55] Für jene Phase charakteristisch ist der Übergang von kleineren Baukörpern zu einem stärker verdichteten Konzept mit Gebäuden, die zwar weiterhin als „Pavillons" bezeichnet wurden, jedoch beträchtliche Ausmaße hatten. Dieses Großprojekt der 1904–23 errichteten Neuen Kliniken des AKH blieb zwar ein Fragment, nichtsdestotrotz zählt es zu den Höhepunkten der Entwicklung des Spitalsbaus in Wien. Die Anlage verkörperte anfangs den damals modernsten Standard in Bautechnik und Medizin. Allerdings zog sich die Planung über Jahrzehnte, währenddessen änderten sich die Konzepte des Krankenhausbaus und die Formen-

organization of the pavilions and a vertical, much denser block system. Given that the pavilion approach required a larger site and would have led to much higher operating costs, it was decided to design the two main buildings as a block; only an isolation pavilion was realized separately.

During the planning of the second construction phase (1909–11), which was earmarked for the erection of the clinics on the Brünnlfeld, the distinguished architect Emil von Förster intervened in order to implement his own ideas. Förster was Head of the Building Department of the Interior Ministry and a Member of the Ministerial Commission and Building Committee for the New Clinics. These roles offered him opportunities to intervene, which he continued to seize upon until shortly before his death in early 1909. By 1908, he had not only drawn up a new general plan but also designed the facades of the clinic buildings of this phase. While not impacting upon the functional organization, Förster's changes to the plans led to the significant displacement of individual buildings. He grouped these symmetrically around the courtyard in such a way that they came close to resembling a perimeter block. This second phase involved the construction of the First Medical Clinic, the Pediatric Clinic, the Clinic for Laryngeal and Nasal Diseases, and three isolation pavilions. (J, K) These buildings were opened at the end of 1911, by which point the entrance building had also been completed.

The third construction phase (1914–23), the planning of which began in 1912, was complicated from the start. The precarious financial situation of the Vienna Hospital Fund led to uncertainty about the future of the project. The phase was to include administration buildings, a kitchen and boiler house, and a further clinic. Having begun in 1914, work on the kitchen complex was made more complicated and delayed by the First World War. After the end of the war, shortages of both labor and materials hampered progress further

and hyperinflation made it impossible to control costs in a serious way. The largest hindrance to the realization was the lack of a financing concept. And latent opposition to the building project had also developed amongst the managers of the Hospital Fund. Finally, when work on the third phase ended in 1923, only the kitchen and boiler house had been completed. The other buildings could not be realized due to the lack of resources and the major project remained a mere torso. The story of the development of the New Clinics exemplifies the problems that faced hospital building in the early 20th century: By the end of the First World War, the basic concept for the complex was already outdated and the paradigm change in hospital building of the interwar years was beginning to emerge. Hence, the buildings erected from the 1960s onwards were laid out in line with a completely different development plan.

Having been incorporated into the General Hospital in 1920, during the final construction phase of the New Clinics, the interiors of the former Garrison Hospital were remodeled in the early 1930s for such new facilities as the School of Nursing. And the building left empty by the closure of the First Gynecological Clinic in 1933 was promptly occupied by the Second Surgical Clinic. Following the assumption of power by the National Socialists, the ownership and management of the General Hospital were transferred to Vienna City Council in 1939. Towards the end of the Second World War, the clinic buildings were damaged by bombing raids and artillery fire. The planning of the necessary expansion of the former First Gynecological Clinic began in 1960. The reconstruction work that was completed in 1966 involved a major intervention in the built substance that ruined the axial symmetry of the complex.

In parallel with this, an architectural competition was held for a new building for the General Hospital (now University Hospital Vienna). The plans for this completely new central hospital and

sprache der Architektur fundamental. Von der anfänglichen Konzeption bis zum Beginn der ersten Bauetappe sollten beinahe 30 Jahre vergehen.

Das enorme Bevölkerungswachstum Wiens im Laufe des 19. Jahrhunderts und epidemisch auftretende Infektionskrankheiten wie die Cholera und die Tuberkulose hatten zu einer chronischen Überbelegung der städtischen Krankenhäuser geführt. Zudem waren in dieser Zeit mehr und mehr spezifische Einrichtungen wie Operationssäle, Labors, klinische Hörsäle, Räume für Diagnosemöglichkeiten und Therapien sowie Ambulatorien nötig geworden. In Reaktion darauf kam es ab den 1880er Jahren zu zahlreichen Spitalsneubauten in Wien. Besonders in den Jahren vor dem Ersten Weltkrieg entstanden bedeutende Großanlagen.

In der Diskussion um den geeigneten Standort der Neuen Kliniken erwog man auch die westliche Peripherie der Stadt, schließlich erschienen preiswerte Liegenschaften im Grünen ideal für die Errichtung von Großanlagen – denken wir an die von Otto Wagner geplante psychiatrische Heil- und Pflegeanstalt Am Steinhof (1905–07), die mit ihren 60 Pavillons wie eine funktionalistisch aufgeteilte Stadt konzipiert war. Auch die Angst vor Ansteckung und die Notwendigkeit, Kranke zu isolieren, hatten seit je zu Einrichtungen außerhalb der Stadtgrenzen geführt; dies galt für die Siechenhäuser des Mittelalters ebenso wie für die späteren Infektionsspitäler. Doch es sprach vieles dafür, die Neuen Kliniken im Bereich des bestehenden „Wohlfahrts-Clusters" am Alsergrund zu situieren. Mit seinen Unikliniken war das Allgemeine Krankenhaus im 19. Jahrhundert zu einem weltweit anerkannten Zentrum medizinischer Forschung und Lehre avanciert. Auf Betreiben der Klinikprofessoren wurde letztlich auch der Bau der Neuen Kliniken auf diesem Areal beschlossen und die dortige Kumulation von Gesundheitseinrichtungen weitergeführt.

Nach einer Planungsphase von gut zwei Jahrzehnten fand

1904–08 die erste Bauperiode des neuen Komplexes statt. Die in dieser Etappe errichteten beiden Universitäts-Frauenkliniken gehen auf den Generalplan von Franz Berger zurück, der damals als Spezialist für Heilanstalten galt. Die Neubauten der I. und II. Frauenklinik waren am Verlauf der Spitalgasse ausgerichtet, die übrigen Gebäude plante Berger auf dem Brünnlfeld und erschloss sie von der Lazarettgasse aus. Aufgrund der Gegebenheiten der jeweiligen Bauplätze waren die beiden Bereiche völlig unterschiedlich strukturiert: Gruppierten sich die Frauenkliniken symmetrisch um den aus Verwaltungsbau und Kirche bestehenden Mitteltrakt des ehemaligen Armenversorgungshauses, so konnte Berger auf dem Brünnlfeld wesentlich freier planen, da die dortige psychiatrische Heilanstalt damals zum Abbruch bestimmt war (letztlich sollte der Bau noch bis 1974 bestehen). Friedrich Schauta und Rudolf Chrobak, die als Gynäkologen den Neubau der Frauenkliniken von medizinischer Seite begleiteten, wogen die Vor- und Nachteile einer horizontalen Anordnung des Pavillonsystems und eines vertikal orientierten, stärker verdichteten Blocksystems gegeneinander ab. Da eine Pavillonbauweise ein ausgedehntes Areal erfordert und erhebliche Betriebskosten mit sich gebracht hätte, entschloss man sich für eine Anlage der beiden Hauptgebäude als Block; lediglich ein Isolierpavillon wurde separat ausgeführt.

In die Planung der zweiten Bauperiode (1909–11), welche die Errichtung der Kliniken auf dem Brünnlfeld vorsah, griff der renommierte Architekt Emil von Förster ein, um seine Vorstellungen zu realisieren. Förster fungierte damals als Leiter der Hochbauabteilung des Innenministeriums und war Mitglied der Ministerialkommission und des Baukomitees für die Neuen Kliniken. Die damit einhergehenden Interventionsmöglichkeiten nahm er bis kurz vor seinem Tod Anfang 1909 wahr. Bis 1908 erstellte er nicht nur einen neuen Generalplan, sondern entwarf auch die Fassaden für die Klinikbauten dieser Etappe. Durch die Planänderungen Försters kam es – bei

J   Neue Kliniken des Allgemeinen Krankenhauses (I. Medizinische Klinik), Lazarettgasse 14, nach 1911, Fotografie (anonym)
The New Clinics of the General Hospital (First Medical Clinic), Lazarettgasse 14, after 1911, photograph (anonymous)

K   Neue Kliniken des Allgemeinen Krankenhauses (Kinderklinik), Spitalgasse, nach 1911, Fotografie (anonym)
The New Clinics of the General Hospital (Pediatric Clinic), Spitalgasse, after 1911, photograph (anonymous)

gleichbleibender Anordnung der Funktionen – zu signifikanten Verschiebungen einzelner Bauten. Er gruppierte die Gebäude nun spiegelbildlich um Höfe, was dem Prinzip einer Blockrandbebauung nahekam. In dieser zweiten Phase wurden die I. Medizinische Klinik, die Kinderklinik sowie die Klinik für Kehlkopf- und Nasenkrankheiten errichtet, außerdem drei Isolierpavillons. (J, K) Ende 1911 konnten diese Gebäude eröffnet werden, zu diesem Zeitpunkt war auch das Einfahrtsgebäude schon fertiggestellt.

Die ab 1912 in Planung befindliche dritte Bauphase (1914–23) gestaltete sich von Anfang an schwierig. Aufgrund der prekären Finanzlage des Wiener Krankenanstaltenfonds war die Fortsetzung des Projekts ungewiss. Administrationsbauten, ein Küchengebäude mit Kesselhaus (Heizhaus) sowie eine weitere Klinik sollten in dieser Etappe ausgeführt werden. Die noch 1914 begonnenen Arbeiten am Küchenkomplex wurden durch den Ersten Weltkrieg erheblich erschwert und verzögert. Nach Kriegsende hemmte der Mangel an Material und Arbeitskräften den Baufortschritt; aufgrund der damaligen Hyperinflation erschien zudem eine seriöse Kalkulation unmöglich. Das größte Problem für die Realisierung war das fehlende Finanzierungskonzept. Zudem hatte sich seitens der Verwaltung des Krankenanstaltenfonds eine latente Opposition gegen das Neubauprojekt gebildet. Letzten Endes wurde in dieser dritten Phase einzig das Küchengebäude samt Kesselhaus realisiert, 1923 waren die Arbeiten abgeschlossen. Die anderen Bauten konnten aufgrund fehlender Mittel nicht ausgeführt werden, somit blieb das Großvorhaben ein Torso. Das Projekt der Neuen Kliniken weist exemplarisch die Probleme des Krankenhausbaus zu Beginn des 20. Jahrhunderts auf: Das zugrundeliegende Konzept der Anlage war nach dem Ersten Weltkrieg bereits veraltet, im Krankenhausbau der Zwischenkriegszeit zeichnete sich ein Paradigmenwechsel ab. Die ab den 1960er Jahren errichteten Neubauten gingen schließlich von einem gänzlich veränderten Bebauungsplan aus.

Während der letzten Bauphase der Neuen Kliniken wurde 1920 das ehemalige Garnisonsspital an das Allgemeine Krankenhaus angegliedert, Anfang der 1930er Jahre adaptierte man seine Räumlichkeiten unter anderem für die Krankenpflegeschule. Nach Auflösung der I. Frauenklinik 1933 übersiedelte die II. Chirurgische Klinik in deren Gebäude. Im Zuge der Machtübernahme der Nationalsozialisten wurde das Allgemeine Krankenhaus 1939 in das Eigentum und die Verwaltung der Stadt Wien übertragen. Gegen Ende des Zweiten Weltkriegs kam es durch Bombenangriffe und Artilleriefeuer zu Schäden an den Klinikgebäuden. 1960 begannen die Planungen zur notwendigen Erweiterung der einstigen I. Frauenklinik. Diese 1966 abgeschlossenen Umbauarbeiten bedeuteten einen gravierenden Eingriff in die Substanz, das axialsymmetrische Konzept der Anlage wurde damit zerstört.

Parallel dazu war bereits der Architektenwettbewerb für den Neubau des Allgemeinen Krankenhauses (heute Universitätsklinikum AKH Wien) durchgeführt worden. Nachdem 1961 die Pläne für dieses von Grund auf neu errichtete Zentralspital und Uniklinikum vorlagen, wurde 1963 mit den Abbrucharbeiten der Neuen Kliniken begonnen. Auf die Abtragung des Haupteinfahrtsgebäudes folgte der Abbruch zweier Isolierpavillons und der Psychiatrischen Klinik, 1986 wurde schließlich das Küchengebäude samt Kesselhaus demoliert. 1988 hatte das Bundesdenkmalamt Teile der Frauenklinik unter Schutz gestellt. Diese nächst der Spitalgasse liegenden Trakte wurden in den Jahren 1993–2004 restauriert und zu Forschungs- und Lehreinrichtungen umgebaut. Im Zuge dieser von der VAMED (Voestalpine Medizintechnik GmbH) durchgeführten Adaptierung brach man auch die beiden hinteren Trakte der II. Frauenklinik sowie die Klinik für Kehlkopf- und Nasenkrankheiten ab.

In einem der erhaltenen denkmalgeschützten Jugendstilbauten sind seit dem Jahr 2004 die Büros des Rektorats der MedUni Wien

university clinic were completed in 1961 and the demolition of the New Clinics began in 1963. Following the removal of the main entrance building and then two isolation pavilions and the Psychiatric Clinic, the kitchen and boiler house were finally demolished in 1986. In 1988, the Federal Monuments Office placed parts of the Gynecological Clinic on the list of protected buildings. This block on Spitalgasse was restored and converted into research and teaching areas between 1993 and 2004. During this adaptation by VAMED (Voestalpine Medizintechnik GmbH), the two rear wings of the Second Gynecological Clinic and the Clinic for Laryngeal and Nasal Diseases were also demolished.

One of these Jugendstil buildings that was listed and, hence, retained has housed the office of the Rectorate of MedUni Vienna since 2004. However, with the exception of these restored blocks, the New Clinics have disappeared from the public eye. Contemporary photographic postcards offer us an excellent impression of the complex: Black-and-white images from shortly before the First World War depict the clinics built during the first two phases and the entrance building. (L, M, N, O) Postcards spread rapidly after 1900. These recorded not only important buildings and other attractions but also changes in the urban landscape and even landmarks such as the New Clinics while they were still under construction. Large publishing houses such as Brüder Kohn or Ledermann sometimes released entire series of Vienna motifs, and hospitals even occasionally commissioned postcards themselves.[56]

These historical images help us to understand both the design of the overall complex and the formal language of the individual buildings: Despite the strict cost savings, the buildings have monumental qualities, with both the triumphal arch and the dome over the main entrance on Lazarettgasse being adapted from the typology of the city gate and motifs from patrician architecture. This entrance, which was approached by the sweep of a curving ramp, almost appeared

ostentatious. The central gateway was reserved for vehicles (besides horse-drawn vehicles, the number of cars was increasing) and the two side entrances for pedestrians. During the first two construction phases, the individual buildings were adorned with avant-corps, some of which were accentuated by pediments. Roof terraces and verandas were created in an attempt to allow the users of the building to experience nature in the city. However, the lack of funds meant that the sculptural additions to the buildings were reduced to a minimum; the Ministry for Culture and Education had explicitly pointed out that the complex consisted not of monumental but, rather, of "functional" buildings.

The formal vocabulary of hygiene
Hospital buildings – like all other public buildings of the time – were built in predetermined architectural styles, which reflected the official aesthetic language of the state. This differentiation between styles became particularly important following the historicist period in the mid-19th century, when several stylistic options were available. While the hospitals and scientific institutions erected around that time display neo-renaissance characteristics (and, thus, a particular affinity with Enlightenment values, rationality, and a trust in science), those constructed after 1900 adopted Jugendstil forms. Franz Berger's design for the two Gynecological Clinics employed modern elements as a leitmotif: decorative tiles, a powerfully cantilevered main cornice, and grating with vegetal motifs along the edges of the roof. (P, Q) These details lent the buildings the air of recreational structures such as sanatoria or villas. However, the dominant theme of hospital building of the period was hygiene, and this shaped the architecture on a number of levels. The latest theories about avoiding infection influenced the design of both the entire hospital complex and its individual elements. Excellently illuminated and ventilated spaces with huge windows on

211

untergebracht. Mit Ausnahme dieser restaurierten Gebäudeflügel sind die Neuen Kliniken jedoch aus der öffentlichen Wahrnehmung verschwunden. Einen guten Eindruck der Anlage bieten zeitgenössische Fotopostkarten: Die kurz vor dem Ersten Weltkrieg entstandenen Schwarzweiß-Aufnahmen zeigen die in den ersten beiden Phasen errichteten Kliniken und das Einfahrtsgebäude. (L, M, N, O) Die Ansichtskarte erlebte nach der Jahrhundertwende eine rasante Verbreitung. Neben zentralen Sehenswürdigkeiten wurden auch urbane Veränderungen festgehalten, so auch im Entstehen begriffene *landmarks* wie die Neuen Kliniken. Große Verlage wie die Brüder Kohn oder Ledermann brachten manchmal ganze Serien von Wien-Motiven auf den Markt, auch Spitäler konnten Auftraggeber bestimmter Ansichtskarten sein.[56]

Sowohl die Gestaltung der Gesamtanlage wie auch die Formensprache der einzelnen Bauten lassen sich anhand der historischen Aufnahmen gut nachvollziehen: Trotz des rigiden Sparkurses hatte man monumentale Akzente gesetzt, der Triumphbogen und die Kuppel der Haupteinfahrt an der Lazarettgasse wandelten den Typus des Stadttores ebenso ab wie Motive herrschaftlicher Architektur. Mit der darauf zuführenden, kurvig einschwingenden Rampe war die Einfahrt beinahe pompös inszeniert. Das Mitteltor hatte man für den Fahrverkehr reserviert (neben Pferdefuhrwerken nahm die Zahl an Automobilen zu), zwei seitliche Eingänge waren für Fußgänger:innen bestimmt. In den beiden ersten Bauperioden wurden die einzelnen Gebäude durch Risalite gegliedert, mitunter fanden sich diese durch Giebel akzentuiert. Mit Dachterrassen und Veranden suchte man das Erlebnis von Natur auch in der Stadt möglich zu machen. Die Bauplastik war wegen der beschränkten Mittel allerdings auf ein Minimum reduziert; seitens des Ministeriums für Kultus und Unterricht hatte man explizit darauf verwiesen, dass es sich bei der Anlage nicht um Monumental-, sondern um „Nutzbauten" handle.

Die Formensprache der Hygiene
Im Krankenhausbau wurden damals – wie bei anderen öffentlichen Bauaufgaben – vorgegebene Architekturstile eingesetzt, die den jeweils „staatstragenden" Gestaltungsmodus widerspiegeln. Relevant wird diese Differenzierung nach Stilen besonders ab der Mitte des 19. Jahrhunderts, der Phase des Historismus, als mehrere Optionen offenstehen. Weisen die zu jener Zeit errichteten Spitäler und wissenschaftlichen Einrichtungen Merkmale der Neorenaissance auf (und damit eine besondere Nähe zu den Werten der Aufklärung, zur Rationalität und zum Vertrauen in die Wissenschaft), so werden nach 1900 Formen des Jugendstils aufgegriffen. Franz Bergers Gestaltung der beiden Frauenkliniken setzt leitmotivisch moderne Elemente ein: Fliesendekor, ein weit vorkragendes Hauptgesims und Gitter mit vegetabilen Motiven zur Begrenzung der Flachdächer. (P, Q) Damit vermitteln die Bauten den Eindruck von Erholungsarchitekturen wie Sanatorien oder Villen. Das dominierende Thema des Krankenhausbaus jener Zeit ist jedoch die Hygiene, und dies prägt die Architektur auf unterschiedlichen Ebenen. Die damaligen Theorien zur Vermeidung von Infektionen wirken sich sowohl auf die gesamte Krankenhausanlage als auch auf einzelne Bauteile aus. Von großen Fenstern beidseitig oder mitunter auch auf drei Seiten belichtete und belüftete Räume bilden weiterhin das Ideal, Säle mit über 20 Betten sind in den Neuen Kliniken die Regel. Über die vordringliche Anforderung nach Luft und Licht hinaus sucht Architektur hygienische Inhalte auch ästhetisch zu vermitteln. Die grünen Kachelbänder der neuen Frauenkliniken sind als Dekor in diesem Sinne zu sehen.

Strukturelle Transformation
Ob die spezifischen Funktionen von Krankenhaus- und Klinikbauten jener Zeit in kompakten Blocks vertikal übereinander angelegt sind oder in einzelnen Pavillons horizontal nebeneinander, ist funktional

two or, sometimes, three sides continued to represent the ideal, with 20 beds being the standard size for a ward in the New Clinics. And, in addition to this vital need for air and light, the architecture also sought to communicate the message of hygiene through aesthetic detail. This is the context for the decoration of the new Gynecological Clinics with strips of green tiles.

Structural transformation
Whether the specific functions of the hospital and clinic buildings of the time were arranged in compact vertical blocks, or alongside each other in horizontal rows of individual pavilions, was of secondary organizational significance. Rapidly developing communication and transport technologies had a much greater impact on the design of the hospital complex. Towards the end of the 19th century, elevators became an increasingly important means of vertical communication. Initially, these were small service elevators that transported food and laundry, while patients continued to be transported up and down stairs sitting in chairs carried by hospital assistants. The first elevators to transport patients lying in beds were limited to surgical stations. But these soon developed into a general means of transport and, by 1900, the elevator had become a standard piece of equipment in a hospital with several stories. Elevators could also be found in each of the buildings of the New Clinics. These radically altered the typology of medical buildings and were soon heralding the emergence of the "high-rise hospital."

It is important to remember that the people most likely to attend hospital until well into the second half of the 19th century came from those layers of society for which a home visit by a doctor was simply unaffordable. In sociological terms, hospitals long remained places for the destitute and for patients with low incomes. They only became attractive to the middle and upper classes following the development of

operating techniques and sterile working methods towards the end of the century.

While it was standard practice to operate on wounded soldiers, the treatment of civilian patients played no more than a minor role until around 1850. However, the introduction of anesthetics from 1846 and the antiseptic and aseptic procedures that (largely) guaranteed sterility drove up success rates and, hence, the general importance of operating techniques. The 1870s brought a series of developments in surgical methods that were also reflected by changes in the equipment found in operating rooms. Theodor Billroth, who headed the Second Surgical Clinic at Vienna's General Hospital from 1867, made a major contribution to these advances in surgery. He developed a series of new operating techniques that significantly broadened the area of intervention of surgeons. The transformation of the status of surgery from a subordinate subject to the most prestigious of all medical disciplines towards the end of the 19th century also led to a rapid growth in the number of operating rooms. The ideal location for an operating room was initially considered to be the ground floor due to the fear that wounds would heal much less successfully at higher levels. It was believed that putrid, "contagious" air would rise upwards and create detrimental conditions on the upper stories.[57] The idea of providing two operating rooms – an aseptic room for clean wounds and a further one for septic wounds – became established around the same time. The development of sterilization techniques was accompanied by the creation of special spaces for the accommodation of specific equipment. Operating rooms were soon surrounded by numerous ancillary spaces – washing, anesthetic, preparation, and recovery rooms – and large elevators for the transport of patients in their beds soon became fixed elements of the hospital infrastructure that were always located close to surgical stations. Before the introduction of high-performance surgery lights, the location of the operating rooms in

L

M

N

O

L–O Neue Kliniken des Allgemeinen Krankenhauses,
    Lazarettgasse 14, nach 1911, Ansichtskarten
The New Clinics of the General Hospital, Lazarettgasse 14, after 1911,
postcards

gesehen sekundär. Vielmehr spielen die sich damals verändernden Kommunikations- und Transportmöglichkeiten eine immer größere Rolle für das jeweilige Anlagenkonzept. Für die Kommunikation in vertikaler Richtung werden zum Ende des 19. Jahrhunderts Aufzüge immer wichtiger. Zunächst sind dies kleine Lastenaufzüge für Essen und Wäsche, Kranke werden damals noch von Dienern in Sesseln durch die Stiegenhäuser getragen. Fahrstühle, die in Betten Liegende befördern, sind zunächst auf die chirurgischen Stationen beschränkt. Bald aber entwickeln sie sich zum allgemeinen Beförderungsmittel, um 1900 gehörten Aufzüge zur Standardausrüstung eines mehrstöckigen Krankenhausbaus. Auch in jedem Gebäude der Neuen Kliniken waren Personenaufzüge installiert. Der Fahrstuhl verändert den Bautypus des Spitals radikal, die Entwicklung zu „Kranken-Hochhäusern" bahnt sich damit an.

Man muss sich vor Augen führen, dass bis in die zweite Hälfte des 19. Jahrhunderts vorwiegend jene Bevölkerungsschichten ein Krankenhaus frequentierten, für die Arztbesuche zuhause nicht leistbar waren. Soziologisch gesehen blieben Spitäler lange ein Ort für Mittellose und Kranke mit geringem Verdienst. Erst mit der Entwicklung der Operationstechniken und steriler Arbeitsmethoden gegen Ende des 19. Jahrhunderts wird das Krankenhaus auch für die mittleren und wohlhabenden Schichten attraktiv.

War die Durchführung chirurgischer Operationen an Kriegsverletzten gängige Praxis, so spielten sie in der Behandlung ziviler Kranker bis gegen 1850 nur eine untergeordnete Rolle. Doch mit der Etablierung der Anästhesie ab 1846 sowie der anti- und aseptischen Verfahren, die (weitgehende) Keimfreiheit garantierten, stieg die Erfolgsquote und damit auch die generelle Bedeutung operativer Techniken. Maßgebliche Entwicklungsschübe in der Chirurgie fanden in den 1870er Jahren statt, was sich auch in der Einrichtung von Operationsräumen manifestierte. Theodor Billroth, ab 1867 Leiter der

II. Chirurgischen Klinik am Wiener AKH, hatte wesentlichen Anteil am Aufschwung der Chirurgie. Er entwickelte eine Reihe neuer Operationstechniken, die das Arbeitsfeld der Chirurgen wesentlich erweiterten. Mit dem gewandelten Status der Chirurgie von einem untergeordneten Fach zur medizinischen Stardisziplin stieg gegen Ende des 19. Jahrhunderts auch die Anzahl der OP-Säle sprunghaft an. Als ideale Lage für einen Operationsraum sah man zunächst das Erdgeschoß an, da man in den oberen Etagen eine schwierige Wundheilung fürchtete. Man glaubte, die verdorbene, „kontagiöse" Luft steige von unten nach oben und sorge in den höher gelegenen Stockwerken für schlechte Verhältnisse.[57] Damals bürgerte sich auch die Anlage zweier Operationsräume ein, eines aseptischen für reine Wunden und eines weiteren für septische. Die Entwicklung von Sterilisierungstechniken zog die Einrichtung eigener Räume zur Unterbringung entsprechender Apparate nach sich. Bald waren die OP-Säle umgeben von zahlreichen Nebenräumen – Wasch-, Narkose-, Vorbereitungs- und Aufwachräumen –, und in unmittelbarer Nähe waren groß dimensionierte Aufzüge zum Transport der Kranken in ihren Betten fix in die Spitalsstruktur integriert. Vor der Einführung leistungsstarker Operationsscheinwerfer war das nordseitige, schattenfreie Tageslicht maßgeblich für die Positionierung der OP-Säle im Bau, die Größe der Fenster spielte eine wichtige Rolle. Die Operationsräume von Unikliniken waren mit Sitzreihen für die Studierenden ausgestattet, und in den klinischen Hörsälen wurden neben den theoretischen Vorlesungen auch Operationen durchgeführt. Die beiden Funktionen finden sich häufig in einem Raum vereint. Historisch gesehen geht dieser Raumtypus mit teleskopartig ansteigenden Sitzreihen auf das Anatomische Theater an der Universität Padua zurück. Der dort 1594 eingerichtete Sektionsraum gilt als Ursprungsort medizinischer Forschung und wurde zum Modell ähnlicher Einrichtungen in ganz Europa.[58]

P

Q

P, Q Neue Kliniken des Allgemeinen Krankenhauses
(Frauenkliniken), Spitalgasse, 1908, Fotografien (anonym)
The New Clinics of the General Hospital (Gynecological Clinics),
Spitalgasse, 1908, photographs (anonymous)

Die Hörsäle der beiden Frauenkliniken stellen eine Besonderheit dar: Ihre amphitheatralisch ansteigenden Sitzreihen aus Eisen entsprechen den Kriterien der Hygiene, die Pultflächen sind zudem mit Linoleum belegt – ein Material, das man damals im Krankenhaus- und Klinikbau sehr schätzte. Der erhaltene Jugendstil-Hörsaal im revitalisierten Gebäude der ehemaligen Frauenkliniken dient heute als Rahmen für besondere Anlässe der MedUni Wien.

Monumente für Mediziner
Die Vorstände der Frauenkliniken hatten zur Eröffnung der Bauten 1908 auch ein Denkmal für ihren Vorgänger Ignaz Philipp Semmelweis gestiftet.[59] Die Bedeutung der von ihm empfohlenen Händedesinfektion zur Verhinderung von Todesfällen durch Sepsis wurde erst von der Nachwelt erkannt. Die Monumente auf dem Areal des heutigen MedUni Campus AKH Wien, des Alten AKH sowie im Arkadenhof der Universität Wien stehen in der Tradition der sich im 19. Jahrhundert entwickelnden Denkmäler für Wissenschaftler und Künstler. Besonders Medizinern wurden in Wien zahlreiche Personendenkmäler gesetzt. Manche sind an das tradierte Vorbild des Herrscherporträts angelehnt (etwa die Büste des Chirurgen Franz Schuh), häufig sind Mediziner jedoch bewusst als bürgerliche Leistungsträger im Anzug dargestellt. Zum Teil verweist die Ikonografie explizit auf die jeweilige Disziplin der Gelehrten: Im Falle Theodor Billroths kam im Jahr 1944 erstmals der Chirurgenkittel in einem überlebensgroßen Monument zu Ehren (Billroth hatte antiseptische Kleidung 1878 verpflichtend im Operationssaal eingeführt), der Kittel steht als Symbol für den gefeierten Fortschritt der Medizin.[60] Mitunter erinnert ein Denkmal auch an ein tragisches Schicksal, wie jenes des Internisten Hermann Franz Müller, der sich 1898 mit dem Pestbazillus angesteckt hatte und als letzter Pesttoter Europas in die Geschichte einging. Von einer Studienreise ins damalige Bombay hatte er Pestkulturen mitgebracht, um sie in Wien

auszuwerten. Der Labordiener des Pathologisch-Anatomischen Instituts infizierte sich beim Kontakt mit den Versuchstieren und erkrankte an Lungenpest. Müller und die Krankenpflegerin, die ihn behandelten, steckten sich ebenfalls an, alle drei verstarben nach wenigen Tagen.

Insgesamt zeugen diese Denkmäler auch davon, dass die wissenschaftliche Elite eine ausschließlich männliche war. Besonders die Medizin galt als maskuline Domäne, hier hielten die patriarchalen Verhältnisse sehr lange an.[61] Neben dem Ausschluss von Frauen wäre auch die nicht unproblematische Geschichte mancher Monumente ein eigenes Kapitel – so geht jenes erwähnte von Billroth etwa auf die NS-Zeit zurück.

Das moderne Krankenhaus

Das ein Fragment gebliebene Projekt der Neuen Kliniken stellt international gesehen keinen Einzelfall dar. Krankenhaus- und Klinikbauten, die kurz vor dem Ersten Weltkrieg begonnen wurden, galten nicht selten bereits in den 1930er Jahren als obsolet. Die Medizintechnik durchlief damals einen rapiden Wandel, was grundlegende Änderungen in der Spitalsgestaltung zur Folge hatte. Parallel dazu fand auf sozialpolitischer Ebene im frühen 20. Jahrhundert ein Paradigmenwechsel von wohltätiger Pflege zu organisierter Gesundheitspolitik und staatlicher Wohlfahrt statt. Hatten bis dahin jene, die es sich leisten konnten, eine Behandlung und Pflege daheim vorgezogen, so stieg nun die Nachfrage nach Spitalsbehandlungen in allen gesellschaftlichen Schichten. Erst ab diesem Zeitpunkt wurde die Institution Krankenhaus zu einem Fixpunkt im Leben des Großteils der Bevölkerung, von der Geburt bis zum Tod. Anfangs bloß karitative Orte für sozial Randständige und bedürftige Kranke, haben sich Krankenhäuser im

a building was largely determined by the need for large, north-facing windows that provided high levels of shadow-free daylight. The operating rooms of the university clinics had rows of seats for students and the clinical lecture theaters also hosted operations as well as theoretical lectures. These two functions were often combined in a single space. From the historical perspective, this spatial typology of telescopically rising rows of seats can be traced back to the anatomy theater of the University of Padua. The dissecting room, which dates from 1594, is regarded as the birthplace of medical research and became a model for similar facilities across Europe.[58]

The lecture theaters of both Gynecological Clinics had a particular feature: The rows of iron seats that formed steeply rising amphitheaters met strict hygiene criteria and the desks were covered with linoleum, a material that was highly regarded by the hospital and clinic builders of the day. The one remaining Jugendstil lecture theater in the refurbished building of the former Gynecological Clinics is now used by MedUni Vienna as a setting for special events.

Monuments for doctors
The opening of the newly built Gynecological Clinics in 1908 was also marked by the endowment by the directors of the clinics of a monument to their predecessor Ignaz Philipp Semmelweis.[59] The important role of Semmelweis's recommendation to disinfect the hands in preventing deaths from sepsis was only recognized after his death. The monuments still found on the site of today's MedUni Campus AKH, the Altes AKH, and the Arkadenhof of the University of Vienna belong to the tradition of creating memorials to scientists and artists that developed during the 19th century. Doctors are particular prominent amongst the monuments to individuals that were installed in Vienna. Some are inspired by the traditional model of the portrait of a ruler (such as the bust of the surgeon Franz Schuh), but doctors

are often very deliberately portrayed as suit-wearing upper middle class high achievers. The iconography of these monuments sometimes explicitly refers to the discipline of the subject: The larger-than-life monument to Theodor Billroth that was completed in 1944 is the first to honor the surgical gown, which symbolizes the medical breakthrough commemorated by the memorial (Billroth had introduced compulsory antiseptic clothing in the operating room in 1878).[60] Some monuments recall a tragic fate, such as that of the internist Hermann Franz Müller, who infected himself with plague bacilli in 1898 and went down in history as Europe's final plague victim. He had brought plague bacteria back from a study visit to Bombay, as it was known at the time, in order to study them in Vienna. The laboratory assistant of the Pathological Anatomical Institute infected himself upon having contact with the laboratory animals and was taken ill with pneumonic plague. Müller and the nurse who treated the assistant also contracted the disease and, within a few days, all three were dead.

Taken together, these monuments also provide evidence of the fact that the scientific elite were exclusively male. Medicine was regarded as a particularly masculine domain and patriarchal conditions persisted for a long time.[61] In addition to this exclusion of women, the not unproblematic history of some of these monuments is another chapter in itself – as exemplified by the abovementioned monument to Billroth that dates back to the Nazi era.

The modern hospital

Seen from an international perspective, it is hardly unusual that just one fragment of the New Clinics still exists today. Hospital and clinic buildings whose construction had begun shortly before the First World War were often already regarded as obsolete by the 1930s. Medical

frühen 20. Jahrhundert zu veritablen Stätten medizinischen Wissens entwickelt.[62]

Mehr als andere Gebäudetypen sind Spitäler und Kliniken integral für die biopolitischen Interessen eines Staates. Und umgekehrt betrachtet schlagen sich Veränderungen im Gesundheitszustand der Bevölkerung und die zunehmend steigende Lebenserwartung in der Anlage dieser Bauten nieder. Besonders deutlich zeigt sich dies in der Zwischenkriegszeit, wo es das Ziel kommunalpolitischer Maßnahmen war, die damals sehr hohe Säuglings- und Kindersterblichkeit zu senken. In diesen Jahren fand nach und nach die Normalisierung von Spitalsgeburten statt. Auch der grassierenden Tuberkulose – auf sie gingen noch Anfang der 1920er Jahre die meisten Todesfälle zurück – suchte man mit eigens konzipierten Gesundheitsbauten zu begegnen. Die Tuberkulosesanatorien der Zwischenkriegszeit mit ihren breiten Schiebefenstern und ausladenden Terrassen stehen sinnbildlich für die Emphase auf Licht, Luft und Sonne; über die Materialien Glas und Stahl reflektieren sie die einstigen Hygienestandards und die medizinisch angestrebte keimfreie Umgebung. In einer Zeit, in der Krankheiten wie Rachitis und Tuberkulose stark verbreitet waren, wurden Spitäler und Sanatorien wie ein medizinisches Instrument konzipiert:[63] Eine nach Süden orientierte Architektur galt als gesundheitsfördernd, Sonnenlicht würde Bakterien töten und den Organismus stärken, frische Luft diene der Erholung der Lunge, so das damalige Credo. Mit dem Aufkommen von Antibiotika wie Streptomycin wurden diese Gesundheitsbauten ab den 1940er Jahren jedoch überflüssig.

In der Zwischenkriegszeit bildete sich auch ein Expertendiskurs zu Fragen des modernen Spitals heraus: Krankenhausfachleute aus Europa und Nordamerika etablierten ein internationales Netzwerk, das 1929 mit der Gründung der International Hospital Association (IHA) seine institutionelle Basis erhielt. Ungeachtet der nationalistischen und totalitaristischen Tendenzen jener Zeit war dieser Verein von liberalen Idealen getragen und organisierte eine Reihe erfolgreicher Konferenzen. Nach der Auftaktveranstaltung 1929 in den USA (Atlantic City, New Jersey) wurde der II. Internationale Hospitalkongress 1931 in Wien ausgetragen.[64] Julius Tandler, der als Leiter des Volksgesundheitsamts 1920 bereits das Krankenanstaltengesetz geschaffen hatte, welches den bis dahin durch wohltätige Fonds finanzierten österreichischen Krankenhäusern die Übernahme durch die Gebietskörperschaften sicherte,[65] hatte 1929 (als nunmehr amtsführender Stadtrat für das Wohlfahrts- und Gesundheitswesen) die Donaumetropole als Austragungsort vorgeschlagen. Das moderne Spital ist gewissermaßen das Produkt dieses internationalen Diskurses. In der vierteljährlich erscheinenden Fachzeitschrift Nosokomeion (1930–39) etwa, die Artikel in fünf Sprachen enthielt, wurden die jeweils neuesten Strömungen im Krankenhauswesen weltweit kommuniziert. Die Modernität eines Spitals bezog sich jedoch nicht allein auf die Ästhetik des Baus. Kriterien wie Effizienz, Rationalität und Produktivität rückten nun in den Vordergrund, die Analogie zu einer Fabrik war in den 1930er Jahren ein gängiger Topos. Ab etwa 1950 avancierten Spitäler zur zentralen Institution im Gesundheitssystem und dominierten auch architektonisch gesehen ganze Stadtviertel.

Räumliche Rekonfiguration
Dieser grundlegenden Neugestaltung von Krankenhaus- und Klinikbauten in der Zeit um 1950 lagen medizintechnische und professionelle Veränderungen zugrunde. Das moderne Spital wurde parallel zum Aufkommen spezifischer Diagnose- und Therapiemöglichkeiten entwickelt. Wandten Mediziner bis zu Beginn des 20. Jahrhunderts vor allem äußerliche Behandlungen an, so verstärkten sich nun die Investigationen im Körperinneren. Mit dem zunehmenden Einsatz von Röntgengeräten und anderen bildgebenden Technologien wie dem Ultraschall, der Computer- und der Magnetresonanztomographie etablier-

technology was advancing rapidly and this was leading to fundamental changes in hospital design. In parallel with this, a sociopolitical paradigm change that took place in the early 20th century led to a transition from charitable care to organized health policies. Whereas those who could afford it had previously preferred to be treated and cared for at home, demand for hospital treatment was now growing at every level of society. This was the moment at which the institution of the hospital began to become a fixture in the lives of most of the population, from the cradle to the grave. Having originated as mere charitable settings for social outsiders and needy patients, hospitals developed in the early 20th century into veritable centers of medical expertise.[62]

More than other building types, hospitals and clinics play an integral role in the biopolitical interests of a state. And, conversely, changes in the state of health of the population and rising life expectancy are reflected in the design of these buildings. This became particularly clear between the wars, when municipal politicians set themselves the objective of reducing the very high mortality rates amongst babies and small children. During these years, hospital births gradually became the norm. Healthcare buildings were also specially designed to address the rampant tuberculosis that was still the leading cause of death in the early 1920s. With their large sliding windows and sweeping terraces, the tuberculosis sanatoria of the interwar years embodied the emphasis on light, air, and sunshine; their use of glass and steel reflected the hygiene standards of their day and the medical aspiration to create a germ-free environment. At a time in which diseases such as rickets and tuberculosis were widespread, hospitals and sanatoria were designed like medical instruments:[63] South-facing architecture was seen as beneficial to health, sunlight would kill bacteria and strengthen the organism, and fresh air would support the recovery of the lungs. These were the principles of the day. However, the introduction of antibiotics such as streptomycin meant that these types of healthcare buildings became redundant after the 1940s.

The interwar years saw the emergence of an expert discussion about aspects of the modern hospital: Hospital specialists from Europe and North America established an international network that was put on an institutional footing in 1929 with the founding of the International Hospital Association (IHA). Despite the nationalist and totalitarian tendencies of the period, the association was underpinned by liberal ideals and organized a series of successful conferences. Following the initial event in the USA (Atlantic City, New Jersey) in 1929, the Second International Hospital Congress was held in Vienna in 1931.[64] Julius Tandler, the author of the Hospitals Act, which ensured that the Austrian hospitals that had previously been financed by charitable funds were taken over by the municipalities and had been drawn up by Tandler in his role as Head of the Public Health Office in 1920,[65] nominated Vienna as the venue in 1929 (when he was Executive City Councilor for Health and Welfare). To some extent, the modern hospital is the product of this international discourse. For example, the specialist quarterly publication Nosokomeion (1930–39), which contained articles in five languages, reported on the latest healthcare trends from around the world. However, the modernity of a hospital was not only a result of its built aesthetic. Such criteria as efficiency, rationality, and productivity now came to the fore and the analogy with the factory was a common topos in the 1930s. After around 1950, hospitals became central institutions in the healthcare system that dominated entire urban districts – including in the architectural sense.

Spatial reconfiguration
This fundamental reshaping of hospital and clinic buildings in the years around 1950 was the result of both medical-technical and professional changes. The modern hospital developed in parallel with the emergence

te man ein zuverlässiges Diagnoseregime. Auch die schon im späten 19. Jahrhundert anhebende Entwicklung in Richtung Labormedizin erfuhr einen starken Impuls, was den Ausbau von Pathologielaboratorien erforderlich machte. Vor allem diese Diagnose- und Therapieräumlichkeiten markierten die erweiterte Rolle des Krankenhauses; die grundlegenden Spitalsabteilungen wurden in dieser Phase rekonfiguriert. Medizinisch gesehen verschob sich der Fokus von der Unterbringung und Pflege Kranker auf die Diagnose und intensive Behandlung. Mit dem Aufkommen pharmazeutischer Therapien bestand nach dem Zweiten Weltkrieg keine Notwendigkeit mehr, Frischluft (und damit auch Pathogene) ins Spital dringen zu lassen. Krankenhausbauten entwickelten sich zu einer geschlossenen Einheit, architektonisches Ideal war nun die hermetisch verschlossene „Box". Damit war die Funktion des Baus nicht mehr von außen erkennbar; Spitäler wurden Hochhäuser, mitunter auch Flachbauten oder eine Kombination aus beidem. Abstrakt wirkende Türme und Blöcke waren die Folge, der Großteil der Krankenhausbauten ab den frühen 1960er Jahren unterschied sich rein äußerlich nicht mehr von einem Bürohochhaus.

Die vertikale Anlage als mehrstöckiger Block und das Prinzip tayloristischer Organisation kamen zuerst in Nordamerika auf, und generell entstanden in den 1920er und 1930er Jahren viele wegweisende Spitalsbauten in den USA. Eines der ersten als Hochhaus konzipierten Krankenhäuser war das 1929 eröffnete Columbia-Presbyterian Medical Center in New York City. Der Konnex zwischen Forschung und Lehre ist im modernen Spital fundamental; integrierte Universitätskliniken garantieren die praktische Ausbildung der medizinischen Profession. Zu den führenden nordamerikanischen Spitälern der Zwischenkriegszeit zählten durchwegs Unikliniken, etwa die Vanderbilt University Medical School in Nashville, Tennessee (1925) oder das New York Hospital – Cornell Medical Center (1932). Diese Lehrkrankenhäuser waren wie eine Stadt für sich konzipiert,

zeitgenössische Stimmen nannten die beeindruckenden Anlagen *citadels of health* oder *cathedrals of healing*.

Das vertikale Bauen, das ab der Mitte des 20. Jahrhunderts die Anlage von Krankenhäusern wesentlich bestimmte, wurde erst möglich durch den elektrischen Fahrstuhl und den Stahlskelettbau.[66] Die ersten Aufzüge kamen in den 1870ern auf (anfangs noch mit Hydraulikbetrieb), durch die Elektrifizierung bald darauf ließen sich bereits zehn, zwölf Etagen befahren. Der zu Beginn der 1880er Jahre in Chicago entwickelte Stahlskelettbau erlaubte es, die potenzielle Geschoßzahl um ein Vielfaches zu erhöhen. Durch den anhebenden Prozess der Technisierung und Elektrifizierung war das Innere von Gebäuden fortan durchzogen von einem komplexen System aus Röhren, Leitungen und Schächten. An dieser profunden Neuorganisation von Bauten hatte der Fahrstuhl maßgeblich Anteil, ihm kam bald die Funktion des Gebäudekerns zu. Besonders im Krankenhaus- und Klinikbau spielt der Aufzug als Transportmittel eine elementare Rolle, die Positionierung der Schächte ist im Planungsprozess essenziell.

Die rational angelegte Spitalsmaschinerie
Die auf solchen Technologien basierende Rationalisierung der Abläufe hat ebenfalls ihren Ursprung in den USA, sie sollte das ökonomische Funktionieren von Gebäuden garantieren. Erst mit dem Einzug effizienter logistischer Systeme ließ sich die viel zitierte „Spitalsmaschinerie" realisieren; bis dahin war der Begriff einer *machine à guérir* eher ein Schlagwort geblieben. Das Erstellen von Netzwerkdiagrammen stand nun am Beginn jeder Krankenhaus- und Klinikplanung. Das Augenmerk galt der Funktion eines Gebäudes als effizientes System, die gesamte Anlage war nun im Wortsinn als *healing machine* konzipiert.

Nicht nur Transport- und Kommunikationssysteme änderten sich in den Jahrzehnten zwischen 1920 und 1960 radikal, auch die

of specific diagnostic and therapeutic methods. While the doctors of the early 20th century had largely applied themselves to external treatments, internal investigation was now becoming much more common. The increasing use of x-ray equipment and other imaging technologies such as ultrasound and computer and magnetic resonance tomography led to the establishment of a reliable diagnostic regime. The trend towards laboratory medicine that had emerged towards the end of the 19th century also received a major boost, which created the need for more pathology laboratories. Above all, these diagnostic and therapeutic spaces underlined the expanded role of the hospital, while this phase also saw the reconfiguration of the basic hospital departments.

In terms of medical practice, the focus shifted from the accommodation and care of the sick to diagnosis and intensive treatment. The advent of pharmaceutical therapies after the Second World War removed the need for allowing fresh air (and hence pathogens) into hospitals. Hospital buildings developed into closed units and the architectural ideal was now the hermetically sealed "box." As a result, the building's function could no longer be read from outside; hospitals became high-rise or, occasionally, low-rise buildings, or a combination of the two. This resulted in abstract towers and slabs and most hospital buildings from the early 1960s could no longer be differentiated, on the outside, from office blocks.

The vertical organization of hospitals as multistory blocks and the application of the principles of Taylorism first emerged in North America and, more generally, many pioneering hospitals were built in the USA in the 1920s and 1930s. One of the first to be designed as a multistory building was the Columbia-Presbyterian Medical Center in New York City, which opened in 1929. The connection between research and teaching is fundamental to the modern hospital; integrated university clinics guarantee the practical training of the

medical profession. The leading North American hospitals of the interwar years were consistently university clinics, such as Vanderbilt University Medical School in Nashville, Tennessee (1925) or New York Hospital – Cornell Medical Center (1932). These teaching hospitals were designed like cities in their own right and contemporary opinion labeled them *citadels of health* or *cathedrals of healing*.

Vertical building, which largely determined hospital design from the mid-20th century, had only been made possible by the electric elevator and steel frame construction.[66] The first (hydraulic) elevators appeared in the 1870s, but the electrification that took place shortly afterwards meant that these could soon climb ten or twelve stories. Steel frame construction, which was developed in Chicago in the early 1880s, led to a huge increase in the potential number of levels in a building. This ongoing process of mechanization and electrification meant that the insides of buildings were soon permeated by a system of pipes, wires, and ducts. The elevator made a major contribution to this fundamental reorganization of buildings and soon provided their core. As a means of transport, elevators play a fundamental role in hospitals and clinics, and the positioning of the shafts is central to the design process.

The rationally designed hospital machine
The rationalization of processes that is driven by such technologies also originated in the USA, where this rationalization was seen as a means of ensuring that buildings functioned economically. But it was only this introduction of efficient logistical systems that enabled the often discussed "hospital machine" to become reality: Until this point, the term *machine à guérir* had largely remained a slogan. The design of every hospital and clinic now began with the preparation of network diagrams. Attention was paid to the functioning of a building as an efficient system and the entire facility was now conceived, literally, as a *healing machine*.

Technologien zur Energieerzeugung sowie jene zur Ver- und Entsorgung durchliefen einen Wandel. Spitalsküchen und -wäschereien wurden nun zentralisiert, effektivere Heiz-, Belüftungs- und Klimatisierungssysteme zogen immer größere, meist unterirdisch angelegte Technikbereiche nach sich. Die Zentralküche und das Kesselhaus, in dem Dampf und Heißwasser aufbereitet werden (zur Sterilisierung sowie zum Kochen und Heizen), sind seither zu gigantischen Maschinenräumen mutiert, auch die notwendigen Kühl- und Lagerräume erreichen industrielle Dimensionen. Damit haben sich Krankenhäuser zu großmaßstäblichen Bauten entwickelt. Auch das Volumen an (Kunststoff-)Abfall stieg exponentiell an, in Spitälern werden Unmengen an medizinischem Müll produziert.⁶⁷ Die notwendigen Anlagen zur Entsorgung evozieren nicht von ungefähr die Anmutung einer Fabrik.

Operationssäle haben im modernen Krankenhaus höchste Relevanz. Der aseptischen (keimfreien) Standards wegen sind sie als geschlossene Systeme angelegt; die anfangs sehr teure Klimatisierung war in der ersten Zeit auf die Operationsräume, Sezierbereiche und Leichenhallen beschränkt. Hatte Ende des 19. Jahrhunderts noch die erforderliche natürliche Belichtung die Lage der Operationssäle im Krankenhaus bestimmt, so rückten sie mit dem Aufkommen von leistungsstarkem künstlichem Licht ins Gebäudeinnere. Da die anfangs weiße Umgebung und das Licht bei den Chirurgen starke Blendung und Kopfschmerzen zur Folge hatte, ging man bald dazu über, Grün (als Komplementärfarbe zu Rot) einzuführen. Dies wurde nicht nur im Operationsbereich rasch zum akzeptierten Standard, sondern generell zum Synonym für Spitalsinterieurs; die Farbe Grün wird seitdem mit der gesamten Institution Krankenhaus bzw. Klinik assoziiert.

Krankenhäuser wurden auch zunehmend wissenszentriert: Diverse Daten der Kranken wurden vor allem von den „Schwestern" vermerkt (die Anrede geht auf Pflegerinnen in konfessionell geprägten Ordensspitälern zurück), die einzelnen Stationen im Haus fungierten

somit als Knoten in einem großen Informationsnetzwerk. Ab den 1950er Jahren wurde der Einsatz von EDV unabdingbar, denn die Archive des Wissens über den Zustand der Patient:innen wuchsen kontinuierlich. Auch bildgebende Technologien entwickelten sich mit der steigenden Relevanz medizinischer Wissenschaft. Die fortschreitende Spezialisierung zog ein entsprechendes Equipment nach sich, die räumlichen und technischen Anforderungen wurden damit immer größer. Um 1950 waren technologiebasierte Diagnosen und Therapien für das moderne Spital unverzichtbar geworden, das gesamte Gebäude wuchs im Maßstab und in seiner Komplexität. Krankenhäuser waren nun mindestens ebenso wissenschaftliche Einrichtungen und nicht mehr allein Orte des Heilens.

Ungeachtet der Größe des Baus bestimmt jedoch das Spitalsbett seit je die Organisation der Pflege. Die im Bett liegenden Kranken sind zentral für die Institution Krankenhaus und den klinischen Unterricht (*bedside teaching*); vom Bett aus präsentieren sich die Körper der Patient:innen dem medizinischen Blick. Zu Beginn des 20. Jahrhunderts wurde das Krankenbett auch zum mobilen Ort der Behandlung: Räder, die durch Lenkrollen bald drehbar waren, ermöglichten das Verschieben der Betten; eigens dimensionierte Aufzüge erlaubten den Transport durch den gesamten Gebäudekomplex. In der rational angelegten Spitalsmaschinerie wird das Bett auch zur Einheit, anhand derer man die Kapazität eines Hauses definiert. Die Anzahl der Betten ist die Determinante für die gesamte Funktion des Spitals: Jeder Krankenhausplan basiert auf dem Bettenmaß, viele Raumtypen sind danach ausgerichtet, Gangbreiten und Aufzüge dahingehend dimensioniert.

Die Umsetzung derart hoher technischer Standards erforderte selbstredend hoch spezialisierte Architekten und Planer. Schon um 1940 zog man für den Planungsprozess evidenzbasierte Diagramme heran; die in den 1960er Jahren schließlich aufgekommene computer-

It was not only transport and communication systems that changed radically in the decades between 1920 and 1960. Technologies for generating energy, supplying media, and removing waste also underwent a transformation. Hospital kitchens and laundries were centralized and more effective heating, ventilation, and air conditioning systems created the need for ever larger plant rooms, which were generally located below ground. The central kitchen and the boiler house, in which steam and hot water were produced (for sterilizing as well as for cooking and heating), have long since become gigantic machine rooms, and the vital cold stores and storage areas have also reached industrial dimensions. The result of all of this is that hospitals have become large-scale structures. The volume of (plastic) refuse has risen exponentially and hospitals produce vast amounts of medical waste.⁶⁷ It is no coincidence that the areas required for managing this garbage create the impression of a factory.

Operating rooms have the upmost importance in the modern hospital. Due to aseptic (sterile) standards they are designed as closed systems; the high cost of the earliest air conditioning systems meant that these were only installed in operating rooms, dissecting areas, and morgues. While the position of the operating rooms in the late 19th-century hospital was still determined by the need for adequate natural lighting, the emergence of high-quality artificial lighting meant that these moved deeper inside buildings. The glare and headaches that affected surgeons due to the combination of the white surroundings and the bright light soon led to the introduction of green (as the complementary color to red). This rapidly became not only the accepted standard in operating areas, but also synonymous with hospital interiors and the color green has been associated with the entire institution of the hospital or clinic ever since.

Hospitals also became increasingly knowledge-based. The wide range of data about the patients that were recorded, principally by the

"sisters" (the form of address goes back to the carers in denominational hospitals run by religious congregations), meant that the individual stations in the building functioned as hubs in a vast information network. From the 1950s onwards, the constant growth of the archive of information about the condition of patients meant that the use of IT became indispensable. The growing importance of medical science also drove the development of imaging technologies. Increasing specialization was accompanied by the appropriate equipment, and spatial and technical requirements expanded accordingly. By 1950, technology-based diagnosis and therapy had become essential for the modern hospital and the entire building grew in both scale and complexity. Hospitals were now just as much scientific institutions as places of healing.

However, regardless of the size of the building it is the hospital bed that has determined the organization of care since the very start. The patients lying in their beds are central for both the hospital as an institution and for clinical education (*bedside teaching*); it is from the bed that patients present their bodies for medical examination. In the early 20th century, the hospital bed also became a mobile place of treatment: Wheels, which could soon be steered in the form of castors, made it possible to relocate beds and specially dimensioned elevators soon enabled them to be transported throughout the entire building. In the rationally designed hospital machine, the bed also becomes the unit that is used to define the capacity of a building. The number of beds is the determinant for the entire functioning of the hospital: Every hospital plan is based on the dimensions of a hospital bed; it determines the layout of many types of space and the sizes of corridors and elevators.

The implementation of such high technical standards naturally required highly specialized architects and planners. Evidence-based diagrams were already being used in the planning process around 1940

gestützte Modellierung von Bewegungsabläufen wurde bald zur Conditio sine qua non der Krankenhaus- und Klinikplanung. Kybernetische Ablaufdiagramme dienen seither zur Optimierung funktioneller Abläufe im Großspital.[68] Eine ganze Industrie der Krankenhausplanung entwickelte sich: Consultants und Fachleute für das Spitalsmanagement, medizinische Berater und Architekten(teams) mit einschlägiger Expertise arbeiteten nun interdisziplinär an der Entwicklung hochkomplexer Spitalsmaschinerien.

Die Krise des modernen Spitals

Angesichts dieser forcierten Ausrichtung an den Kriterien der Effizienz und Rationalität überrascht es nicht, dass der menschliche Faktor und die symbolische Identität eines Krankenhausbaus mehr und mehr ins Hintertreffen gerieten. Schon in den 1960er Jahren wurde die fehlende Humanität monolithischer Spitalsblöcke beklagt, die ingenieurbasierten Lösungen technischer Funktionalität evozierten erste kritische Stimmen. Das Krankenhaus der Nachkriegsmoderne galt als unmenschlich und technokratisch; die Logik der Effizienz privilegierte die enge Expertensicht der Planer, die Perspektive der Patient:innen wurde tendenziell vernachlässigt. Bereits in den 1960ern war die moderne Spitalsbewegung also in die Krise geraten, die Qualitäten der Heilung fanden sich zunehmend in Frage gestellt. Die der Integration diverser Behandlungsformen geschuldete Größenausdehnung der Bauten zeitigte unübersehbar Probleme; im Architekturdiskurs monierte man auch die formalen Mängel medizinisch-klinischer Monolithe. Das moderne Spital schien einen Endpunkt erreicht zu haben, was ästhetische Aspekte anlangt. Seitdem begann man bisherige Krankenhauskonzepte in jeder Hinsicht zu überdenken. Dass dieser Prozess keineswegs als abgeschlossen gilt, zeigt die Tatsache, dass in den letzten 20 Jahren eine Menge an Büchern über humanes Spitalsdesign erschienen ist. Ende 2022 tagten Vertreter:innen führender europäi-

scher Universitätskliniken in Wien, um unter dem Schlagwort *healing architecture* bessere bauliche Maßnahmen für die Zukunft zu diskutieren.[69] Weiterhin besteht die Herausforderung für die Krankenhausplanung also darin, bei aller betriebswirtschaftlichen Effizienz auch den speziellen Bedürfnissen kranker Menschen Rechnung zu tragen.[70]

Das Neue AKH als Bau der Superlative

Das Neue Wiener Allgemeine Krankenhaus (heute Universitätsklinikum AKH Wien) lässt sich als Inbegriff einer modernen *healing machine* betrachten. Als wahrer „Mammutbau" stellt dieser Komplex ein weithin sichtbares Monument für die öffentliche Gesundheit dar. Die beiden Bettentürme prägen das Weichbild von Wien, von umliegenden Aussichtspunkten betrachtet dominieren die dunklen Kuben das urbane Gefüge. Zur Zeit seiner Errichtung ein Bau der Superlative, zählt dieses „Megabuilding" selbst heute noch zu Europas größten Spitälern.

Die Planung dieses Wiener Zentralspitals geht auf die späten 1950er Jahre zurück. Das erste Neubauprojekt, das vom Ende des 19. Jahrhunderts datiert, blieb durch den Ausbruch des Ersten Weltkriegs stecken. Und auch in den Jahren unmittelbar nach 1945 war an ein Großbauvorhaben nicht zu denken — waren doch erst die Bombenschäden zu beheben.[71] Damals bildeten die alte josephinische Anlage und die Neuen Kliniken einen 3.000 Betten umfassenden Spitalskomplex. Die Aufteilung auf mehrere, teils durch städtische Hauptverkehrsstraßen voneinander getrennte Gebäude erschwerte die interdisziplinäre Zusammenarbeit, den Lehrbetrieb und die Administration am Allgemeinen Krankenhaus immens. Nach dem Zweiten Weltkrieg griff man den Gedanken eines Neubaus abermals auf. Ziel war eine Zusammenführung der verstreuten Unikliniken in einem

and the computer-aided modeling of movement patterns that eventually followed in the 1960s soon became the *conditio sine qua non* of hospital and clinic design. Cybernetic flow charts have been used ever since for the optimization of functional processes in large hospitals.[68] An entire industry of hospital planning emerged: consultants and specialists in hospital management, medical advisors, and (teams of) architects with relevant expertise were now working together on the interdisciplinary development of highly-complex hospital machines.

The crisis of the modern hospital

In view of this intensified focus on the criteria of efficiency and rationality it is no surprise that the human factor and the symbolic identity of a hospital were increasingly overlooked. Monolithic hospital blocks were already being denounced for their lack of humanity in the 1960s, and the first critical voices were being raised against engineering-based solutions that were driven by technical functionality. The postwar modern hospital was seen as inhuman and technocratic; its logic of efficiency paid more attention to the narrow expert opinion of the planner while the perspective of the patient was generally ignored. As a result, the modern hospital movement found itself in crisis in the 1960s, with the quality of healing being increasingly called into question. The enormous expansion of the buildings that became necessary due to the integration of various forms of treatment created obvious problems; even the architectural debate featured criticism of the formal deficiencies of these medical-clinical monoliths. The modern hospital appeared to have reached an aesthetic full stop. Ever since this point, we have been reevaluating every aspect of these earlier hospital concepts. And the fact that this process is far from complete is demonstrated by the number of books about humane hospital design that have been published in the past 20 years. At the end of 2022, representatives of

leading European university clinics came together in Vienna at an event entitled *healing architecture* in order to discuss better building measures for the future.[69] The challenge for hospital planners continues to be the need to balance the special requirements of sick people with all the demands of economic efficiency.[70]

The new General Hospital as a building without equal

The new Vienna General Hospital (now University Hospital Vienna) can be seen as the epitome of a modern *healing machine*. A veritable "mammoth structure," the complex is a monument to public health that can be seen from far and wide. The dark cubes of the two ward towers shape the Vienna skyline, dominating the urban fabric from every vantage point in the surrounding area. Unparalleled in scale at the time of its realization, this "megabuilding" remains one of Europe's largest hospitals to this day.

The design of this Viennese central hospital dates back to the late 1950s. The first project for a new building, which was drawn up at the end of the 19th century, was halted by the outbreak of the First World War. And realizing a major project in the years immediately following 1945 was out of the question due to the priority that had to be given to repairing the damage done to the city by bombing raids.[71] Back then, the old Josephine ensemble and the New Clinics combined to form a hospital complex with 3,000 beds. The division of this complex into a number of buildings, some separated by busy urban traffic corridors, severely compromised interdisciplinary cooperation, teaching activities, and the administration of the General Hospital. After the Second World War, however, the idea of a new building was revived. The objective was to unite the scattered university clinics in a single major complex, where the concentration of specialist expertise would generate

einzigen großen Komplex, um durch die Konzentration fachlicher Expertise Synergieeffekte in der Forschung und medizinischen Betreuung zu generieren. Bereits 1955 entschieden die Republik Österreich und die Stadt Wien, die Kosten für die Planung und Ausführung eines neuen Universitätskrankenhauses jeweils zur Hälfte zu übernehmen. Dieser Entschluss bildete die Basis für die Zusammenarbeit der beiden Gebietskörperschaften an diesem Projekt. Die neue Anlage sollte nun nicht mehr in Form von Pavillons, sondern als Zentralbau errichtet werden.

Wurde anfangs eine Situierung des Neuen AKH auf einem Gebiet außerhalb der Stadt erwogen, so fiel die Wahl schließlich auf das vorhandene Areal der alten psychiatrischen Kliniken am Brünnlfeld und der 1904–23 errichteten Neuen Kliniken. Aufgrund der zentralen Lage schien der Bauplatz ideal für die gewünschte Nutzung als Schwerpunktkrankenhaus der Stadt Wien, als überregionales Krankenhaus mit allen Fachdisziplinen, als Universitätsklinikum sowie als Ausbildungs- und Unterrichtskrankenhaus. Langfristig gesehen sollte hier jedenfalls eine geschlossene Universitätsstadt entstehen.[72] Auch die Möglichkeiten der Verkehrserschließung schienen in diesem Teil von Wien-Alsergrund optimal.

Die Logistik des Raumes
Für den Neubau des Allgemeinen Krankenhauses – Universitätskliniken (wie es damals hieß) konstituierte sich 1958 die aus Spitzenvertretern des Bundes und der Stadt Wien zusammengesetzte Arbeitsgemeinschaft ARGE-AKH. Festgelegt wurde die gesamte Neuplanung des AKH, doch sollte anfangs nur eine erste Baustufe im Bereich der alten Kliniken am Brünnlfeld verwirklicht werden. Die vor dem Ersten Weltkrieg errichteten Neuen Kliniken dagegen wurden adaptiert und sollten einstweilen weiter bestehen. Die projektierte Größe erforderte eine primär logistische Perspektive auf die künftigen

Abläufe im Neuen AKH – lässt sich doch Architektur generell als ein „operatives Gefüge" verstehen, das soziale Begegnungen und Arbeitsprozesse regelt. Derart komplexe, hoch technisierte Vorhaben wie Krankenhaus- und Klinikbauten bedürfen in besonderem Maß einer „Logistik des Raumes".[73] Ein bis dahin in dieser Größenordnung weltweit noch nie dagewesenes Vorhaben wie der Neubau des AKH in Wien erforderte eine umfassende Organisationsstruktur. Daher beauftragte man den Tübinger Arzt und Funktionsplaner Hans-Ulrich Riethmüller 1959 damit, ein Raum- und Funktionsprogramm zu erstellen, für das er sämtliche Arbeitsprozesse in den Blick nahm und davon ausgehend das Abteilungssystem etablierte.[74] Diese „zeitbasierte" Entwurfstheorie, die sich an funktionalen Abläufen und Choreografien der Bewegung orientiert, war für die Architektur-Avantgarde des 20. Jahrhunderts bestimmend. Insbesondere mit dem Beginn der Moderne wird Architektur eine Agentin der Mobilisierung; in einer der Standardgeschichten moderner Baukunst, Sigfried Giedions *Space, Time and Architecture* (1941),[75] ist dieser Aspekt raumzeitlicher Bewegung leitendes Motiv.

Aus den Preisträgern des 1960 ausgelobten internationalen Architekturwettbewerbs – damals der größte in Europa – wurde eine neunköpfige Arbeitsgemeinschaft gebildet, an die der Auftrag zur Planung des Neuen AKH erging.[76] Der erste Entwurf von 1964 sah einen Flachkörper mit aufgesetzter Bettenhausscheibe vor, in der Ausführungsplanung des Jahres 1966 wurde diese jedoch in zwei Bettenhäuser separiert. Die Errichtung der Gesamtanlage sollte in vier Bauabschnitten erfolgen, wobei die letzte und längste von 1971–82 den Bau des Hauptgebäudes (bestehend aus dem Flachbau mit den beiden Bettenhäusern und einer Reihe ausgegliederter Gebäude) umfasste, während der Planung „Kern der Anlage" genannt.[77] Es bedurfte einer ganzen Armee an Planungsmanagern, Baustatikern, Logistikfachleuten, Konstruktionsphysikern und medizinisch-technischen Beratern,

synergies in the areas of both research and medical care. In 1955, the Austrian Government and Vienna City Council agreed to equally share the costs of the design and execution of a new university hospital. This decision formed the basis for the cooperation between the two administrative bodies on the project. The new complex should be built in the form of a centralized structure rather than pavilions.

While initial consideration was given to locating the new general hospital – the Neues AKH – outside the city, it was eventually decided to use the area occupied by the former psychiatric clinics on Brünnlfeld and the New Clinics, which had been built between 1904 and 1923. This central location seemed ideal for the site of Vienna City Council's main hospital, which is also a trans-regional facility that offers all medical specialties, a university clinic, and a teaching and training hospital. The long-term vision was to transform the site into a self-contained university city.[72] And the possibilities offered by the transport infrastructure in this part of Vienna-Alsergrund also appeared to be optimal.

Spatial logistics
In 1958, the planned construction of the General Hospital – University Clinics (as it was then called) led to the creation of the ARGE-AKH consortium, which consisted of leading representatives of the Federal Government and Vienna City Council. But although it had been decided to build a completely new general hospital, the initial plan was to realize a first phase that would replace the former clinics on Brünnlfeld. Those New Clinics that dated from before the First World War were to be retained for the present and were adapted accordingly. The planned dimensions of the new hospital placed the logistical planning of the processes in the Neues AKH at the heart of the project – in line with the understanding of architecture as an "operational framework" that manages social interactions and working processes.

Complex, highly-technical undertakings such as hospital and clinic buildings require a special degree of "spatial logistics."[73] A project like the Neues AKH, with its globally unprecedented scale, demanded a comprehensive organizational structure. Hence, the Tubingen-based doctor and functional planner Hans-Ulrich Riethmüller was commissioned in 1959 to draw up a spatial and functional program, which he produced by examining all the working processes of the facility as a means of establishing a system of departments.[74] This "time-based" design theory, which focuses on functional processes and choreographies of movement, was decisive for the 20th-century architectural avant-garde. The beginning of the modern era cemented the role of architecture as an agent of mobilization; this notion of space- and time-based movement is a leading motif in one of the standard works on modern architecture, Sigfried Giedion's *Space, Time and Architecture* (1941).[75]

The winners of the international architectural competition of 1960 – Europe's largest to date – were brought together in a ninemember consortium, which was commissioned to plan the Neues AKH.[76] Presented in 1964, the first design envisaged a low volume, upon which a stack of wards was placed, but these were subsequently divided into two ward blocks in the execution project of 1966. The overall complex was to be built in four phases, the last and longest of which would be the realization of the main building or, as it became known during construction, the "core of the complex" (the low volume, the two ward blocks, and a series of separated structures) between 1971 and 1982.[77] An entire army of design managers, structural engineers, logistics experts, building physicists, and medical-technical consultants was required in order to execute the building project, which was easily the largest of the Second Republic. A specially developed "planning and building process" enabled design and construction to take place simultaneously: The design was used as the basis of a shell & core

um dieses mit Abstand größte Hochbauprojekt der Zweiten Republik durchzuführen. Ein eigens entwickeltes „Planungsbauverfahren" erlaubte ein simultanes Planen und Konstruieren: Vom Entwurf ausgehend wurde ein roher Errichtungsplan erstellt, der dann ein mehrjähriges Genehmigungsverfahren durchlief; im nächsten Schritt erfolgten Entwurf und Planung der Räume.[78] Eine modulare Struktur und ein Konstruktionsraster von 4,5 Metern (basierend auf den Maßen eines Krankenbetts) bildeten die Parameter dieses Prozesses; durch das Erfordernis des *bedside teaching* sind die Krankenzimmer in Unikliniken generell etwas größer dimensioniert. Nicht von ungefähr kam der medizinischen Fakultät in dieser Phase der Planung eine Sonderrolle zu. Die schiere Größe des Projekts war eine logistische Herausforderung sondergleichen, weltweit hatte man bis dahin noch nie ein Spital in diesen Dimensionen konzipiert.

Der AKH-Skandal
Doch nicht nur das AKH als „Megabuilding" stellt ein Objekt der Superlative dar. Auch der damit verbundene Bauskandal ging als bislang größter der Zweiten Republik in die Geschichte ein. Die sich zunehmend komplizierter gestaltende Planung und Überwachung öffnete der Korruption Tür und Tor. Bereits 1975 wurde klar, dass es keine Finanzaufsicht für die Aktivitäten im Zuge der Errichtung gab, was die Gründung der AKH Wien Planungs- und Errichtungs-Aktiengesellschaft (AKPE) zur Folge hatte, die den effizienten Ablauf des Konstruktionsprozesses sicherstellen sollte. Nichtsdestotrotz folgte wenig später das böse Erwachen, als herauskam, dass unzählige involvierte Interessenvertreter den Baufortgang (mit Absicht oder nicht) gebremst oder blockiert hatten.[79] Für die Jahre 1980/81 wurde daher ein Baustopp verhängt; das AKH galt als Synonym für Korruption und dominierte die damalige Medienberichterstattung.

Der Investigativjournalist Alfred Worm hatte den „AKH-Skandal"

aufgedeckt, eine Mischung aus Malversationen und explodierenden Kosten.[80] Der nächste Skandal kam auf, als sich herausstellte, dass auch die AKPE enorme Summen unterschlagen und Vetternwirtschaft mit ausgewählten Bauunternehmen betrieben hatte. Die Errichtungskosten betrugen am Ende das Mehrfache des ursprünglich veranschlagten Budgets. Zwar fassten der Direktor der AKPE und einige seiner Kollegen für ihre Mitschuld lange Gefängnisstrafen aus, doch das öffentliche Vertrauen in die Verantwortlichen für den Bau erlitt dennoch erheblichen Schaden.

Kritik am „Monsterkrankenhaus"
Die Kritik am Neubau des Allgemeinen Krankenhauses hat ihre eigene Geschichte, besonders in einem spezialisierten Architekturdiskurs wurde das Vorhaben kontrovers diskutiert. Schon in den 1960ern hatte in der progressiven Wiener Architekturszene eine prononcierte Funktionalismus-Kritik eingesetzt – man denke an die utopischen Projekte damaliger Architekten- und Künstlergruppen wie Haus-Rucker-Co oder die von Friedensreich Hundertwasser propagierte Begrünung von Bauten, die damals noch sehr befremdlich erschien. Besonders in den Jahren zwischen 1968 und 1978 folgte eine generelle Ernüchterung auf die Euphorie, was den Glauben an Fortschritt, Technologie und das Wirtschaftswachstum betrifft. Mit der ersten bemannten Mondlandung im Jahr 1969 war ein Schritt in das Weltall getan; bald darauf warnte der Club of Rome vor Ressourcenverschwendung und präsentierte 1972 seinen Report über *Die Grenzen des Wachstums*. Die „Ölpreisschocks" der Jahre 1973 und 1979/80 lösten in Industrieländern starke Rezessionen aus; 1978 fand in Österreich eine Volksabstimmung über die Inbetriebnahme des bereits fertiggestellten Kernkraftwerks Zwentendorf statt, eine breite Anti-Atomkraft-Bewegung war nicht mehr bereit, die Risiken der Modernisierung zu tragen.[81]

execution plan, which was then subject to an approvals process that lasted several years; the next step was the design and planning of the individual spaces.[78] A modular structure and a building grid of 4.5 meters (that was based on the dimensions of a hospital bed) formed the parameters of this process; the requirements of *bedside teaching* mean that patients' rooms in university clinics tend to be somewhat larger. It is no coincidence that the Medical Faculty had a special role in this phase of the planning. The sheer size of the project – nowhere in the world had a hospital of this size ever been planned – represented an unprecedented logistical challenge.

The AKH scandal
But the General Hospital – the AKH, as it is known by all Viennese – was not only without equal as a "megabuilding." The associated building scandal also went down in history as the largest of the Second Republic to date. Increasingly complicated planning and monitoring processes opened the door to corruption. The recognition that there was a lack of financial control of the building work led, in 1975, to the establishment of the AKH Wien Planungs- und Errichtungs-Aktiengesellschaft (AKPE), whose role would be to ensure the efficiency of the construction process. However, this was soon followed by a rude awakening as it became clear that many of the involved stakeholders had (intentionally or otherwise) slowed down or even blocked the progress of construction.[79] This led to the stoppage of building work in 1980/81; the AKH became a synonym for corruption and dominated the headlines of the day.

The investigative journalist Alfred Worm had uncovered the "AKH scandal," a combination of corrupt behavior and exploding costs.[80] The next scandal arose when it became clear that the AKPE had also misappropriated huge sums and engaged in cronyism with selected construction companies. The final building costs exceeded the

originally proposed budget many times over. And while the Director of the AKPE and some of his colleagues were given long prison terms for complicity, public trust in those responsible for the building had been seriously damaged.

Criticism of the "monster hospital"
The criticism of the new building of the General Hospital has a history of its own, with the project being the subject of a particularly contentious specialist architectural debate. The critique of functionalism had already become a distinct feature of the progressive architecture scene of 1960's Vienna – as exemplified by the utopian projects of contemporary groups of architects or artists such as Haus-Rucker-Co or the greening of buildings promoted by Friedensreich Hundertwasser, which still seemed very strange at the time. The years between 1968 and 1978 in particular witnessed a general disillusionment with the previous euphoria regarding progress, technology, and economic growth. The first manned landing on the Moon in 1969 had been one large leap in space but this was soon followed by the warnings about our waste of resources delivered by the Club of Rome in 1972 in its report *The Limits to Growth*. The "oil price shocks" of 1973 and 1979/80 led to deep recessions in industrialized countries; in 1978, a referendum held in Austria about the startup of the already completed nuclear power plant in Zwentendorf showed that a broad anti-nuclear power movement was no longer willing to bear the risks of modernization.[81]

Against this background, it is no surprise that the AKH was also subject to massive criticism in the mid-1970s and that many people no longer regarded it as appropriate. Three of the four building phases had already been completed and the central complex (the low volume with the two ward blocks) was under construction. Rethinking the overall project in this phase had become impossible, it had passed the financial

Vor diesem Hintergrund überrascht es nicht, dass Mitte der 1970er Jahre auch das AKH massiver Kritik ausgesetzt war und es vielen als nicht mehr adäquat galt. Drei der vier Errichtungsphasen waren damals schon abgeschlossen, der zentrale Komplex (der Flachbau mit den zwei Bettentürmen) befand sich noch mitten im Bau. Das Gesamtprojekt in dieser Phase nochmals zu überdenken, war unmöglich geworden, finanziell gab es kein Zurück, und auch architekturmäßig ließ sich nicht mehr viel modifizieren. Für Architekten und Planer war dies generell eine Zeit der technologischen Umbrüche: Computer und CAD-Programme für den Entwurf standen damals noch nicht zur Verfügung, während die Entwicklung medizinisch-technischer Geräte rasend schnell vonstattenging. Man suchte daher eine effiziente Lösung für das Gesamtvorhaben und beauftragte 1982 die VAMED (Voestalpine Medizintechnik GmbH) damit, die Errichtung zu beaufsichtigen und eine transparente organisatorische und finanzielle Abwicklung zu garantieren.

Die Fertigstellung des Neuen AKH geschah also in einer Zeit, in der der Modernismus bereits mit wachsender Kritik seitens der (selbsternannten) Postmodernisten konfrontiert war. Wie andere Megabauten, die zwischen den späten 1950er und den 1970er Jahren errichtet worden waren, galt das Wiener AKH vielen als Ikone eines ideologisch fehlgeleiteten Modernismus. Effizienzsteigerung, Kostenreduktion und Funktionalität standen in dieser Zeit an oberster Stelle, nicht die menschlichen Bedürfnisse nach Tageslicht und natürlicher Belüftung.[82] Noch im Jahr 1981 machten sich Spitalsfachleute für den Abbruch des bereits fertiggestellten Rohbaus stark und plädierten für eine neue Anlage im Pavillonstil: „Monsterkrankenhäuser" stünden einer humanen Behandlung entgegen, man prophezeite ein „Abgleiten in die Mechanik der Apparatemedizin" und fragte sich, ob „die Dienstnehmer die Vollklimatisierung und fehlende Kommunikation überhaupt verkraften". Angesichts der befürchteten „Krisenanfälligkeit der komplizierten Gesamtanlage" wurden ernsthafte Zweifel geäußert, dieses überdimensionierte Spital jemals betreiben zu können.[83]

Die Qualität von „big buildings"
Und doch existiert dieser Bau nun schon seit vielen Jahrzehnten, seine schiere Größe hat wohl seine Demolierung verhindert. Das AKH Wien ließe sich – im positiven Sinn – auch als ein Monument für die Ideale und Ziele der Zeit seiner Planung betrachten, zeugt es doch vom letzten Versuch des Staates, seinen Bürger:innen Wohlfahrt qua Architektur zukommen zu lassen. Das großmaßstäbliche Projekt wurde als Lösung aller gesundheitlichen (und damit verbundenen technischen) Probleme gesehen. Mit seiner Logik der Modernisierung und Zentralisierung steht es gleichsam am Endpunkt einer kritischen Auseinandersetzung mit Gesellschaft und kann als ein klassisches Sozialprojekt der Nachkriegsmoderne gelten.[84]

Als eine „Stadt in der Stadt" entspricht das Neue AKH auch jenem Typus von Architektur, den Rem Koolhaas 1994 in seiner „Theorie der Bigness" skizzierte:[85] Wenngleich als klobig und schwerfällig diskreditiert, sei Bigness ultimative Architektur, denn die erforderliche Komplexität mobilisiere die gesamte Intelligenz des Konstruierens. Ein *big building*, das eine bestimmte kritische Masse erreicht, zeichnet sich nicht durch die Geste eines einzelnen Architekten aus. Ja, es wäre verfehlt, von „Baukunst" zu sprechen, denn die Kriterien guter Komposition und Proportion greifen hier nicht. Vielmehr fungieren Aufzugsschächte als strukturierende Elemente, die mechanische Verbindungen innerhalb des Gebäudes etablieren. Das Innere und das Äußere solcher Bauten sind voneinander separiert, die Fassade lässt nicht mehr erahnen, was sich dahinter abspielt. Allein durch ihre Größe, so Koolhaas weiter, sind *big buildings* jenseits von Gut und Böse zu sehen; sie fügen sich nicht in den städtebaulichen Kontext, sondern sind Entitäten für sich.

---

point of no return, and there was also little that could still be modified in architectural terms. For architects and planners, this was generally a period of technical breakthroughs: Computers and CAD design programs were still not available, but medical-technical equipment was developing at a startling pace. This led to the search for an efficient solution for the overall project that ended in 1982 with the commissioning of VAMED (Voestalpine Medizintechnik GmbH) to monitor the construction and ensure the transparency of the organizational and financial implementation.

Hence, the Neues AKH was completed at a time in which Modernism was already being confronted by growing criticism from (self-proclaimed) postmodernists. Like other megabuildings that were realized between the late 1950s and the 1970s, Vienna's AKH was seen by many as an icon of an ideologically misguided Modernism. This was a period in which priority had been given to increased efficiency, reduced costs, and functionality rather than the human need for daylight and natural ventilation.[82] As early as 1981, hospital experts argued loudly for the demolition of the already completed shell & core structure and for its replacement by a new complex designed in the pavilion style: "Monster hospitals" stood in the way of humane treatment and experts predicted a "slide towards the machine of high-tech medicine" and asked whether "the employees will even be able to put up with the ubiquitous air conditioning and lack of communication." In view of the feared "susceptibility of the complicated overall complex to a crisis," serious doubts were expressed as to whether it would ever be possible to operate this over-dimensioned hospital.[83]

The quality of "big buildings"
And yet this building is still standing after many decades, possibly because its very size makes it difficult to demolish. Thinking positively, University Hospital Vienna can also be seen as a monument to the ideals and aims of the period in which it was planned and as an embodiment of the last attempt of the state to provide welfare combined with architecture. The large-scale project was regarded as the solution to all medical (and related technical) problems. With its logic of modernization and centralization it feels like the final act of a critical analysis of society and can be regarded as a classic social project of the postwar modern era.[84]

As a "city within the city," the Neues AKH also conforms to the architectural typology outlined by Rem Koolhaas in 1994 in his "Theory of Bigness":[85] Even if it is attacked as clumsy and cumbersome, bigness is the ultimate architecture because it is accompanied by a complexity that mobilizes the entire intelligence of the building process. A *big building* that achieves a certain critical mass is not characterized by the gesture of any single architect. Indeed, it would be wrong to speak of architecture as "the art of building," because the criteria of good composition and proportion do not apply. Elevator shafts play a much more important role as structuring elements that establish mechanical connections within a building. The interior and exterior of such a building are separate issues; the facade no longer tells us what is happening behind it. Koolhaas argued that size alone puts *big buildings* beyond discussions of good or evil; rather than merging into the urban context they are entities in themselves.

When the megastructure of the Neues AKH was completed after a total of 30 years on site, the modernist era was long over. The start of occupation of the main building in 1989 was followed by the successive startups of the individual clinics and the official opening of the complex in 1994. Despite the massive criticism during its construction, the building is widely accepted today and regarded as a model of success. And University Hospital Vienna also enjoys an international reputation as a model of medical-technical expertise. The internal logistics

Als nach 30 Jahren Gesamtbauzeit die Megastruktur des AKH realisiert worden war, war die modernistische Ära schon lange vorüber. Nach Beginn der Besiedelung des Hauptgebäudes 1989 erfolgte sukzessive die Inbetriebnahme der einzelnen Kliniken, 1994 fand schließlich die offizielle Eröffnung des Neuen AKH statt. Ungeachtet der massiven Kritik während der Errichtung erfreut sich der Bau bis heute hoher Akzeptanz und wird als Erfolgsmodell betrachtet. Auch international gilt das Universitätsklinikum AKH Wien als Parade-beispiel für medizinisch-technische Kompetenz. Die Logistik im Haus zeugt von der Verdichtung möglichst vieler Funktionen auf wenig Raum, insbesondere in den diversen Transport- und Versorgungs-systemen zeigt sich die gern zitierte Maschinenanalogie. Architektur dieser Art steuert Prozesse, sie lenkt den Fluss von Materialien und Information – und ist somit unabdingbar für den Workflow des Krankenhaus- und Klinikbetriebs. Der Großteil dieser inneren Abläufe, die logistische Dimension des AKH ist allerdings verborgen – anders als im zur gleichen Zeit entstandenen Universitätsklinikum Aachen (1971–85), dessen Äußeres wie eine elegante Ölraffinerie wirkt und das als (mittlerweile denkmalgeschütztes) Beispiel einer „technischen Moderne" gilt. Wie das Pariser Centre Pompidou (1971–77) fungiert das Aachener Uniklinikum als selbstreferenzielle Maschine. Hightech wird als Inbild von Kompetenz und Perfektion vorgeführt: Die Gebäu-detechnik ist ebenso sichtbar wie die Struktur des Stahlbetonskeletts, die Versorgungsmedien verlaufen teils unverkleidet entlang der Decken.[86]

Einblick in die Blackbox AKH
Im Universitätsklinikum AKH Wien jedoch bleibt das, was die „Maschi-ne" am Laufen hält, größtenteils unsichtbar. Vor allem die unterirdisch gelegene Technikzentrale dürfen nur wenige Befugte betreten. Wenn Stefan Oláh diese Anlagen in seinen Fotografien sichtbar macht, öffnet er gleichsam die Blackbox des AKH. Diese der Technikgeschichte entlehnte Metapher steht für ein Objekt, dessen innere Abläufe (weitgehend) unbekannt sind. Von Interesse ist nur jene Funktionali-tät, die diese Blackbox nach außen hin garantiert, ihr Output gewisser-maßen. Einige der Fotoaufnahmen gewähren uns Einsicht in diese verborgenen Teile: Wir sehen Wasserzisternen, die auf den ersten Blick wie unterirdische Swimmingpools wirken, jedoch als Reservoir für Trink-, Brauch- und Löschwasser dienen. Zahllose Röhren zur Versor-gung mit Wasser, Wärme und Luft durchziehen die Gebäudetechnik im Untergeschoß. In den eingehausten, konstant auf 50 Grad Celsius beheizten Motorenraum für die Notstromaggregate blicken wir ebenso wie in die Kältezentrale. Hunderte Kartons mit Hygieneartikeln stapeln sich auf Paletten in eigenen Lagern; eine Batterie frisch bezogener Betten steht jederzeit bereit, ebenso wie Rollcontainer, voll mit Wäsche-transportsäcken, gereinigten Kitteln und Laken. Auch die im Dunkeln tätigen beiden „Robots", die so zügig wie zackig Medikamente sortieren, kommen dadurch ans Licht. Desgleichen Besonderheiten wie die Anlagen zur Bettensterilisation, die an überdimensionierte Spül-maschinen erinnern. Auch in der Küche des Hauses wirkt alles gigantisch: Die unterirdische Zufahrt zur Lebensmittelanlieferung mutet wie ein Industriebereich an, und dementsprechend sind auch die Kühlräume dimensioniert. Schöpflöffel haben den Durchmesser von Schüsseln, und die Kochkessel fassen so viel, dass sie nur durch einen Kippmechanismus entleert werden können.

Aufgrund der Größe des Baus sind mechanische Transport-systeme unerlässlich: Neben den öffentlichen Personenaufzügen und den Förderbändern im Foyer durchziehen im Verborgenen drei weitere Anlagen das Haus: die automatische Transportanlage für Speisen, Geschirr und Wäsche, die Kleinbehältertransportanlage für Laborpro-ben und Präparate, Blutkonserven, Ersatzteile und Kleingeräte sowie einige voneinander unabhängige Rohrpostsysteme zur dringlichen

---

exemplify the concentration of a maximum number of functions in a minimum space, and the widely quoted machine analogy is clearly reflected in the various transport and supply systems. This sort of architecture manages processes and steers the flow of material and information, which makes it indispensable for the workflow of the hospital and clinic operations. However, most of these internal processes, the logistical dimension of University Hospital Vienna, are hidden – unlike those of University Hospital Aachen (1971–85), which was built at the same time, resembles an elegant oil refinery, is regarded as an example of "technical modernism," and is now even a listed building. Like the Centre Pompidou in Paris (1971–77), University Hospital Aachen functions as a self-referential machine. High-tech architecture is presented as the epitome of competence and perfection: The building technology is just as visible as the reinforced concrete structural frame, while supply lines – some exposed – run across the ceilings.[86]

An insight into the black box of University Hospital Vienna
In comparison, the things that keep the "machine" of University Hospital Vienna running are generally invisible. And very few people are permitted to enter the plant rooms in the basement. When Stefan Oláh visualizes these areas in his photographs, it is as if he is opening the black box of the University Hospital Vienna. This metaphor, which is borrowed from the history of technology, describes an object whose internal processes are (largely) unknown. We are only interested in the external functionality guaranteed by this object – in, as it were, its output. Some of the photographs offer us a glimpse of these hidden parts: We see water tanks that, at first glance, look like underground swimming pools but are actually reservoirs for drinking, process, and extinguishing water. Countless pipes carrying water, heat, and air pass through these underground plant rooms. We see into the machine rooms that contain the emergency generators, which are constantly heated to 50 degrees Celsius, and the refrigeration equipment. Hundreds of boxes containing sanitary products are piled on palettes in dedicated storerooms; a battery of freshly made beds is ready for action at any time, as are trolleys filled with laundry bags and freshly washed surgical gowns and bed sheets. And light is also shed on the two robots that work in the dark, smartly and swiftly sorting medicines, or special features such as the bed sterilization stations that resemble oversized dishwashers. Everything appears equally gigantic in the hospital kitchen: The underground entrance where the food is delivered has an industrial quality and the same applies to the dimensioning of the cold stores. The ladles are the size of dishes and the cooking pots contain so much food that they can only be emptied with the help of a tilting mechanism.

The size of the building means that mechanical transportation systems are indispensable: Alongside the public passenger lifts and travelators in the foyer, three further hidden conveying systems traverse the building: the automatic transport system for food, dishes, and laundry, the system for transporting small containers for laboratory specimens and compounds, blood products, small pieces of equipment, and replacement parts, and a series of independent pneumatic postal systems for the urgent delivery of samples. While the large containers only move orthogonally, the smaller vehicles mounted on rollers change their direction all the time. Centrally controlled by an IT system, these containers follow circular routes that take in every functional area (the network for transporting small containers has around 140 stations and a total length of 12 kilometers). The stream of images in this book reproduces the simultaneity of these widely different processes in University Hospital Vienna. Taken as a whole, these supply channels represent a highly complex undertaking that interacts with the architecture. In a certain way, the various transport systems form the

Übermittlung von Proben. Während sich die größeren Container nur in der Waag- und Senkrechten bewegen, ändern die kleinen, auf Reitern montierten Vehikel ihre Ausrichtung permanent. Die vom zentralen IT-System gesteuerten Behältnisse bewegen sich zirkulären Mustern entlang zu allen funktionellen Bereichen (das Streckennetz der Kleinbehältertransportanlage etwa ist 12 Kilometer lang und verbindet an die 140 Stationen). Diese Gleichzeitigkeit der unterschiedlichsten Abläufe im Universitätsklinikum AKH Wien findet sich durch den Bilderfluss hier im Buch simuliert. In Summe stellen diese Versorgungskanäle ein höchst komplexes Unterfangen dar, das mit der Architektur interagiert. Die diversen Transportsysteme bilden gewissermaßen die Blutgefäße des Hauses; medizinische Spitzenleistungen verdanken sich nicht zuletzt auch einer effizienten Logistik wie dieser.

Die Mängel des Megabaus
Ungeachtet dessen weist das AKH doch gewisse Defizite auf; die räumliche Qualität der Architektur bleibt hinter der funktionellen zurück. Die enorme Tiefe des Baus erfordert eine Unzahl an Gängen, die Zugangswege zu den inneren Bereichen nehmen beinahe die Hälfte der Gesamtfläche ein. Dadurch, dass das Gebäude über keine Innenhöfe verfügt, haben über 90 Prozent der Räumlichkeiten des AKH keine Fenster. Nur die Krankenzimmer der Bettentürme sowie ständig besetzte Serviceräume sind zum Tageslicht hin orientiert, und auch die Mall im Bereich des Haupteingangs ist als ein atmosphärisch angenehmer Raum gestaltet. In der im Haus untergebrachten Universitätsbibliothek der MedUni Wien dagegen zeigen sich deutlich die Mängel, die Lesesäle weisen kein einziges Fenster auf. Für das im Haus beschäftigte Personal birgt die Arbeit in den künstlich beleuchteten Untersuchungszimmern und Labors auf Dauer gesundheitliche Risiken; die Aufenthaltszeit der Patient:innen dagegen ist mittlerweile ohnehin auf ein Minimum reduziert. Nach wie vor gilt die bestmögliche

Versorgung als oberstes Ziel; ein „Erholungsheim" kann und soll ein hoch spezialisiertes Uniklinikum nicht sein (um einen an der Planung beteiligten Architekten zu zitieren).[87] Angesichts der Größe und Komplexität der räumlichen Struktur ist ein klares Informationsdesign unabdingbar; ohne das Leitsystem aus Farbcodes und Lettern wäre die Orientierung in den labyrinthischen Gängen kaum möglich. Manche Zonen erinnern an klassische Transiträume wie Flughäfen, Bahnhöfe, Einkaufszentren („Nicht-Orte" nannte der Anthropologe Marc Augé diese Bereiche ohne besondere Identität). Unweigerlich sind die Hinweistafeln stellenweise zu einem Schilderwald verdichtet, von dem Pfeile in alle Richtungen weisen. Und manche zusätzliche Ziffern- und Buchstabenkombination auf den Türen dient wohl nur der internen Identifizierung.

Ist die Größe des AKH Wien in mancher Hinsicht problematisch, so stellt sie doch einen enormen Vorteil für ein Universitätsklinikum dar. Die hohe Zahl stationär wie ambulant behandelter Kranker bietet eine Kumulation unterschiedlichster Fälle für Studienzwecke und somit optimale Bedingungen für die klinische Forschung. Aktuell werden gut 2.000 Patient:innen stationär versorgt, und rund 9.000 Mitarbeiter:innen sind in den diversen Bereichen des Universitätsklinikums AKH tätig. Somit befinden sich an die 11.000 Personen täglich im Haus. Zusätzlich wird das Zentralspital von rund 3.000 ambulant Behandelten pro Tag frequentiert. Angesichts der geschilderten Dimensionen überrascht es nicht, dass der Energiebedarf des AKH Wien jenem einer Kleinstadt entspricht.

Derzeit ist es schwierig zu sagen, wann es sein Limit erreicht haben wird; bis jetzt funktioniert im Wesentlichen alles bestens. Der Konstruktionsraster, auf dem seine Architektur basiert, erlaubt rasch und unkompliziert räumliche Modifikationen, die laufend notwendig sind. Die hauseigenen Lager halten alle Elemente dieses Modulsystems ständig bereit. Dass sich die Medizintechnik wesentlich schneller

---

arteries of the building and the excellent medical care delivered by the hospital also owes much to this efficient logistical infrastructure.

The defects of the megabuilding
Regardless of all this, University Hospital Vienna also exhibits certain defects; the spatial qualities of the architecture fail to match its functional qualities. The enormous depth of the building requires so many corridors that these access routes account for almost half of its total area. As the building has no internal courtyards, more than 90 percent of the rooms have no windows. Only the patient rooms in the ward blocks and permanently occupied service rooms are oriented towards daylight, while the entrance mall is also designed to offer an agreeable atmosphere. Conversely, the lack of a single window in the reading rooms of the university library of MedUni Vienna, which is also located in the building, provides clear evidence of its deficits. Long periods of working in artificially illuminated consulting rooms and laboratories represent a risk to the health of the building's staff. In contrast with this, the length of time that patients stay in the hospital has already been reduced to a minimum. The primary objective of the facility is to provide optimum treatment; a highly-specialized university hospital cannot and should not be what one of the architects who worked on the design called a "rest home."[87] The size and complexity of the spatial structure means that the information systems must be clearly designed; without the color codes and letters of the guidance system, it would almost be impossible to orient oneself in the labyrinth of corridors. Some zones recall classic transit spaces such as airports, stations, and shopping centers (places without a particular identity that the anthropologist Marc Augé has described as "non-places"). Inevitably, these information panels occasionally cluster together and form a forest of signs, from which arrows point in every direction. And some of the additional combinations of numbers and letters that

are found on doors can only possibly serve as a form of internal identification.

Even if the size of University Hospital Vienna has certain negative consequences, this brings huge advantages in its role as a university clinic. The large numbers of both inpatients and outpatients offer an accumulation of widely differing cases that can be used for the purposes of study and, hence, create optimal conditions for clinical research. Over 2,000 inpatients are currently cared for and around 9,000 employees are active in the various departments of University Hospital Vienna. In other words, 11,000 people are in the building every day. In addition to this, around 3,000 outpatients are treated daily. In the light of such numbers it is no surprise that the energy requirements of University Hospital Vienna are similar to those of a small city.

It is currently difficult to say when the complex will reach its limits; so far, most things continue to work very well. The structural grid underlying the architecture allows the regularly required spatial modifications to be carried out rapidly and without complication. All the elements of this modular system are permanently available in the building's own store. The fact that the rate of development of medical technology far outstrips the speed with which we can build has posed a general challenge to hospital and clinic designers for decades.

A permanent state of change
Ever more rapid functional change has created a situation in which today's hospital and clinic complexes are permanent building sites – they are often being demolished, converted, expanded, and newly built simultaneously. Change is, essentially, a permanent condition. This photographic documentation of the buildings of University Hospital Vienna, which Stefan Oláh produced over almost three years, illustrates this sense of rapid transformation: The former First Medical Clinic (part of the New Clinics), which was still in place in 2020, now only exists as

entwickelt, als gebaut werden kann, stellt generell seit Jahrzehnten die größte Herausforderung bei der Planung von Spitälern und Kliniken dar.

Veränderung als Dauerzustand
Der immer raschere Funktionswandel hat dazu geführt, dass Krankenhaus- und Klinikareale heute permanente Baustellen sind – meist wird gleichzeitig abgerissen, umgebaut, erweitert, neu errichtet. Die ständige Veränderung stellt im Grunde den Dauerzustand dar. Stefan Oláhs sich über knapp drei Jahre erstreckende fotografische Dokumentation der Gebäudeteile des Universitätsklinikums AKH Wien führt diesen raschen Wandel vor Augen: Die 2020 noch bestehende ehemalige I. Medizinische Klinik (ein Teil der Neuen Kliniken) existiert mittlerweile nur noch als bildliches Motiv, und auch das einstige Personalwohnhaus ("Schwesternheim") – zur Zeit seiner Errichtung zentrales Element der Krankenhausplanung – wurde kürzlich abgerissen. Die große Baugrube in unmittelbarer Nähe zum Spitalsareal, inzwischen MedUni Campus AKH genannt, weist dagegen bereits auf die Errichtung des neuen MedUni Campus Mariannengasse voraus. Die Bildmotive im Buch bilden somit einen zeitlichen Schnitt, sie zeigen die besonders im 9. Wiener Gemeindebezirk verdichtete medizinische Geschichte.

Die Wiener Universitätsmedizin im 21. Jahrhundert

Vom späten 18. bis zum frühen 20. Jahrhundert fungierte die Wiener medizinische Fakultät als Schrittmacher der globalen Verbreitung wissenschaftsbasierter Medizin. Nicht von ungefähr sprach man von einer eigenen Wiener Schule. Vor allem in den Jahren zwischen 1900 und dem Beginn des Ersten Weltkriegs stellte die Wiener Fakultät eine Institution von Weltruf dar. Das überaus dichte Netz an medizinischen Einrichtungen und akademischen Institutionen im „Medizinerviertel" förderte nicht nur die Zusammenarbeit unter den Ärzten, sondern generell jene zwischen Naturwissenschaft und Medizin. Vier Nobelpreise wurden in den ersten Jahrzehnten des 20. Jahrhunderts an in Wien tätige Wissenschaftler verliehen,[88] eine Reihe weiterer Mediziner waren dafür nominiert.[89] Noch um 1930 zählte die Wiener Fakultät mit gut 300 Hochschullehrern neben jener in Berlin zu den größten des deutschsprachigen Raums. In Wien waren die medizinischen Fächer jedoch in stärkerem Maße spezialisiert; diese schon im frühen 19. Jahrhundert einsetzende Fächergliederung zeugt von der größeren Modernität der Wiener Unikliniken. Diese neueren Fächer waren großteils die Domäne jüdischer Wissenschaftler, dementsprechend schwer wogen die Folgen der erzwungenen Entlassungen nach dem „Anschluss" an das Deutsche Reich. Aus rassistischen oder politischen Gründen wurde der Lehrkörper 1938 um mehr als die Hälfte dezimiert, die besten Köpfe wurden vertrieben. Von diesem intellektuellen Kahlschlag, der schon in den 1920er Jahren schleichend eingesetzt hatte, erholte sich die medizinische Fakultät nur langsam. Nach dem Zweiten Weltkrieg brauchte es lange, um wieder das Niveau der einstigen Wiener Spitzenmedizin zu erreichen.[90] Die universitären Strukturen der Nachkriegsjahrzehnte waren verknöchert und internationale Zusammenarbeit rar. Auch die auf die Zeit der Monarchie zurückgehenden Doppelkliniken agierten eher in interner Konkurrenz, anstatt einander komplementär zu ergänzen. Wohl tat sich das AKH damals durch seine Erfolge in der Transplantationsmedizin oder durch die Entwicklung des „Kunstherzens" hervor, doch erst ab Mitte der 1990er Jahre zeichnete sich ein deutlicher Aufholprozess in Richtung internationaler Standards ab:[91] Mit der Übersiedlung in das Neue AKH fand ein Umbruch für die medizinische Forschung statt, die bis dahin in Wien bestehenden Doppelkliniken wurden abgeschafft und alle diagnostischen Leistungen in Form eigener Kliniken bzw. klinischer

a visual motif, and the former staff residence (the "nurses home") – which, upon construction, was a central element of the hospital layout – was also recently demolished. In contrast, the huge construction pit adjacent to the hospital complex, which is now known as the MedUni Campus AKH, hints at the construction of the new MedUni Campus Mariannengasse. In this way, the images in the book form a chronological cross-section that reveal the dense medical history that is unique to Vienna's 9th District.

University medicine in Vienna in the 21st century

Between the late 18th and the early 20th centuries, Vienna's Medical Faculty set the pace for the worldwide spread of knowledge-based medicine. It comes as no surprise that people spoke about a Vienna School. The Vienna faculty enjoyed a global reputation, particularly in the years between 1900 and the outbreak of the First World War. The extremely close-knit network of medical facilities and academic institutions in the "Doctors' Quarter" promoted cooperation not only amongst these doctors but also, more generally, between science and medicine. Four Nobel Prizes were awarded to Vienna-based scientists during the early decades of the 20th century,[88] and a number of further doctors were nominated.[89] Around 1930, when its teaching staff numbered over 300, the faculty in Vienna was, alongside its counterpart in Berlin, one of the largest in the German-speaking region. However, Vienna had a higher degree of medical specialization; the division of medicine into different fields, which had developed from the early 19th century, bore witness to the more modern approach of Vienna's university clinics. These newer specializations were largely the domains of Jewish scientists, as a result of which the consequences of the forced dismissals that followed the "Anschluss" with the Third Reich were particularly severe. More than half of the teaching staff were removed in 1938 for racist or political reasons and the best minds were driven abroad. The Medical Faculty was slow to recover from this process of intellectual decimation, which had begun insidiously back in the 1920s. After the Second World War, it took many years for Viennese medicine to return to its former level of excellence.[90] The university structures of the postwar decades were extremely outdated and international cooperation was rare. Even the double clinics, which dated back to the Monarchy, tended to compete with rather than complement each other. The General Hospital may have distinguished itself due to its successes in transplantation medicine and the development of the "artificial heart," but it was not until the mid-1990s that the institution clearly began catching up with international standards:[91] The move into the Neues AKH brought radical change to medical research, the double clinics that had existed up to that point were phased out, and all diagnostic services were centralized in the form of dedicated clinics or clinical institutes. The availability of new research space was accompanied by a noticeable increase in the quality of clinical research and there was also a strong growth in the quantity of research during the 1990s. In the years since then, Vienna's scientific culture has returned to an international level and established its own research profile, leading to a qualitative improvement that has been significantly driven by increasing interdisciplinarity and international cooperation.

Academic investigation of the "dark" period between 1938 and 1945 has also been actively pursued since the 1990s; ever since it was founded, MedUni Vienna has launched initiatives designed to address its difficult legacy.[92] The "Memorial of Remembrance," which is dedicated to the teachers and students of the former Medical Faculty who were banished or murdered under National Socialism, was unveiled on the campus in 2008 and the pages missing from this book

Institute zentralisiert. Mit den nun zur Verfügung stehenden For-
schungsflächen ging eine merkliche Qualitätssteigerung der klinischen
Forschung einher, und auch quantitativ stieg der Output in den 1990er
Jahren stark an. Die wissenschaftliche Kultur hat sich seither dem
internationalen Niveau angepasst, ein eigenes Forschungsprofil wurde
etabliert, zunehmende Interdisziplinarität und Kooperationen auf
internationaler Basis trugen maßgeblich zu diesem Qualitätsschub bei.

Auch die wissenschaftliche Auseinandersetzung mit den „dunklen" Jahren 1938–45 wird seit den 1990er Jahren aktiv betrieben; die
MedUni Wien hat seit ihrem Bestehen sichtbare Initiativen zur Aufarbeitung ihres schwierigen Erbes gesetzt.[92] 2008 wurde auf dem Campus
das „Mahnmal gegen das Vergessen" enthüllt, das den im Nationalsozialismus vertriebenen oder ermordeten Lehrenden und Studierenden der damaligen medizinischen Fakultät gewidmet ist; die aus dem
Buch fallenden Seiten stehen symbolisch für den großen Verlust an
Wissen. Als Anerkennung der großen Leistungen des Psychoanalytikers
und Kulturtheoretikers Sigmund Freud wurde 2018 eine überlebens-
große Statue auf dem Gelände vor dem Rektorat der Medizinischen
Universität aufgestellt. Der Entwurf für dieses Denkmal datiert aus dem
Jahr 1936, als Freud für einen befreundeten Künstler posierte; der
jetzige Bronzeguss wurde nach dem Gipsmodell hergestellt.

Die dynamische Entwicklung der MedUni Wien
Gehörte die medizinische Fakultät von 1365 bis 2003 (also fast 650
Jahre lang) zur Universität Wien, so erlangte sie 2004 als neu eingerichtete Medizinische Universität hochschulpolitische Autonomie.[93] Mit
dem Universitätsgesetz 2002 wurden viele Bereiche des österreichischen Universitätsrechts neu strukturiert, seither gelten Universitäten
als vollrechtsfähig. Der Bund ist zu ihrer Finanzierung verpflichtet,
schließt mit ihnen jedoch Leistungsvereinbarungen ab. Mit dieser
Ausgestaltung als Universität setzte an der MedUni Wien eine äußerst

dynamische Entwicklung ein. Die Zahl der Fachpublikationen stieg
rasant, desgleichen der Impact-Faktor, der als bibliografisches Quali-
tätskriterium über die Zitationen Auskunft gibt. In der Messperiode
2004–08 lag die MedUni Wien mit ihrer Forschungsleistung sogar
knapp 30 Prozent über dem weltweiten Schnitt. Ein neues, zeitgemäßes
Curriculum wurde etabliert, das laufend Ergänzung um neue Studien-
angebote erfährt – jüngst etwa „Gender Medicine", „Medizinische
Informatik", „Molecular Precision Medicine" sowie „Transkulturelle
Medizin und Diversity Care". Unter den Studierenden beträgt die
Frauenquote inzwischen exakt die Hälfte; das Schließen des noch
bestehenden Gender-Gaps auf den höheren Ebenen der MedUni Wien
sieht der aktuelle Entwicklungsplan für die kommenden Jahre vor.[94]

2014 wurde das zehnjährige Bestehen der Medizinischen
Universität gefeiert, 2024 steht das 20-jährige Jubiläum an. Mit ihrer in
das Mittelalter reichenden Vergangenheit darf sie sich zu den ältesten
Ausbildungsstätten zählen; zugleich ist sie heute eine der jüngsten
medizinischen Universitäten. Mit rund 8.000 Studierenden gilt die
MedUni Wien nicht nur als größte im deutschsprachigen Raum,
sondern auch weltweit als eine der renommiertesten. Dies zeigen nicht
zuletzt die Platzierungen in den einschlägigen internationalen Rankings: 2023 wurde sie unter die 100 besten Medical Schools weltweit
gereiht;[95] auf der Rangliste des US-Nachrichtenmagazins *Newsweek*
und des Datenproviders Statista rangierten die MedUni Wien und das
Universitätsklinikum AKH Wien im Jahr 2023 auf Platz 30, im Jahr
zuvor sogar auf Platz 24 der 250 besten Spitäler der Welt.[96]

Im Unterschied zur US-amerikanischen Hochschullandschaft
stellen solche Leistungsvergleiche im mitteleuropäischen Kontext ein
eher junges Phänomen dar. Auch wenn sich über die Methoden und
Kriterien dieser Rankings streiten ließe, sind quantitative Bewertungs-
verfahren für ein erfolgreiches Agieren in globalen Wissenschafts-
systemen heute unerlässlich. Gemäß der Devise „Leistungsfähigkeit

---

symbolize the resulting huge loss of knowledge. In recognition of his
extraordinary achievements, a larger-than-life statue of the
psychoanalyst and cultural theorist Sigmund Freud was erected in front
of the Rectorate of the Medical University in 2018. The design for the
monument dates from 1936, when Freud posed for an artist friend; the
current bronze cast was made using the earlier plaster model.

The dynamic development of MedUni Vienna
Having belonged to the University of Vienna from 1365 to 2003
(e.g., for almost 650 years), the Medical Faculty gained academic autonomy in 2004 as the newly established Medical University.[93] The
University Act of 2002 restructured many areas of Austrian university
law and universities have enjoyed complete legal capacity ever since.
The Federal Government is obliged to provide financing, on the basis
of which performance agreements are concluded. The new university
status of MedUni Vienna triggered a period of extremely dynamic
development. The number of specialist publications rose rapidly, as
did the impact factor, a bibliographic quality criterion that provides
information about the citing of such publications. In the period of
measurement 2004–08, the research performance of MedUni Vienna
was even almost 30 percent above the global average. A new up-to-date
curriculum was established and this is constantly being updated with
new courses – including, most recently, "Gender Medicine," "Medical
IT," "Molecular Precision Medicine," and "Transcultural Medicine and
Diversity Care." Exactly half of all students are now women; and the
latest development plan for the next few years envisages the closing of
the remaining gender gap at the higher levels of MedUni Vienna.[94]

The Medical University of Vienna marked its tenth birthday in
2014 and the 20th anniversary is being celebrated in 2024. Thanks to a
history stretching back to the Middle Ages it is both one of the oldest
educational institutions and one of the youngest medical universities.

With around 8,000 students, MedUni Vienna is not only the largest in
the German-speaking region, but also one of the most prestigious
worldwide. This is also reflected by the relevant international rankings:
In 2023, it was rated as one of the world's best 100 medical schools;[95]
MedUni Vienna and University Hospital Vienna occupied 30th place in
the ranking of the US news magazine *Newsweek* and data provider
Statista in 2023 and, in the year before, were even ranked 24th amongst
the world's best 250 hospitals.[96]

In contrast with the university landscape in the USA, such
performance comparisons are a much more recent phenomenon in the
Central European context. But even if we can argue about the methods
and criteria employed by such rankings, quantitative evaluation
processes are indispensable if one wants to successfully operate in
today's global scientific system. New governance models for universities
have been developed, which – in line with the motto "performance
through autonomy" – grant much more room for maneuver to
universities that are prepared to accept reform. This process has been
accompanied in many places by great optimism and has had an
extremely positive impact on the image of the most successful areas
of research and teaching.[97] The most recent recognition clearly
demonstrates that MedUni Vienna, together with its clinics in
University Hospital Vienna, is not only Austria's leading provider of
state-of-the-art medicine but also a global *center of excellence* with the
potential to develop further. Since 2016, the Medical University and
University Hospital Vienna have also been run as a joint operation –
and research-led teaching and international benchmarks have ensured
that this cooperation is a success.

An infrastructure for the medicine of the future
Top quality research, teaching, and patient care also require
appropriate spatial conditions. Between now and 2030, the Medical

durch Eigenverantwortung" wurden neue hochschulpolitische Governance-Modelle entwickelt, die reformwilligen Universitäten einen beträchtlich erweiterten Spielraum gewähren. Vielerorts ging dies mit einer enormen Aufbruchstimmung einher und zeitigte äußerst positive Effekte für die Profilierung der leistungsstärksten Bereiche in Forschung und Lehre.[97] Die jüngste Anerkennung zeigt doch deutlich, dass die MedUni Wien mit ihren Kliniken am AKH nicht nur das führende spitzenmedizinische Zentrum Österreichs darstellt, sondern auch ein globales *center of excellence* mit Potenzial zur Weiterentwicklung. Seit dem Jahr 2016 werden die Medizinische Universität und das AKH Wien auch als gemeinsamer Betrieb geführt, forschungsgeleitete Lehre und internationale Qualitätsstandards bilden die Basis dieser erfolgreichen Kooperation.

Infrastruktur für die Medizin der Zukunft
Forschung, Lehre und Krankenversorgung auf höchstem Niveau hängen nicht zuletzt von adäquaten räumlichen Voraussetzungen ab. Bis 2030 investieren die Medizinische Universität und das Universitätsklinikum AKH Wien in bedeutende Um- und Neubauprojekte am gemeinsamen Standort MedUni Campus AKH: Langfristig werden dort möglichst alle der derzeit auf viele Gebäudeteile verstreuten Organisationseinheiten räumlich konzentriert, um optimale Rahmenbedingungen für die Medizin der Zukunft zu schaffen.[98] Die bauliche Fertigstellung des MedUni Campus Mariannengasse ist für 2026 geplant,[99] die bis dato versprengten vorklinischen Einrichtungen werden in diesem neuen Kompetenzzentrum für Grundlagenforschung gebündelt. Dieser moderne, offene Campus in unmittelbarer Nähe zum Universitätsklinikum AKH Wien soll nicht nur den interdisziplinären Austausch fördern, sondern mit seiner Glasfassade auch die architektonische Visitenkarte der MedUni Wien bilden. Ebenfalls in Bau ist derzeit das Eric Kandel Institut – Zentrum für Präzisionsmedizin, das

der Erforschung der Möglichkeiten personalisierter Medizin dienen wird. Mit diesem neuen Forschungsgebäude, das Raum für hoch spezialisierte Technologien wie Genomsequenzierung bietet und der fortschreitenden Digitalisierung in der Medizin Rechnung trägt, wird auch die Vorreiterrolle des Wissenschaftsstandorts Wien gesichert. Ein weiteres großes Zukunftsprojekt der MedUni Wien ist das Center for Translational Medicine, dessen Eröffnung für 2025 vorgesehen ist. Es soll helfen, neue Erkenntnisse der Grundlagenforschung schnell und effizient in die klinische Forschung überzuführen. Räumlich zwischen dem AKH Wien und dem MedUni Campus Mariannengasse situiert, wird es als Drehscheibe zwischen Labor, Klinik und Lehre fungieren. Weiters in Planung ist das Ignaz Semmelweis Institut für Infektionsforschung (ISI), das jene Spezialfächer beheimaten soll, die im Rahmen von Infektionskrankheiten eine besondere Rolle spielen (Infektiologie, Epidemiologie, Public Health). Das Coronavirus SARS-COV-2 hat uns in den letzten Jahren vor Augen geführt, dass wir uns in einem „pandemischen Zeitalter" befinden.[100] In Kooperation mit vier österreichischen Partneruniversitäten wird sich das Semmelweis Institut der Erforschung neuer lebensbedrohlicher Infektionskrankheiten widmen. Auch ein Zentrum für Technologietransfer wird demnächst errichtet; mittelfristig soll die MedUni Wien zu einem „Hub" der digitalen Medizin ausgebaut werden.

Vor kurzem abgeschlossen wurde der Neubau für die Labortierzucht und -haltung in Himberg bei Wien. In diesem Hightechgebäude ist unter anderem ein Hybrid-Operationssaal mit avancierter Bildgebung eingerichtet, die Anlage wird als Test- und Trainingszentrum für neue medizinische Produkte wie Herzklappen und Stents genutzt.

Das kulturhistorische Erbe
Nach vierjähriger Renovierung wurde im Herbst 2022 auch das Josephinum wiedereröffnet. Der historische Hörsaal, der in der

University and University Hospital Vienna are investing in a series of conversion and new-build projects on their joint campus, the MedUni Campus AKH: Over the long term, the organizational units that are currently distributed across many buildings will be concentrated together as much as possible, in order to create an optimal framework for the medicine of the future.[98] The construction of the MedUni Campus Mariannengasse is scheduled for completion in 2026,[99] at which point the previously scattered preclinical facilities will be clustered in this new competence center for basic research. This modern and open campus, which is located very close to University Hospital Vienna, should not only encourage interdisciplinary exchange but also provide MedUni Vienna with an architectural visiting card in the shape of its glass facade. A further facility that is currently under construction is the Eric Kandel Institute – Center for Precision Medicine, which will facilitate research into the possibilities offered by personalized medicine. This new research building, which offers space for highly specialized technologies such as genome sequencing and is a response to the increasing digitalization of medicine, will also help to safeguard the pioneering role of Vienna as a research location. A further major forward-looking project of MedUni Vienna is the Center for Translational Medicine, which is scheduled to open in 2025. This should increase the speed and efficiency with which new findings from basic research are taken up by clinical researchers. Located directly between University Hospital Vienna and the MedUni Campus Mariannengasse, this institute will act as an interface between laboratory-based, clinical, and teaching activities. A further facility that is currently being planned is the Ignaz Semmelweis Institute for Infection Research (ISI), which will provide a home to all those specialist areas that play a vital role in the context of infectious diseases (infectiology, epidemiology, and public health). During recent years, the coronavirus SARS-COV-2 made it clear that we find ourselves in a

"pandemic age."[100] The Semmelweis Institute will devote itself to research into new, life-threatening infectious diseases in cooperation with four Austrian partner universities. A Center for Technology Transfer will also soon be created and, in the medium term, MedUni Vienna should develop into a "hub" for digital medicine.

The construction of a new building for the breeding and husbandry of laboratory animals in Himberg bei Wien was recently completed. This high-tech complex, whose facilities include a hybrid operating room with advanced imaging technology, will act as a testing and training center for new medical products such as cardiac valves and stents.

The cultural-historical legacy
The Josephinum reopened in autumn 2022 after four years of renovation work. The historic lecture theater, which had been sub-divided by a mezzanine during the postwar period, was restored to its original form in a process that included the rediscovery of the original wall painting. This high, light-filled space now offers a special setting for events. Due to its medical-historical collections, the Josephinum also embodies the history of the Medical University. It is one of the rare medical institutions worldwide that have such a rich cultural legacy. And there are also few medical-historical institutions in Europe that are also connected with a museum. The newly developed museum concept is based on the idea of a constantly changing permanent exhibition; the famous anatomical wax models continue to form the highlight of the collection. The Institute for the History of Medicine, which has been located in the building since 1920, remains as important as ever; since 2016 it has formed part of the organizational unit Ethics, Collections, and History of Medicine.

The entire site occupied by the former General Hospital was transferred to the ownership of the University of Vienna in 1988.

Nachkriegszeit durch eine Zwischendecke unterteilt worden war, wurde rückgebaut, wodurch auch die bauzeitlichen Wandmalereien freigelegt werden konnten. Für Veranstaltungen bildet dieser lichte, hohe Raum einen besonderen Rahmen. Das Josephinum repräsentiert mit seinen medizinhistorischen Sammlungen auch die Geschichte der Medizinischen Universität. Diese gehört weltweit zu den raren medizinischen Einrichtungen, die über ein derart reiches kulturelles Erbe verfügen. Zudem gibt es in Europa nur wenige medizinhistorische Institute, die auch mit einem Museum verbunden sind. Das neu entwickelte Museumskonzept basiert auf der Idee einer sich ständig wandelnden Dauerausstellung; die berühmten anatomischen Wachsmodelle bilden nach wie vor das Highlight der Sammlung. Das seit 1920 im Haus angesiedelte Institut für Geschichte der Medizin bleibt unverändert wichtig; seit dem Jahr 2016 bildet es einen Teil der Organisationseinheit Ethik, Sammlungen und Geschichte der Medizin.

Das gesamte Areal des Alten Allgemeinen Krankenhauses war bereits 1988 in den Besitz der Universität Wien übergegangen. Nach Absiedelung der letzten Uniklinik in den Neubau des AKH wurde der josephinische Gebäudekomplex für die Unterbringung der bislang auf mehrere Standorte verteilten geistes- und kulturwissenschaftlichen Institute adaptiert.[101] In ihrer spartanischen Einfachheit hat die Anlage des einstigen Zentralspitals ihre Wandlungsfähigkeit einmal mehr unter Beweis gestellt, die Trakte mit ihren saalartigen Räumen erwiesen sich als ideal für eine Revitalisierung. Der seit dem Jahr 1998 bestehende „Campus Altes AKH" bildet heute einen wichtigen Schauplatz akademischen Lebens der Universität.

Medizinische Exzellenz
Im Zuge der Coronavirus-Pandemie ist Gesundheit ins Zentrum der gesellschaftlichen Debatte gerückt und damit die Rolle der MedUni Wien als wissenschaftlicher Leitinstitution des Landes. In der

derzeitigen Phase eines globalen disruptiven Wandels infolge der zweiten (post-)industriellen Revolution bedarf es des nötigen Raums, um die Forschungsaktivitäten im Bereich digitaler Medizin weiter auszubauen. Die projektierten Zentren bieten nicht nur ein Arbeitsumfeld auf dem neuesten Stand der Technologie; ihre Gestaltung fördert auch die Zusammenarbeit in interdisziplinären Teams. Die neu entstehende Architektur des MedUni Campus AKH Wien und des MedUni Campus Mariannengasse wird als Agentin wissenschaftlicher Entwicklungen wirken und identitätsstiftend für das Selbstverständnis der Wiener Universitätsmedizin sein. Nicht zuletzt trägt dieses neue Ensemble mit dazu bei, den Life-Science-Standort Österreich international besser sichtbar zu machen. Der medizinischen Fakultät bzw. der MedUni Wien ist es in den letzten Jahrzehnten gelungen, mit ihrem Universitätsklinikum AKH Wien eines der weltweit erfolgreichsten Gesundheitssysteme zu etablieren. Der räumlich zusammengeführte Forschungs- und Lehrkomplex in Wien-Alsergrund wird die Rolle der MedUni Wien als führender Healthcare-Player weiterhin sichern. Diese exzellente medizinische Versorgung ist nicht von ungefähr einer der Gründe, weshalb Wien seit 15 Jahren unangefochten als Stadt mit der weltweit höchsten Lebensqualität gilt.[102]

1   Ist (so gut wie) ausschließlich von männlichen Akteuren die Rede, wird im Folgenden die grammatikalisch männliche Form verwendet, überall sonst die inklusive Version mit Doppelpunkt oder ein genderneutraler Ausdruck. – Hier ist natürlich insbesondere die Medizinhistorikerin Erna Lesky zu nennen, die zwar ein Medizinstudium an der Wiener medizinischen Fakultät absolviert hatte, sich aber bald der Geschichte der Medizin zuwandte und sich 1957 in diesem Fach habilitierte; ab 1960 hatte sie die erste Professur für Medizingeschichte an der Universität Wien inne.
2   Siehe etwa: *Im Krankenhaus*, hg. von der Alfried Krupp von Bohlen und Halbach-Stiftung, mit Fotografien von Elisabeth Neudörfl, Ludwig Kuffer, Andreas Langfeld und Texten von Hanna Engelmeier, Armin Nassehi, Thomas Hettche, Leipzig 2018; *Im Krankenhaus. Der Patient zwischen Technik und Zuwendung. Bilder aus dem Alfried Krupp Krankenhaus*, hg. von Timm Rautert, Regine Hauch und der Alfried Krupp von Bohlen und Halbach-Stiftung, Berlin u. a. 1993.

Following the move of the final university clinic to the Neues AKH, the Josephine building complex was adapted to accommodate the humanities departments that had previously been distributed across a number of locations.[101] The design of the former central hospital, with all its spartan simplicity, once again demonstrated its great adaptability as the blocks and their hall-like spaces were found to be ideal subjects for revitalization. The "Campus Altes AKH," which opened in 1998, now provides a key setting for the academic life of the university.

Medical excellence
During the coronavirus pandemic, health – and hence the role of MedUni Vienna as one of the country's leading scientific institutions – became a focus of debate. In the current phase of the global disruptive transformation that was triggered by the second (post-)industrial revolution, there is a pressing need for spaces in which we can further expand research into digital medicine. The planned centers not only offer a working environment with state-of-the-art technology; their design also encourages cooperation within interdisciplinary teams. The emerging architecture of the MedUni Campus AKH and the MedUni Campus Mariannengasse will act as an agent for scientific development and as a symbol of the self-image of university medicine in Vienna. And, last but not least, this new ensemble will help to increase awareness of Austria's role as a life sciences location. In recent years, the Medical Faculty and MedUni Vienna have established – together with their teaching hospital, University Hospital Vienna, – one of the world's most successful health systems. The spatially concentrated research and teaching complex in Vienna-Alsergrund will continue to safeguard the role of MedUni Vienna as a leading healthcare player. It is no coincidence that this excellent medical provision is one of the reasons why Vienna has spent the past 15 years as the unchallenged holder of the title of the most livable city in the world.[102]

1   While these were almost exclusively male, it is essential to recall the role of such figures as the medical historian Erna Lesky, who studied medicine at Vienna's Medical Faculty but soon turned her attention to the history of medicine, the area in which she qualified as a lecturerer in 1957; she became the University of Vienna's first Professor of the History of Medicine in 1960.
2   See, for example, *Im Krankenhaus*, edited by the Alfried Krupp von Bohlen und Halbach-Stiftung, with photographs by Elisabeth Neudörfl, Ludwig Kuffer, and Andreas Langfeld, and texts by Hanna Engelmeier, Armin Nassehi, and Thomas Hettche, Leipzig, 2018; *Im Krankenhaus. Der Patient zwischen Technik und Zuwendung. Bilder aus dem Alfried Krupp Krankenhaus*, edited by Timm Rautert, Regine Hauch, and the Alfried Krupp von Bohlen und Halbach-Stiftung, Berlin et al. 1993.
3   This approach corresponds with that of the US-American photographer Walker Evans: "Absence was a phenomenon he knew and liked. […] He was also devoted to photographing empty rooms, whose spaces and furnishings suggested absent inhabitants." In: Svetlana Alpers, *Walker Evans. Starting from Scratch*, Princeton, 2020, 10.
4   Cf. Hans-Georg Hofer, Lutz Sauerteig, Perspektiven einer Kulturgeschichte der Medizin, in: *Medizinhistorisches Journal*, no. 42, 2007, 105–41; Ralf Bröer (ed.), *Eine Wissenschaft emanzipiert sich. Die Medizinhistoriographie von der Aufklärung bis zur Postmoderne* (Neuere Medizin- und Wissenschaftsgeschichte – Quellen und Studien, vol. 9), Pfaffenweiler, 1999, 3–15.
5   Cf. Bruno Latour, *Science in Action. How to Follow Scientists and Engineers through Society*, Cambridge, Massachusetts, 1987.
6   Cf. Susanne Hauser, Christa Kamleithner, Roland Meyer (eds.), *Architekturwissen. Grundlagentexte aus den Kulturwissenschaften, vol. 1: Zur Ästhetik des sozialen Raumes*, Bielefeld, 2011.
7   Cf. Peter Payer, *Der Gestank von Wien. Über Kanalgase, Totendünste und andere üble Geruchskulissen*, Vienna, 1997.
8   Cf. Beatriz Colomina, Le lit à l'ère de la Covid-19, in: Cynthia Fleury, SCAU, *Soutenir. Ville, architecture et soin*, exh. cat. Pavillon de l'Arsenal, Paris, Paris, 2022, 51–54.
9   Cf. Philipp Meuser, Vom Patientenzimmer zur Wellness-Suite, in: Meuser (ed.), *Krankenhausbauten / Gesundheitsbauten. Handbuch und Planungshilfe, vol. 1: Allgemeinkrankenhäuser und Gesundheitszentren*, Berlin, 2011, 11.
10   Cf. Peter Galison, Buildings and the Subject of Science, in: Galison, Emily Thompson (eds.), *The Architecture of Science*, Cambridge – London, 1999, 1–21, here 3.
11   With regard to the development of the hospital from the typology of the hospice I refer to the following overviews: John D. Thompson, Grace Goldin, *The Hospital. A Social and Architectural History*, New Haven – London, 1975; Nikolaus Pevsner, *A History of Building Types*, Princeton, 1976, 139–58; Axel Hinrich Murken, Vom Armenhospital zum Großklinikum. *Die Geschichte des Krankenhauses vom 18. Jahrhundert bis zur Gegenwart*, 3rd ed., Cologne, 1995, 9–35; Karl Heinz Tragl, *Chronik der Wiener Krankenanstalten*, Vienna et al., 2007, 25–32; Pierre-Louis Laget, Claude Laroche, Isabelle Duhau, et al., *L'Hôpital en France. Du Moyen Âge à nos jours. Histoire & architecture* (Cahiers du Patrimoine, no 116), 2nd ed., Lyon, 2016, 24–114; Ernst Seidl (ed.), *Lexikon der Bautypen. Funktionen und Formen der Architektur*, Stuttgart, 2012, 227–31

3 Eine Haltung, die mit jener des US-amerikanischen Fotografen Walker Evans korrespondiert: „Absence was a phenomenon he knew and liked. […] He was also devoted to photographing empty rooms, whose spaces and furnishings suggested absent inhabitants." In: Svetlana Alpers, *Walker Evans. Starting from Scratch*, Princeton 2020, S. 10.
4 Vgl. Hans-Georg Hofer, Lutz Sauerteig, Perspektiven einer Kulturgeschichte der Medizin, in: *Medizinhistorisches Journal*, Nr. 42, 2007, S. 105–141; Ralf Bröer (Hg.), *Eine Wissenschaft emanzipiert sich. Die Medizinhistoriographie von der Aufklärung bis zur Postmoderne* (Neuere Medizin- und Wissenschaftsgeschichte – Quellen und Studien, Bd. 9), Pfaffenweiler 1999, S. 3–15.
5 Vgl. Bruno Latour, *Science in Action. How to Follow Scientists and Engineers Through Society*, Cambridge, Massachusetts, 1987.
6 Vgl. Susanne Hauser, Christa Kamleithner, Roland Meyer (Hg.), *Architekturwissen. Grundlagentexte aus den Kulturwissenschaften, Bd. 1: Zur Ästhetik des sozialen Raumes*, Bielefeld 2011.
7 Vgl. Peter Payer, *Der Gestank von Wien. Über Kanalgase, Totendünste und andere üble Geruchskulissen*, Wien 1997.
8 Vgl. Beatriz Colomina, Le lit à l'ère de la Covid-19, in: Cynthia Fleury, SCAU, *Soutenir. Ville, architecture et soin*, Ausst.-Kat. Pavillon de l'Arsenal, Paris, Paris 2022, S. 51–54.
9 Vgl. Philipp Meuser, Vom Patientenzimmer zur Wellness-Suite, in: ders. (Hg.), *Krankenhausbauten / Gesundheitsbauten. Handbuch und Planungshilfe, Bd. 1: Allgemeinkrankenhäuser und Gesundheitszentren*, Berlin 2011, S. 11.
10 Vgl. Peter Galison, Buildings and the Subject of Science, in: ders., Emily Thompson (Hg.), *The Architecture of Science*, Cambridge – London 1999, S. 1–21, hier S. 3.
11 Was die Herausbildung des Krankenhauses aus dem Typus des Hospitals betrifft, beziehe ich mich auf folgende Überblickswerke: John D. Thompson, Grace Goldin, *The Hospital. A Social and Architectural History*, New Haven – London 1975; Nikolaus Pevsner, *A History of Building Types*, Princeton 1976, S. 139–158; Axel Hinrich Murken, *Vom Armenhospital zum Großklinikum. Die Geschichte des Krankenhauses vom 18. Jahrhundert bis zur Gegenwart*, 3. Aufl., Köln 1995, S. 9–35; Karl Heinz Tragl, *Chronik der Wiener Krankenanstalten*, Wien u. a. 2007, S. 25–32; Pierre-Louis Laget, Claude Laroche, Isabelle Duhau et al., *L'Hôpital en France. Du Moyen Âge à nos jours. Histoire & architecture* (Cahiers du Patrimoine, n° 116), 2. Aufl., Lyon 2016, S. 24–114; Ernst Seidl (Hg.), *Lexikon der Bautypen. Funktionen und Formen der Architektur*, Stuttgart 2012, S. 227–231 (Hospital), 302–304 (Krankenhaus); Philipp Meuser (Hg.), *Krankenhausbauten / Gesundheitsbauten. Handbuch und Planungshilfe, Bd. 1: Allgemeinkrankenhäuser und Gesundheitszentren, Bd. 2: Spezialkliniken und Fachabteilungen*, Berlin 2011.
12 Vgl. Wolfgang Uwe Eckart, *Geschichte, Theorie und Ethik der Medizin*, 7., völlig neu bearb. Aufl., Berlin – Heidelberg 2013, S. 153.
13 Krankenhäuser in Österreich und in der deutschsprachigen Schweiz werden bis heute meist auch Spitäler genannt. In der offiziellen Bezeichnung solcher Einrichtungen findet sich dieser Begriff jedoch selten.
14 Vgl. Peter Payer, *Der Gestank von Wien*, S. 43.
15 Vgl. Alain Corbin, *Le miasme et la jonquille. L'odorat et l'imaginaire social (XVIIIe–XIXe siècles)*, Paris 1982 (dt. *Pesthauch und Blütenduft. Eine Geschichte des Geruchs*, Berlin 2005).
16 Michel Foucault, Blandine Barret-Kriegel, Anne Thalamy et al., *Les machines à guérir (aux origines de l'hôpital moderne)*, 2. Aufl., Brüssel – Lüttich 1979.
17 Michel Foucault, *Naissance de la Clinique*, Paris 1963 (dt. *Die Geburt der Klinik. Eine Archäologie des ärztlichen Blicks*, München 1973). Vgl. auch: Clemens Kammler, Rolf Parr, Ulrich Johannes Schneider (Hg.), *Foucault-Handbuch. Leben – Werk – Wirkung*, Stuttgart – Weimar 2008, S. 32–37.
18 Vgl. Herwig Czech, Medizin, Macht und Polizey. Joseph II. und die Erste Wiener Medizinische Schule, in: Christiane Druml (Hg.), *Das neue Josephinum. Medizinhistorisches Museum Wien*, Wien 2022, S. 53–69.
19 Michel Foucault, *Histoire de la sexualité 1: La volonté de savoir*, Paris 1976 (dt. *Sexualität und Wahrheit, Bd. 1: Der Wille zum Wissen*, Frankfurt am Main 1977).
20 Vgl. Thomas Lemke, *Biopolitik zur Einführung*, Hamburg 2013.
21 Vgl. Wolfgang Eric Wagner, Doctores – Practicantes – Empirici. Die Durchsetzung der Medizinischen Fakultäten gegenüber anderen Heilergruppen in Paris und Wien im späten Mittelalter, in: Rainer Christoph Schwinges (Hg.), *Universität im öffentlichen Raum* (Veröffentlichungen der Gesellschaft für Universitäts- und Wissenschaftsgeschichte, Bd. 10), Basel 2008, S. 15–43.
22 Mit den von Kaiser Joseph II. erlassenen sogenannten Toleranzpatenten 1781/82 wurden auch jüdische Studenten zum Medizinstudium zugelassen, Frauen konnten sich erst ab 1900 an der medizinischen Fakultät der Universität Wien inskribieren. Andere, subtilere Formen von Diskriminierung (im Studium, beim Erlangen von Stellen und in der Berufsausübung) wurden indessen weiterhin praktiziert.
23 Vgl. Karl Heinz Tragl, *Chronik der Wiener Krankenanstalten*, S. 26.
24 Vgl. Erna Lesky, Gerard van Swieten. Auftrag und Erfüllung, in: dies, Adam Wandruszka (Hg.), *Gerard van Swieten und seine Zeit. Internationales Symposium, veranstaltet von der Universität Wien im Institut für Geschichte der Medizin, 8.–10. Mai 1972*, Wien u. a. 1973, S. 11–62.
25 Vgl. Christoph Gnant, Die Universität Wien im 18. Jahrhundert. Entkirchlichung – Verstaatlichung – Ausbau, in: Julia Rüdiger, Dieter Schweizer (Hg.), *Stätten des Wissens. Die Universität Wien entlang ihrer Bauten 1365–2015*, Wien u. a. 2015, S. 87–99.
26 Zur Gründung des Wiener Allgemeinen Krankenhauses bzw. der Anlage des gesamten josephinischen Komplexes siehe: Dieter Jetter, *Wien von den Anfängen bis um 1900* (Geschichte des Hospitals, Bd. 5), Wiesbaden 1982, S. 21–90; Helmut Wyklicky, Manfred Skopec (Hg.), *200 Jahre Allgemeines Krankenhaus in Wien*, Wien 1984; Axel Hinrich Murken, *Vom Armenhospital zum Großklinikum*, S. 36–38; Helmut Wyklicky, *200 Jahre Allgemeines Krankenhaus* (Schriftenreihe Österreichische Universitätstexte), Wien 1993; Gabriela Schmidt, Die Wiener Medizinische Fakultät und das Allgemeine Krankenhaus, in: Alfred Ebenbauer, Wolfgang Greisenegger, Kurt Mühlberger (Hg.), *Universitätscampus Wien, Bd. 1: Historie und Geist*, Wien 1998, S. 7–35; Hellmut Lorenz, Das Alte Allgemeine Krankenhaus in Wien. Baugestalt und Baugeschichte, in: Alfred Ebenbauer, Wolfgang Greisenegger, Kurt Mühlberger (Hg.), *Universitätscampus Wien, Bd. 1*, S. 37–55; Karl Heinz Tragl, *Chronik der Wiener Krankenanstalten*, S. 33–60; Hellmut Lorenz: Der josephinische Bautenkomplex. Allgemeines Krankenhaus, Garnisonsspital, Narrenturm und Josephinum, in: Julia Rüdiger, Dieter Schweizer (Hg.), *Stätten des Wissens*, S. 101–111.

(hospice), 302–04 (hospital); Philipp Meuser (ed.), *Krankenhausbauten / Gesundheitsbauten. Handbuch und Planungshilfe, vol. 1: Allgemeinkrankenhäuser und Gesundheitszentren, vol. 2: Spezialkliniken und Fachabteilungen*, Berlin, 2011.
12 Cf. Wolfgang Uwe Eckart, *Geschichte, Theorie und Ethik der Medizin*, 7th, completely new ed., Berlin – Heidelberg, 2013, 153.
13 Hospitals in Austria and the German-speaking regions of Switzerland are generally known as *Spitäler*. However, this term is rarely found in official descriptions of such institutions.
14 Cf. Peter Payer, *Der Gestank von Wien*, 43.
15 Cf. Alain Corbin, *Le miasme et la jonquille. L'odorat et l'imaginaire social (XVIIIe–XIXe siècles)*, Paris, 1982 (Eng. *The Foul and the Fragrant. Odor and the French Social Imagination*, Harvard, 1986).
16 Michel Foucault, Blandine Barret-Kriegel, Anne Thalamy, et al., *Les machines à guérir (aux origines de l'hôpital moderne)*, 2nd ed., Brussels – Liege, 1979.
17 Michel Foucault, *Naissance de la Clinique*, Paris 1963 (Eng. *The Birth of the Clinic. An archaeology of medical perception*, London, 1973). Cf also: Clemens Kammler, Rolf Parr, Ulrich Johannes Schneider (eds.), *Foucault-Handbuch. Leben – Werk – Wirkung*, Stuttgart – Weimar, 2008, 32–37.
18 Cf. Herwig Czech, Medizin, Macht und Polizey. Joseph II. und die Erste Wiener Medizinische Schule, in: Christiane Druml (ed.), *Das neue Josephinum. Medizinhistorisches Museum Wien*, Vienna, 2022, 53–69.
19 Michel Foucault, *Histoire de la sexualité 1: La volonté de savoir*, Paris 1976 (Eng. *The History of Sexuality, vol. 1: The Will to Knowledge*, London, 1976).
20 Cf. Thomas Lemke, *Biopolitik zur Einführung*, Hamburg, 2013.
21 Cf. Wolfgang Eric Wagner, Doctores – Practicantes – Empirici. Die Durchsetzung der Medizinischen Fakultäten gegenüber anderen Heilergruppen in Paris und Wien im späten Mittelalter, in: Rainer Christoph Schwinges (ed.), *Universität im öffentlichen Raum* (Veröffentlichungen der Gesellschaft für Universitäts- und Wissenschaftsgeschichte, vol. 10), Basel, 2008, 15–43.
22 The so-called Tolerance Patents, which were issued by Emperor Joseph II in 1781/82, also enabled Jewish students to study medicine, whereas women could only enroll in the Medical Faculty of the University of Vienna from 1900. However, other more subtle forms of discrimination (during the course, when applying for a post, or when practicing) continued.
23 Cf. Karl Heinz Tragl, *Chronik der Wiener Krankenanstalten*, 26.
24 Cf. Erna Lesky, *Gerard van Swieten. Auftrag und Erfüllung, in: Lesky, Adam Wandruszka (eds.), Gerard van Swieten und seine Zeit. Internationales Symposium, veranstaltet von der Universität Wien im Institut für Geschichte der Medizin, 8.–10. Mai 1972*, Vienna et al., 1973, 11–62.
25 Cf. Christoph Gnant, Die Universität Wien im 18. Jahrhundert. Entkirchlichung – Verstaatlichung – Ausbau, in: Julia Rüdiger, Dieter Schweizer (eds.), *Stätten des Wissens. Die Universität Wien entlang ihrer Bauten 1365–2015*, Vienna et al., 2015, 87–99.
26 For more about the founding of Vienna's General Hospital and the design of the entire Josephine complex see: Dieter Jetter, *Wien von den Anfängen bis um 1900* (Geschichte des Hospitals, vol. 5), Wiesbaden, 1982, 21–90; Helmut Wyklicky, Manfred Skopec (eds.), *200 Jahre Allgemeines Krankenhaus in Wien*, Vienna, 1984; Axel Hinrich Murken, *Vom Armenhospital zum Großklinikum*, 36–38; Helmut Wyklicky, *200 Jahre Allgemeines Krankenhaus* (a series of published texts from Austrian universities), Vienna, 1993; Gabriela Schmidt, Die Wiener Medizinische Fakultät und das Allgemeine Krankenhaus, in: Alfred Ebenbauer, Wolfgang Greisenegger, Kurt Mühlberger (eds.), *Universitätscampus Wien, vol. 1: Historie und Geist*, Vienna, 1998, 7–35; Hellmut Lorenz, Das Alte Allgemeine Krankenhaus in Wien. Baugestalt und Baugeschichte, in: Alfred Ebenbauer, Wolfgang Greisenegger, Kurt Mühlberger (eds.), *Universitätscampus Wien, vol. 1*, 37–55; Karl Heinz Tragl, Chronik der Wiener Krankenanstalten, 33–60; Hellmut Lorenz: Der josephinische Bautenkomplex. Allgemeines Krankenhaus, Garnisonsspital, Narrenturm und Josephinum, in: Julia Rüdiger, Dieter Schweizer (eds.), *Stätten des Wissens*, 101–11.
27 *Direktiv-Regeln zur künftigen Einrichtung der hiesigen Spitäler und allgemeinen Versorgungshäuser*, Vienna, April 16, 1871.
28 Cf. Monika Czernin, *Der Kaiser reist inkognito. Joseph II. und das Europa der Aufklärung*, Munich, 2021, 240–43.
29 Johann Hunczovsky, *Medicinisch-chirurgische Beobachtungen auf seinen Reisen durch England und Frankreich, besonders ueber die Spitäler*, Vienna, 1783.
30 *Nachricht an das Publikum über die Einrichtung des Hauptspitals in Wien: bei dessen Eröffnung von der Oberdirektion herausgegeben*, Vienna, 1784.
31 Cf. Robert Wischer, Hans-Ulrich Riethmüller, *Zukunftsoffenes Krankenhaus. Fakten, Leitlinien, Bausteine*, Vienna, 2007, 22.
32 Cf. Beatrix Patzak, *Faszination und Ekel. Das Pathologisch-anatomische Bundesmuseum im Wiener Narrenturm*, Graz, 2009.
33 Cf. Robert Wischer, Hans-Ulrich Riethmüller, *Zukunftsoffenes Krankenhaus*, 20–22.
34 Cf. Helmut Wyklicky, *Das Josephinum. Biographie eines Hauses. Die medicinisch-chirurgische Josephs-Akademie seit 1785. Das Institut für Geschichte der Medizin seit 1920*, Vienna, 1985; Markus Swittalek, *Das Josephinum. Aufklärung. Klassizismus. Zentrum der Medizin*, technical dissertation (unpublished), Vienna, 2011; Christiane Druml, Moritz Stipsicz (eds.), *Das Josephinum. 650 Jahre Wiener Medizingeschichte. Mythos und Wahrheit*, Vienna, 2014; Hellmut Lorenz, Der josephinische Bautenkomplex. Allgemeines Krankenhaus, Garnisonsspital, Narrenturm und Josephinum, in: Julia Rüdiger, Dieter Schweizer (eds.), *Stätten des Wissens*, 101–11, here 108–10.
35 Cf. Anna Ehrlich, *Ärzte, Bader, Scharlatane. Die Geschichte der Heilkunst in Österreich*, Vienna, 2007, 180.
36 Cf. Erna Lesky, *Das Wiener Institut für Geschichte der Medizin im Josephinum*, Vienna, 1979.
37 Cf. Christiane Druml, Das Josephinum – historisches Eingangstor zur Wiener Medizin, in: Druml (ed.), *Das neue Josephinum*, 19–51.
38 Cf. Axel Hinrich Murken, *Vom Armenhospital zum Großklinikum*, 38 f.
39 Cf. Anke Pieper, Johann Peter Frank. Vom Arzt zum Gesundheitspolitiker. Eine europäische Karriere zwischen Aufklärung, Revolution und Reaktion, in: *Deutsches Ärzteblatt*, vol. 100, nos. 28–29, 7/14/2003, A 1952 f., here A 1952, and www.aerzteblatt.de/pdf.asp?id=37740 (9/22/2023).

27 *Direktiv-Regeln zur künftigen Einrichtung der hiesigen Spitäler und allgemeinen Versorgungshäuser*, Wien, 16. April 1871.
28 Vgl. Monika Czernin, *Der Kaiser reist inkognito. Joseph II. und das Europa der Aufklärung*, München 2021, S. 240–243.
29 Johann Hunczovsky, *Medicinisch-chirurgische Beobachtungen auf seinen Reisen durch England und Frankreich, besonders ueber die Spitäler*, Wien 1783.
30 *Nachricht an das Publikum über die Einrichtung des Hauptspitals in Wien: bei dessen Eröffnung von der Oberdirektion herausgegeben*, Wien 1784.
31 Vgl. Robert Wischer, Hans-Ulrich Riethmüller, *Zukunftsoffenes Krankenhaus. Fakten, Leitlinien, Bausteine*, Wien 2007, S. 22.
32 Vgl. Beatrix Patzak, *Faszination und Ekel. Das Pathologisch-anatomische Bundesmuseum im Wiener Narrenturm*, Graz 2009.
33 Vgl. Robert Wischer, Hans-Ulrich Riethmüller, *Zukunftsoffenes Krankenhaus*, S. 20–22.
34 Vgl. Helmut Wyklicky, *Das Josephinum. Biographie eines Hauses. Die medicinisch-chirurgische Josephs-Akademie seit 1785. Das Institut für Geschichte der Medizin seit 1920*, Wien 1985; Markus Swittalek, *Das Josephinum. Aufklärung. Klassizismus. Zentrum der Medizin*, techn. Diss. (unveröff.), Wien 2011; Christiane Druml, Moritz Stipsicz (Hg.), *Das Josephinum. 650 Jahre Wiener Medizingeschichte. Mythos und Wahrheit*, Wien 2014; Hellmut Lorenz, Der josephinische Bautenkomplex. Allgemeines Krankenhaus, Garnisonsspital, Narrenturm und Josephinum, in: Julia Rüdiger, Dieter Schweizer (Hg.), *Stätten des Wissens*, S. 101–111, hier S. 108–110.
35 Vgl. Anna Ehrlich, *Ärzte, Bader, Scharlatane. Die Geschichte der Heilkunst in Österreich*, Wien 2007, S. 180.
36 Vgl. Erna Lesky, *Das Wiener Institut für Geschichte der Medizin im Josephinum*, Wien 1979.
37 Vgl. Christiane Druml, Das Josephinum – historisches Eingangstor zur Wiener Medizin, in: dies. (Hg.), *Das neue Josephinum*, S. 19–51.
38 Vgl. Axel Hinrich Murken, *Vom Armenhospital zum Großklinikum*, S. 38 f.
39 Vgl. Anke Pieper, Johann Peter Frank. Vom Arzt zum Gesundheitspolitiker. Eine europäische Karriere zwischen Aufklärung, Revolution und Reaktion, in: *Deutsches Ärzteblatt*, Jg. 100, Heft 28–29, 14.7.2003, S. A 1951 f. bzw. www.aerzteblatt.de/pdf.asp?id=37740 (22.9.2023).
40 Vgl. Erna Lesky, *Die Wiener medizinische Schule im 19. Jahrhundert*, Graz – Köln 1965, S. 79.
41 Vgl. Anna Ehrlich, *Ärzte, Bader, Scharlatane*, S. 232 f.
42 Vgl. Kurt Mühlberger, Auf dem Weg zu einer „neuen Universität". Die Zeit der Reformen 1849–1873, in: Julia Rüdiger, Dieter Schweizer (Hg.), *Stätten des Wissens*, S. 139–146, hier S. 144.
43 Vgl. Erna Lesky, *Die Wiener medizinische Schule im 19. Jahrhundert*, S. 111 f.
44 Vgl. Redaktion der allgemeinen Wiener medizinischen Zeitung (Hg.), *Die feierliche Eröffnung des Pathologisch-Anatomischen und des Chemischen Institutes im k. k. Allgemeinen Krankenhause am 24. Mai 1862*, Wien 1862, S. 7 und 12.
45 Vgl. Maria Rentetzi, The city as a context for scientific activity: creating the Mediziner-Viertel in fin-de-siècle Vienna, in: *Endeavour*, Vol. 28 (1), March 2004, S. 39–44.
46 Ausführlich dazu: Thomas Meisel, Vormärz, Revolution 1848 und Verlust der Alten Universität sowie: Kurt Mühlberger, Auf dem Weg zu einer „neuen Universität". Die Zeit der Reformen 1849–1873, beide in: Julia Rüdiger, Dieter Schweizer (Hg.), *Stätten des Wissens*, S. 123–136 bzw. 139–146.
47 Vgl. Werner Ogris, *Die Universitätsreform des Ministers Leo Graf Thun-Hohenstein. Festvortrag anlässlich des Rektorstages im großen Festsaal der Universität Wien am 12. März 1999* (Wiener Universitätsreden, Neue Folge, Bd. 8), Wien 1999.
48 Vgl. Julia Rüdiger, Der kleine Monumentalbau. Das Chemische Institut als erster Universitätsbau nach 1848, in: dies., Dieter Schweizer (Hg.), *Stätten des Wissens*, S. 159–167.
49 Vgl. Klaus Taschwer, Terror gegen das Anatomische Institut von Julius Tandler, 1920–1934, in: *650 plus – Geschichte der Universität Wien*, https://geschichte.univie.ac.at/de/artikel/terror-gegen-das-anatomische-institut-von-julius-tandler (17.10.2022).
50 Vgl. Oliver Hochadel, Wie Wien zum Laboratorium wurde, in: *Der Standard*, 7.11.2020, www.derstandard.at/story/2000121090936/wie-wien-zum-laboratorium-wurde (22.9.2023).
51 Mitchel G. Ash, Metropolitan Scientific Infrastructures and Spaces of Knowledge in Vienna, 1848–1918. An Introduction, in: ders. (Hg.), *Science in the Metropolis. Vienna in Transnational Context, 1848–1918* (Routledge Studies in Cultural History), New York – London 2021, S. 1–21, hier S. 14.
52 Vgl. Doris Bachmann-Medick, Spatial Turn, in: dies., *Cultural Turns. Neuorientierungen in den Kulturwissenschaften*, Reinbek bei Hamburg 2006, S. 284–328.
53 Vgl. Peter Galison, Emily Thompson (Hg.), *The Architecture of Science*.
54 Die Wiener Spitalstadt, in: *Neue Freie Presse*, 20.6.1904, S. 5 f., hier S. 5.
55 Im Folgenden beziehe ich mich wesentlich auf: Dieter Jetter, *Wien von den Anfängen bis um 1900*, S. 91–101; Monika Keplinger, *Die „Neuen Kliniken" des Wiener Allgemeinen Krankenhauses (1904–1923). Fragment einer Krankenstadt* (Enzyklopädie des Wiener Wissens, Bd. 21), Weitra 2014; dies., *Die „Neuen Kliniken" des Wiener Allgemeinen Krankenhauses. Situierung – Bautypen – Formensprachen*, phil. Diss., Wien 2010.
56 Vgl. „Großstadt im Kleinformat. Die Wiener Ansichtskarte", Ausstellung im Wien Museum MUSA, 4.5.–24.9.2023.
57 Vgl. Axel Hinrich Murken, *Vom Armenhospital zum Großklinikum*, S. 147.
58 Vgl. Wolf Dirk Rauh, Die Funktionsstelle Operation, in: Philipp Meuser (Hg.), *Krankenhausbauten / Gesundheitsbauten, Bd. 1*, S. 72–77.
59 Vgl. Monika Keplinger, *Die „Neuen Kliniken" des Wiener Allgemeinen Krankenhauses (1904–1923)*, S. 226 f.
60 Vgl. Julia Rüdiger, Fallstudien zur Ikonografie und Funktion des Medizinerdenkmals in Wien, in: dies., Dieter Schweizer (Hg.), *Stätten des Wissens*, S. 73–93.
61 Vgl. Mary Hunter, *The face of medicine. Visualising medical masculinities in late nineteenth-century Paris*, Manchester 2016.

40 Cf. Erna Lesky, *Die Wiener medizinische Schule im 19. Jahrhundert*, Graz – Cologne, 1965, 79.
41 Cf. Anna Ehrlich, *Ärzte, Bader, Scharlatane*, 232 f.
42 Cf. Kurt Mühlberger, Auf dem Weg zu einer „neuen Universität". Die Zeit der Reformen 1849–1873, in: Julia Rüdiger, Dieter Schweizer (eds.), *Stätten des Wissens*, 139–46, here 144.
43 Cf. Erna Lesky, *Die Wiener medizinische Schule im 19. Jahrhundert*, 111 f.
44 Cf. Redaktion der allgemeinen Wiener medizinischen Zeitung (eds.), *Die feierliche Eröffnung des Pathologisch-Anatomischen und des Chemischen Institutes im k. k. Allgemeinen Krankenhause am 24. Mai 1862*, Vienna, 1862, 7 & 12.
45 Cf. Maria Rentetzi, The city as a context for scientific activity: creating the Mediziner-Viertel in fin-de-siècle Vienna, in: *Endeavour*, vol. 28 (1), March 2004, 39–44.
46 For more details: Thomas Meisel, Vormärz, Revolution 1848 und Verlust der Alten Universität and: Kurt Mühlberger, Auf dem Weg zu einer „neuen Universität". Die Zeit der Reformen 1849–1873, both in: Julia Rüdiger, Dieter Schweizer (eds.), *Stätten des Wissens*, 123–36 & 139–46.
47 Cf. Werner Ogris, *Die Universitätsreform des Ministers Leo Graf Thun-Hohenstein. Festvortrag anlässlich des Rektorstages im großen Festsaal der Universität Wien am 12. März 1999* (Wiener Universitätsreden, Neue Folge, vol. 8), Vienna, 1999.
48 Cf. Julia Rüdiger, Der kleine Monumentalbau. Das Chemische Institut als erster Universitätsbau nach 1848, in: Rüdiger, Dieter Schweizer (eds.), *Stätten des Wissens*, 159–67.
49 Cf. Klaus Taschwer, Terror gegen das Anatomische Institut von Julius Tandler, 1920–1934, in: *650 plus – Geschichte der Universität Wien*, https://geschichte.univie.ac.at/de/artikel/terror-gegen-das-anatomische-institut-von-julius-tandler (10/17/2022).
50 Cf. Oliver Hochadel, Wie Wien zum Laboratorium wurde, in: *Der Standard*, 11/7/2020, www.derstandard.at/story/2000121090936/wie-wien-zum-laboratorium-wurde (9/22/2023).
51 Mitchel G. Ash, Metropolitan Scientific Infrastructures and Spaces of Knowledge in Vienna, 1848–1918. An Introduction, in: Ash (ed.), *Science in the Metropolis. Vienna in Transnational Context, 1848–1918* (Routledge Studies in Cultural History), New York – London, 2021, 1–21, here 14.
52 Cf. Doris Bachmann-Medick, Spatial Turn, in: Bachmann-Medick, *Cultural Turns. Neuorientierungen in den Kulturwissenschaften*, Reinbek bei Hamburg, 2006, 284–328.
53 Cf. Peter Galison, Emily Thompson (eds.), *The Architecture of Science*.
54 Die Wiener Spitalstadt, in: *Neue Freie Presse*, 6/20/1904, 5 f., here 5.
55 In the following pages I principally refer to: Dieter Jetter, *Wien von den Anfängen bis um 1900*, 91–101; Monika Keplinger, *Die „Neuen Kliniken" des Wiener Allgemeinen Krankenhauses (1904–1923). Fragment einer Krankenstadt* (Enzyklopädie des Wiener Wissens, vol. 21), Weitra, 2014; Keplinger, *Die „Neuen Kliniken" des Wiener Allgemeinen Krankenhauses. Situierung – Bautypen – Formensprachen*, philosophical dissertation, Vienna, 2010.
56 Cf. „Großstadt im Kleinformat. Die Wiener Ansichtskarte", Exhibition in the Wien Museum MUSA, 5/4–9/24/2023.
57 Cf. Axel Hinrich Murken, *Vom Armenhospital zum Großklinikum*, 147.
58 Cf. Wolf Dirk Rauh, Die Funktionsstelle Operation, in: Philipp Meuser (ed.), *Krankenhausbauten / Gesundheitsbauten*, vol. 1, 72–77.
59 Cf. Monika Keplinger, *Die „Neuen Kliniken" des Wiener Allgemeinen Krankenhauses (1904–1923)*, 226 f.
60 Cf. Julia Rüdiger, Fallstudien zur Ikonografie und Funktion des Medizinerdenkmals in Wien, in: Rüdiger, Dieter Schweizer (eds.), *Stätten des Wissens*, 73–93.
61 Cf. Mary Hunter, *The face of medicine. Visualising medical masculinities in late nineteenth-century Paris*, Manchester, 2016.
62 In the following pages I refer to two recent overviews of the fundamental transformation of the hospital: Jeanne Kisacky, *Rise of the Modern Hospital. An Architectural History of Health and Healing, 1870–1940*, Pittsburgh, 2017, and Julie Willis, Philip Goad, Cameron Logan, *Architecture and the Modern Hospital. Nosokomeion to Hygeia*, London – New York, 2019.
63 The best-known examples of such healthcare buildings are surely the Sanatorium Zonnestraal in Hilversum, Netherlands (Johannes Duiker, Bernard Bijvoet, 1928), the Paimio Sanatorium in Finland (Alvar Aalto, 1929–33), and Waiblingen District Hospital near Stuttgart (Richard Döcker, 1926–28). The Tuberculosis Pavilion of Vienna City Council's Lainz Hospital (Fritz Judtmann, Egon Riss, 1929/30) also corresponds with this typology. Such hospitals and sanatoria were very important for the architecture of the modern movement.
64 Krankenkassen und Krankenhaus. Der Internationale Hospitalkongreß, in: *Arbeiter-Zeitung*, 6/13/1931, 6.
65 Cf. Karl Heinz Tragl, *Chronik der Wiener Krankenanstalten*, 19.
66 Cf. Andreas Bernard, *Die Geschichte des Fahrstuhls. Über einen beweglichen Ort der Moderne*, Frankfurt am Main, 2006.
67 Cf. Sarah Hodges, Hospitals as factories of medical garbage, in: *Anthropology & Medicine*, vol. 24 (3), December 2017, 319–33.
68 Cf. Linus Hofrichter, Krankenhausarchitektur – Gestaltungsqualität und die Berücksichtigung medizinischer Ablaufprozesse sind kein Widerspruch, in: Hermann Stockhorst, Linus Hofrichter, Andreas Franke (eds.), *Krankenhausbau. Architektur und Planung, bauliche Umsetzung, Projekt- und Betriebsorganisation*, Berlin, 2019, 137–54.
69 Cf. Markus Müller (ed.), *Auf dem Weg in die digitale Zukunft der Medizin. Medizinische Universität Wien – Jahresbericht 2022*, Vienna, 2023, 50.
70 Cf. Das Kranke(n)Haus. *Wie Architektur heilen hilft*, book accompanying the exhibition in the architecture museum of the Technical University of Munich (Pinakothek der Moderne), Berlin, 2023.
71 Cf. Der Neubau des Allgemeinen Krankenhauses Wien (Universitätskliniken), in: *Der Aufbau. Fachschrift für Planen, Bauen und Wohnen*, vol. 21. (1966), no. 6/7, 218–33.
72 Cf. Hans Denk et al., *Neubau Allgemeines Krankenhaus der Stadt Wien – Universitätskliniken*, Vienna – Munich, 1971, 36.
73 Cf. Susanne Hauser, Christa Kamleithner, Roland Meyer (eds.), *Architekturwissen. Grundlagentexte aus den Kulturwissenschaften, vol. 2: Zur Logistik des sozialen Raumes*, Bielefeld, 2013, 14–24.

62 Im Folgenden beziehe ich mich auf zwei aktuelle Überblickswerke, in denen die grundlegende Transformation des Spitals dargestellt wird: Jeanne Kisacky, *Rise of the Modern Hospital. An Architectural History of Health and Healing, 1870–1940*, Pittsburgh 2017; Julie Willis, Philip Goad, Cameron Logan, *Architecture and the Modern Hospital. Nosokomeion to Hygeia*, London – New York 2019.
63 Die bekanntesten Beispiele solcher Gesundheitsbauten sind sicherlich das Sanatorium Zonnestraal im niederländischen Hilversum (Johannes Duiker, Bernard Bijvoet, 1928), das Paimio Sanatorium in Finnland (Alvar Aalto, 1929–33) und das Bezirkskrankenhaus Waiblingen bei Stuttgart (Richard Döcker, 1926–28). Auch der Tuberkulosepavillon des Krankenhauses der Stadt Wien in Lainz (Fritz Judtmann, Egon Riss, 1929/30) entspricht diesem Typus. Für die Architekturmoderne waren Spitäler und Sanatorien wie diese von fundamentaler Bedeutung.
64 Krankenkassen und Krankenhaus. Der Internationale Hospitalkongreß, in: *Arbeiter-Zeitung*, 13.6.1931, S. 6.
65 Vgl. Karl Heinz Tragl, *Chronik der Wiener Krankenanstalten*, S. 19.
66 Vgl. Andreas Bernard, *Die Geschichte des Fahrstuhls. Über einen beweglichen Ort der Moderne*, Frankfurt am Main 2006.
67 Vgl. Sarah Hodges, Hospitals as factories of medical garbage, in: *Anthropology & Medicine*, Vol. 24 (3), December 2017, S. 319–333.
68 Vgl. Linus Hofrichter, Krankenhausarchitektur – Gestaltungsqualität und die Berücksichtigung medizinischer Ablaufprozesse sind kein Widerspruch, in: Hermann Stockhorst, Linus Hofrichter, Andreas Franke (Hg.), *Krankenhausbau. Architektur und Planung, bauliche Umsetzung, Projekt- und Betriebsorganisation*, Berlin 2019, S. 137–154.
69 Vgl. Markus Müller (Hg.), *Auf dem Weg in die digitale Zukunft der Medizin. Medizinische Universität Wien – Jahresbericht 2022*, Wien 2023, S. 50.
70 Vgl. *Das Kranke(n)Haus. Wie Architektur heilen hilft*, Begleitbuch zur Ausstellung im Architekturmuseum der Technischen Universität München (Pinakothek der Moderne), Berlin 2023.
71 Vgl. Der Neubau des Allgemeinen Krankenhauses Wien (Universitätskliniken), in: *Der Aufbau. Fachschrift für Planen, Bauen und Wohnen*, 21. Jg. (1966), Nr. 6/7, S. 218–233.
72 Vgl. Hans Denk et al., *Neubau Allgemeines Krankenhaus der Stadt Wien – Universitätskliniken*, Wien – München 1971, S. 36.
73 Vgl. Susanne Hauser, Christa Kamleithner, Roland Meyer (Hg.), *Architekturwissen. Grundlagentexte aus den Kulturwissenschaften, Bd. 2: Zur Logistik des sozialen Raumes*, Bielefeld 2013, S. 14–24.
74 Hans-Ulrich Riethmüller, *Raum- und Funktions-Programm 1959 für den Neubau des Allgemeinen Krankenhauses (Univ.-Kliniken) in Wien*, Tübingen 1960.
75 Sigfried Giedion, *Space, Time and Architecture. The growth of a new tradition*, Cambridge 1941.
76 Wolfgang Bauer, Hannes Lintl, Georg Lippert, Felix Kässens, Georg Köhler, Alexander Marchart, Otto Mayr, Roland Moebius, Otto Nobis.
77 Vgl. Voestalpine Medizintechnik GmbH (VAMED) (Hg.), *Das Wiener Allgemeine Krankenhaus – Universitätskliniken*, Wien 1994, S. 36 f.
78 Vgl. Unique and Superlative. Excerpts from a lecture on the Vienna AKH General hospital held by Roland Moebius, in: Stefan Gruber, Antje Lehn, Lisa Schmidt-Colinet, Angelika Schnell (Hg.), *Big! Bad? Modern. Four Megabuildings in Vienna*, Zürich 2015, S. 194–196.
79 Vgl. Matthias Oltay, Dawid Klich, The Vienna General Hospital – The Health Machine, in: Stefan Gruber et al. (Hg.), *Big! Bad? Modern*, S. 274–281.
80 Alfred Worm, *Der Skandal. AKH: Story, Analyse, Dokumente. Europas größter Krankenhausbau*, Wien 1981.
81 Vgl. Michael Zinganel, Good and Evil Monsters of Modernity, in: Stefan Gruber et al. (Hg.), *Big! Bad? Modern*, S. 197–200. – Dieses Großbauvorhaben, das als weltweit einziges Kernkraftwerk niemals seinen Betrieb aufgenommen hat, gilt als Wendepunkt im damaligen Demokratiebewusstsein und bildete einen entscheidenden Beitrag zur Etablierung des Umweltschutzgedankens.
82 Vgl. Ziele und Probleme im Krankenhausbau, in: *Der Aufbau*, 21. Jg. (1966), Nr. 6/7, S. 213.
83 Alfred Worm, „Einstellen!" Spitalsexperten erläutern, warum das größte und teuerste Spital der Welt, das AKH in Wien, nicht – zumindest nicht so – weitergebaut werden darf, in: *Profil*, 23. März 1981, S. 18–23.
84 Vgl. Angelika Schnell, Antje Lehn, Introduction, in: Stefan Gruber et al. (Hg.), *Big! Bad? Modern*, S. 12 f.
85 Rem Koolhaas, Bigness or the problem of Large (1994), in: Office for Metropolitan Architecture (OMA), Rem Koolhaas, Bruce Mau, *S, M, L, XL [small, medium, large, extra-large]*, hg. von Jennifer Sigler, Fotografien von Hans Werlemann, New York 1995, S. 495–516.
86 Vgl. Julie Willis, Philip Goad, Cameron Logan, *Architecture and the Modern Hospital*, S. 182 f. und 221. – Als „bedeutendstes Zeugnis der Hightech-Architektur in Deutschland" steht das Universitätsklinikum Aachen seit 2008 unter Schutz. Durch die damit verbundenen Auflagen gestalten sich Sanierungsvorhaben und Zubauten jedoch schwierig, die Unterschutzstellung bildet ein gravierendes Hemmnis für die künftige Entwicklung der Aachener Universitätsmedizin. Vgl. Wissenschaftsrat (Hg.), *Stellungnahme zur Weiterentwicklung der Universitätsmedizin der Rheinisch-Westfälischen Technischen Hochschule Aachen*, Rostock 2019, www.wissenschaftsrat.de/download/2019/8040-19.pdf?__blob=publicationFile&v=1 (22.9.2023).
87 Vgl. Unique and Superlative. Excerpts from a lecture on the Vienna AKH General hospital held by Roland Moebius, in: Stefan Gruber et al. (Hg.), *Big! Bad? Modern*, S. 194–196, hier S. 195.
88 Der Nobelpreis für Physiologie oder Medizin erging 1914 an Robert Bárány für seine experimentelle Erforschung des Gleichgewichtsorgans, 1927 an Julius Wagner-Jauregg für den Einsatz der Malariatherapie bei der Behandlung von Psychosen, 1930 an Karl Landsteiner für die Entdeckung der Blutgruppen und 1936 an Otto Loewi für seine Erkenntnisse zur chemischen Übertragung von Nervenimpulsen.
89 So auch Sigmund Freud, Adolf Lorenz, Clemens von Pirquet u. a.
90 Vgl. Michael Hubenstorf, Ende einer Tradition und Fortsetzung als Provinz. Die Medizinischen Fakultäten der Universitäten Berlin und Wien 1925–1950, in: Christoph Meinel, Peter Voswinckel (Hg.), *Medizin, Naturwissenschaft, Technik und Nationalsozialismus. Kontinuitäten und Diskontinuitäten*, Stuttgart 1994, S. 33–53.

74 Hans-Ulrich Riethmüller, *Raum- und Funktions-Programm 1959 für den Neubau des Allgemeinen Krankenhauses (Univ.-Kliniken) in Wien*, Tubingen, 1960.
75 Sigfried Giedion, *Space, Time and Architecture. The growth of a new tradition*, Cambridge, 1941.
76 Wolfgang Bauer, Hannes Lintl, Georg Lippert, Felix Kässens, Georg Köhler, Alexander Marchart, Otto Mayr, Roland Moebius, and Otto Nobis.
77 Cf. Voestalpine Medizintechnik GmbH (VAMED) (ed.), Das Wiener Allgemeine Krankenhaus – Universitätskliniken, Vienna, 1994, 36 f.
78 Cf. Unique and Superlative. Excerpts from a lecture on the Vienna AKH General Hospital held by Roland Moebius, in: Stefan Gruber, Antje Lehn, Lisa Schmidt-Colinet, and Angelika Schnell (eds.), *Big! Bad? Modern. Four Megabuildings in Vienna*, Zurich, 2015, 194–96.
79 Cf. Matthias Oltay, Dawid Klich, The Vienna General Hospital – The Health Machine, in: Stefan Gruber et al. (eds.), *Big! Bad? Modern*, 274–81.
80 Alfred Worm, *Der Skandal. AKH: Story, Analyse, Dokumente. Europas größter Krankenhausbau*, Vienna, 1981.
81 Cf. Michael Zinganel, Good and Evil Monsters of Modernity, in: Stefan Gruber et al. (eds.), *Big! Bad? Modern*, 197–200. This major project, the only nuclear power station worldwide that never started operating is regarded as a turning point for the democratic awareness at the time and made a key contribution to the establishment of the idea of environmental protection.
82 Cf. Ziele und Probleme im Krankenhausbau, in: *Der Aufbau*, vol. 21. (1966), no. 6/7, 213.
83 Alfred Worm, „Einstellen!" Spitalsexperten erläutern, warum das größte und teuerste Spital der Welt, das AKH in Wien, nicht – zumindest nicht so – weitergebaut werden darf, in: *Profil*, March 23, 1981, 18–23.
84 Cf. Angelika Schnell, Antje Lehn, Introduction, in: Stefan Gruber et al. (eds.), *Big! Bad? Modern*, 12 f.
85 Rem Koolhaas, Bigness or the problem of Large (1994), in: Office for Metropolitan Architecture (OMA), Rem Koolhaas, Bruce Mau, *S, M, L, XL [small, medium, large, extra-large]*, ed. Jennifer Sigler, photographs by Hans Werlemann, New York, 1995, 495–516.
86 Cf. Julie Willis, Philip Goad, Cameron Logan, Architecture and the Modern Hospital, 182 f. & 221. As "the most important example of high-tech architecture in Germany," University Hospital Aachen has been listed since 2008. However, the restrictions imposed by this listing make refurbishment work and extensions difficult to realize and it is a serious obstacle to the future development of university medicine in Aachen. Cf. Wissenschaftsrat (ed.), *Stellungnahme zur Weiterentwicklung der Universitätsmedizin der Rheinisch-Westfälischen Technischen Hochschule Aachen*, Rostock, 2019, www.wissenschaftsrat.de/download/2019/8040-19.pdf?__blob=publicationFile&v=1 (9/22/2023).
87 Cf. Unique and Superlative. Excerpts from a lecture on the Vienna AKH General hospital held by Roland Moebius, in: Stefan Gruber et al. (eds.), *Big! Bad? Modern*, 194–96, here 195.
88 The Nobel Prize for Physiology or Medicine was awarded in 1914 to Robert Bárány for his experimental research into the vestibular system, in 1927 to Julius Wagner-Jauregg for the use of malaria therapy in the treatment of psychoses, in 1930 to Karl Landsteiner for the discovery of the blood groups, and in 1936 to Otto Loewi for his findings on the chemical transmission of nerve impulses.
89 Such as Sigmund Freud, Adolf Lorenz, Clemens von Pirquet, et al.
90 Cf. Michael Hubenstorf, Ende einer Tradition und Fortsetzung als Provinz. Die Medizinischen Fakultäten der Universitäten Berlin und Wien 1925–1950, in: Christoph Meinel, Peter Voswinckel (eds.), *Medizin, Naturwissenschaft, Technik und Nationalsozialismus. Kontinuitäten und Diskontinuitäten*, Stuttgart, 1994, 33–53.
91 Cf. Wolfgang Schütz, Markus Müller, Forschung – der mühsame Weg zurück, in: Birgit Nemec, Hans-Georg Hofer, Felicitas Seebacher, and Wolfgang Schütz (eds.), *Medizin in Wien nach 1945. Strukturen, Aushandlungsprozesse, Reflexionen* (650 Jahre Universität Wien – Aufbruch ins neue Jahrhundert, vol. 6), Vienna, 2022, 163–83.
92 See, for example: *Die Wiener Medizinische Fakultät 1938 bis 1945*, brochure accompanying the exhibition in the Josephinum, Vienna, 2018.
93 The former Medical Faculties in Innsbruck and Graz were also transformed into Medical Universities at the same time.
94 Cf. *Entwicklungsplan der Medizinischen Universität Wien 2022–2027* (Mitteilungsblatt der Medizinischen Universität Wien, Studienjahr 2020/2021, 5th part, no. 5), Vienna, 2020.
95 *QS World University Rankings by Subject 2023: Medicine*, www.topuniversities.com/university-rankings/university-subject-rankings/2023/medicine (9/20/2023).
96 The World's Best Hospitals 2022, www.newsweek.com/worlds-best-hospitals-2022 (9/22/2023). A total of 2,200 clinics in 27 countries were evaluated. Alongside first-class care, research, and innovation, stability is also included as a hallmark of the ranked clinics.
97 Cf. Wilhelm Krull, *Die vermessene Universität. Ziel, Wunsch und Wirklichkeit*, Vienna, 2017.
98 Cf. Markus Müller (ed.), *Auf dem Weg in die digitale Zukunft der Medizin*, 16–19; *Entwicklungsplan der Medizinischen Universität Wien 2022–2027*; https://bauprojekte.meduniwien.ac.at (11/14/2023).
99 www.medunicampus-mariannengasse.at
100 Nathan Wolfe, *The Viral Storm. The Dawn of a New Pandemic Age*, London, 2011.
101 Cf. Alfred Ebenbauer, Wolfgang Greisenegger, Kurt Mühlberger (eds.), *Universitätscampus Wien, vol. 1*; Elmar Schübl, Vom Alten Allgemeinen Krankenhaus zum Universitäts-Campus Wien, in: Julia Rüdiger, Dieter Schweizer (eds.), *Stätten des Wissens*, 301–08.
102 Cf. *The Global Liveability Index 2023*, www.eiu.com/n/campaigns/global-liveability-index-2023/ (9/22/2023). Vienna has headed these rankings since 2009. In the areas of "Healthcare," "Education," and "Infrastructure," the city was most recently awarded a maximum of 100 points.

91   Vgl. Wolfgang Schütz, Markus Müller, Forschung – der mühsame Weg zurück, in: Birgit Nemec, Hans-Georg Hofer, Felicitas Seebacher, Wolfgang Schütz (Hg.), *Medizin in Wien nach 1945. Strukturen, Aushandlungsprozesse, Reflexionen* (650 Jahre Universität Wien – Aufbruch ins neue Jahrhundert, Bd. 6), Wien 2022, S. 163–183.

92   Siehe etwa: *Die Wiener Medizinische Fakultät 1938 bis 1945*, Broschüre zur Ausstellung im Josephinum, Wien 2018.

93   Auch die einstigen medizinischen Fakultäten in Innsbruck und Graz wurden zeitgleich in medizinische Universitäten umgewandelt.

94   Vgl. *Entwicklungsplan der Medizinischen Universität Wien 2022–2027* (Mitteilungsblatt der Medizinischen Universität Wien, Studienjahr 2020/2021, 5. Stück, Nr. 5), Wien 2020.

95   *QS World University Rankings by Subject 2023: Medicine*, www.topuniversities.com/university-rankings/university-subject-rankings/2023/medicine (20.9.2023).

96   *The World's Best Hospitals 2022*, www.newsweek.com/worlds-best-hospitals-2022 (22.9.2023). – Insgesamt 2.200 Kliniken aus 27 Ländern wurden hierfür bewertet. Neben erstklassiger Pflege, Forschung und Innovation ist auch die Beständigkeit als ein Markenzeichen der gereihten Kliniken angeführt.

97   Vgl. Wilhelm Krull, *Die vermessene Universität. Ziel, Wunsch und Wirklichkeit*, Wien 2017.

98   Vgl. Markus Müller (Hg.), *Auf dem Weg in die digitale Zukunft der Medizin*, S. 16–19; Entwicklungsplan der Medizinischen Universität Wien 2022–2027; https://bauprojekte.meduniwien.ac.at (14.11.2023).

99   www.medunicampus-mariannengasse.at

100   Nathan Wolfe, *The Viral Storm. The Dawn of a New Pandemic Age*, London 2011 (dt. *Die Wiederkehr der Seuchen*, Hamburg 2012).

101   Vgl. Alfred Ebenbauer, Wolfgang Greisenegger, Kurt Mühlberger (Hg.), *Universitätscampus Wien, Bd. 1*; Elmar Schübl, Vom Alten Allgemeinen Krankenhaus zum Universitäts-Campus Wien, in: Julia Rüdiger, Dieter Schweizer (Hg.), *Stätten des Wissens*, S. 301–308.

102   Vgl. *The Global Liveability Index 2023*, www.eiu.com/n/campaigns/global-liveability-index-2023 (22.9.2023). – Seit 2009 figuriert Wien an der Spitze dieses Rankings. Für die Bereiche „Healthcare", „Education" und „Infrastructure" wurde zuletzt die maximale Punktezahl von 100 vergeben.

Bildindex

Photo Index

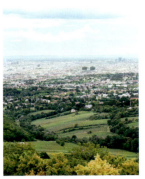

11   Blick vom Kahlenberg
View from Kahlenberg

13   MedUni Campus AKH

14   Grünes Bettenhaus,
        MedUni Campus AKH
Green ward block, MedUni
Campus AKH

15   MedUni Campus AKH

16   Energiezentrale,
        AKH Wien
Energy supply center, University
Hospital Vienna

17   Feuerwache, AKH Wien
Fire station, University Hospital
Vienna

18   Gebäudetechnik,
        AKH Wien
Building services, University
Hospital Vienna

19   Energieversorgung,
        MedUni Campus AKH
Energy supply infrastructure,
MedUni Campus AKH

20   MedUni Campus AKH

21   Logistik, AKH Wien
Logistics infrastructure,
University Hospital Vienna

22   Küche, AKH Wien
Kitchen, University Hospital
Vienna

23   Küche, AKH Wien
Kitchen, University Hospital
Vienna

24   Küche, AKH Wien
Kitchen, University Hospital
Vienna

25   Küche, AKH Wien
Kitchen, University Hospital
Vienna

27   Gebäudetechnik,
        AKH Wien
Building services, University
Hospital Vienna

28   Gebäudetechnik,
        AKH Wien
Building services, University
Hospital Vienna

29 Gebäudetechnik,
    AKH Wien
Building services, University
Hospital Vienna

30 Gebäudetechnik,
    AKH Wien
Building services, University
Hospital Vienna

31 Gebäudetechnik,
    AKH Wien
Building services, University
Hospital Vienna

32 Gebäudetechnik,
    AKH Wien
Building services, University
Hospital Vienna

33 Gebäudetechnik,
    AKH Wien
Building services, University
Hospital Vienna

35 Gebäudetechnik,
    AKH Wien
Building services, University
Hospital Vienna

36 Gebäudetechnik,
    AKH Wien
Building services, University
Hospital Vienna

37 Gebäudetechnik,
    AKH Wien
Building services, University
Hospital Vienna

38 Gebäudetechnik,
    AKH Wien
Building services, University
Hospital Vienna

39 Gebäudetechnik,
    AKH Wien
Building services, University
Hospital Vienna

40 Gebäudetechnik,
    AKH Wien
Building services, University
Hospital Vienna

41 Gebäudetechnik,
    AKH Wien
Building services, University
Hospital Vienna

42 Technischer Leitstand,
    AKH Wien
Technical control station, University Hospital Vienna

43 Technischer Leitstand,
    AKH Wien
Technical control station, University Hospital Vienna

44 Gebäudetechnik,
    AKH Wien
Building services, University
Hospital Vienna

45 Gebäudetechnik,
    AKH Wien
Building services, University
Hospital Vienna

46   Gebäudetechnik,
      AKH Wien
Building services, University
Hospital Vienna

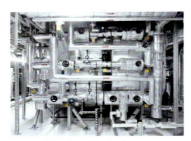

47   Core Facility Labortier-
      zucht und -haltung,
      Himberg
Core Facility Laboratory Animal
Breeding and Husbandry,
Himberg

48   Logistik, AKH Wien
Logistics infrastructure,
University Hospital Vienna

49   Gebäudetechnik,
      AKH Wien
Building services, University
Hospital Vienna

51   Wasserspeicher,
      AKH Wien
Water tank, University Hospital
Vienna

52   Desinfektionsanlage,
      AKH Wien
Disinfection facility, University
Hospital Vienna

53   Logistik, AKH Wien
Logistics infrastructure,
University Hospital Vienna

54   Apotheke, AKH Wien
Pharmacy, University Hospital
Vienna

55   Apotheke, AKH Wien
Pharmacy, University Hospital
Vienna

57   Logistik, AKH Wien
Logistics infrastructure,
University Hospital Vienna

58   Logistik, AKH Wien
Logistics infrastructure,
University Hospital Vienna

59   Logistik, AKH Wien
Logistics infrastructure,
University Hospital Vienna

60   Logistik, AKH Wien
Logistics infrastructure,
University Hospital Vienna

61   Logistik, AKH Wien
Logistics infrastructure,
University Hospital Vienna

62   Logistik, AKH Wien
Logistics infrastructure,
University Hospital Vienna

63   Logistik, AKH Wien
Logistics infrastructure,
University Hospital Vienna

64   Logistik, AKH Wien
Logistics infrastructure,
University Hospital Vienna

65   Apotheke, AKH Wien
Pharmacy, University Hospital
Vienna

67   Zentrum für Anatomie
      und Zellbiologie
Center for Anatomy and
Cell Biology

68   Zentrum für Pathophysio-
      logie, Infektiologie und
      Immunologie
Center for Pathophysiology,
Infectiology, and Immunology

69   Zentrum für Pathobio-
      chemie und Genetik
Center for Pathobiochemistry
and Genetics

70   Josephinum

71   Zentrum für Pathobio-
      chemie und Genetik
Center for Pathobiochemistry
and Genetics

72   Erschließung, AKH Wien
Circulation areas, University
Hospital Vienna

73   Erschließung, AKH Wien
Circulation areas, University
Hospital Vienna

74   Core Facility Labortierzucht
      und -haltung, Himberg
Core Facility Laboratory Animal
Breeding and Husbandry,
Himberg

75   Core Facility Labortierzucht
      und -haltung, Himberg
Core Facility Laboratory Animal
Breeding and Husbandry,
Himberg

76   Universitätszahnklinik
      Wien
University Clinic of Dentistry

77   Erschließung, AKH Wien
Circulation areas, University
Hospital Vienna

78   Betriebsrestaurant,
      AKH Wien
Staff restaurant, University
Hospital Vienna

79   Erschließung, AKH Wien
Circulation areas, University
Hospital Vienna

81   Erschließung, AKH Wien
Circulation areas, University
Hospital Vienna

237

82   Leitstelle, AKH Wien
Control room, University
Hospital Vienna

83   Aufenthaltsbereich,
AKH Wien
Waiting area, University
Hospital Vienna

85   Näherei, AKH Wien
Sewing room, University
Hospital Vienna

86   Erschließung, AKH Wien
Circulation areas, University
Hospital Vienna

87   Operationssaal, AKH Wien
Operating room, University
Hospital Vienna

88   Umkleidebereich,
AKH Wien
Changing area, University
Hospital Vienna

89   Umkleidebereich,
AKH Wien
Changing area, University
Hospital Vienna

90   Operationssaal, AKH Wien
Operating room, University
Hospital Vienna

91   Operationssaal, AKH Wien
Operating room, University
Hospital Vienna

93   Operationssaal, AKH Wien
Operating room, University
Hospital Vienna

94   Reinigungsstützpunkt,
AKH Wien
Cleaning base, University
Hospital Vienna

95   Sterilgutlager, AKH Wien
Sterile goods store, University
Hospital Vienna

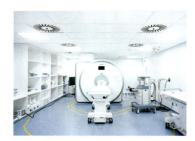

96   Operationssaal, AKH Wien
Operating room, University
Hospital Vienna

97   Operationssaal, AKH Wien
Operating room, University
Hospital Vienna

98   Zentrum für Biomedizini-
sche Forschung und Trans-
lationale Chirurgie, Himberg
Center for Biomedical Research
and Translational Surgery,
Himberg

99   Operationssaal, Universi-
tätszahnklinik Wien
Operating room, University
Clinic of Dentistry

100   Klinisches Institut für
       Labormedizin, AKH Wien
Department of Laboratory Medicine, University Hospital Vienna

101   Biobank, Klinisches
       Institut für Pathologie,
       AKH Wien
Biobank, Department of
Pathology, University Hospital
Vienna

103   Biobank, Klinisches
       Institut für Pathologie,
       AKH Wien
Biobank, Department of
Pathology, University Hospital
Vienna

104   Klinisches Institut
       für Pathologie, AKH Wien
Department of Pathology,
University Hospital Vienna

105   Klinisches Institut
       für Pathologie, AKH Wien
Department of Pathology,
University Hospital Vienna

106   Kommunikation,
       AKH Wien
Communication infrastructure,
University Hospital Vienna

107   Apotheke, AKH Wien
Pharmacy, University Hospital
Vienna

108   Intensivzimmer,
       AKH Wien
Intensive care unit, University
Hospital Vienna

109   Bettenzimmer, AKH Wien
Patient room, University
Hospital Vienna

110   Hubschrauberlandeplatz,
       AKH Wien
Helicopter landing pad,
University Hospital Vienna

111   Rotes Bettenhaus,
       MedUni Campus AKH
Red ward block, MedUni
Campus AKH

112   Rotes Bettenhaus,
       MedUni Campus AKH
Red ward block, MedUni
Campus AKH

113   Baufeld Süd, MedUni
       Campus AKH
Southern building plot, MedUni
Campus AKH

114   Aufgang Hörsaalzentrum,
       MedUni Campus AKH
Vertical circulation, lecture
theater center, MedUni Campus
AKH

115   CeMM – Forschungszen-
       trum für Molekulare Medi-
       zin, MedUni Campus AKH
CeMM – Research Center
for Molecular Medicine, MedUni
Campus AKH

117   Exzellenzzentrum
       Hochfeld MR, MedUni
       Campus AKH
High Field MR Center, MedUni
Campus AKH

239

119   Teaching Center, MedUni Campus AKH

120   Teaching Center, MedUni Campus AKH

121   Ehemalige Pflegeschule, MedUni Campus AKH
Former nursing school, MedUni Campus AKH

123   Baugrube, MedUni Campus Mariannengasse
Construction pit, MedUni Campus Mariannengasse

124   Eingangstor, Altes AKH Wien
Entrance gate, Altes AKH

125   Denkmal Theodor Billroth, Altes AKH Wien
Theodor Billroth Monument, Altes AKH

125   Denkmal Hermann Franz Müller, Altes AKH Wien
Hermann Franz Müller Monument, Altes AKH

125   Denkmal Ignaz Semmelweis, MedUni Campus AKH
Ignaz Semmelweis Monument, MedUni Campus AKH

125   Denkmal Joseph II., Altes AKH Wien
Joseph II Monument, Altes AKH

126   Denkmal Ignaz Semmelweis, MedUni Campus AKH
Ignaz Semmelweis Monument, MedUni Campus AKH

126   Denkmal Wilhelm Türk, MedUni Campus AKH
Wilhelm Türk Monument, MedUni Campus AKH

126   Denkmal Franz Schuh, Altes AKH Wien
Franz Schuh Monument, Altes AKH

126   Denkmal Ottokar Chiari, MedUni Campus AKH
Ottokar Chiari Monument, MedUni Campus AKH

127   Denkmal Sigmund Freud, MedUni Campus AKH
Sigmund Freud Monument, MedUni Campus AKH

127   Mahnmal gegen das Vergessen, MedUni Campus AKH
The Memorial of Remembrance, MedUni Campus AKH

128   Universitätszahnklinik Wien
University Clinic of Denistry

129 Narrenturm, Altes AKH
Wien
Narrenturm, Altes AKH

131 Zentrum für
Hirnforschung
Center for Brain Research

132 Zentrum für
Hirnforschung
Center for Brain Research

133 Zentrum für
Hirnforschung
Center for Brain Research

134 Zentrum für
Hirnforschung
Center for Brain Research

135 Core Facility Imaging,
Anna Spiegel Forschungs-
gebäude
Core Facility Imaging,
Anna Spiegel Research Building

136 Core Facility Proteomics,
Anna Spiegel Forschungs-
gebäude
Core Facility Proteomics,
Anna Spiegel Research Building

137 Core Facility Proteomics,
Anna Spiegel Forschungs-
gebäude
Core Facility Proteomics,
Anna Spiegel Research Building

138 Core Facility Proteomics,
Anna Spiegel Forschungs-
gebäude
Core Facility Proteomics,
Anna Spiegel Research Building

139 Core Facility Imaging,
Anna Spiegel Forschungs-
gebäude
Core Facility Imaging,
Anna Spiegel Research Building

140 Core Facility Imaging,
Anna Spiegel Forschungs-
gebäude
Core Facility Imaging,
Anna Spiegel Research Building

141 Core Facility Imaging,
Anna Spiegel Forschungs-
gebäude
Core Facility Imaging,
Anna Spiegel Research Building

143 Zentrum für Anatomie
und Zellbiologie
Center for Anatomy and
Cell Biology

144 Hörsaal, Zentrum für
Physiologie und Pharma-
kologie
Lecture theater, Center for
Physiology and Pharmacology

145 Emanuel Merck
Auditorium, Zentrum für
Pathobiochemie und
Genetik
Emanuel Merck Auditorium,
Center for Pathobiochemistry
and Genetics

146 Ehemaliger Hörsaal,
Zentrum für
Gerichtsmedizin
Former lecture theater, Center
for Forensic Medicine

241

147 Hörsaalzentrum,
AKH Wien
Lecture theater center,
University Hospital Vienna

149 Jugendstilhörsaal, MedUni
Campus AKH
Jugendstil lecture theater,
MedUni Campus AKH

150 Hörsaal Borschkegasse
Lecture theater, Borschkegasse

151 Zentrum für Patho-
biochemie und Genetik
Center for Pathobiochemistry
and Genetics

152 Zentrum für Anatomie
und Zellbiologie
Center for Anatomy and
Cell Biology

153 Zentrum für Anatomie
und Zellbiologie
Center for Anatomy and
Cell Biology

155 Universitätszahnklinik
Wien
University Clinic of Dentistry

156 Zentrum für Anatomie
und Zellbiologie
Center for Anatomy and
Cell Biology

157 Zentrum für Anatomie
und Zellbiologie
Center for Anatomy and
Cell Biology

158 Zentrum für
Gerichtsmedizin
Center for Forensic Medicine

159 Zentrum für Anatomie
und Zellbiologie
Center for Anatomy and
Cell Biology

160 Universitätsbibliothek,
AKH Wien
University Library, University
Hospital Vienna

161 Universitätsbibliothek,
AKH Wien
University Library, University
Hospital Vienna

162 Zentrum für Anatomie
und Zellbiologie
Center for Anatomy and
Cell Biology

163 Lesesaal, Josephinum
Reading room, Josephinum

165 Zentrum für
Gerichtsmedizin
Center for Forensic Medicine

166 Josephinum – Medizin-
historisches Museum Wien
Josephinum – Medical History
Museum Vienna

167 Josephinum – Medizin-
historisches Museum Wien
Josephinum – Medical History
Museum Vienna

168 Historischer Hörsaal,
Josephinum
Historical lecture theater,
Josephinum

169 Josephinum

171 Zentrum für
Hirnforschung
Center for Brain Research

172 Medizinisches Dokumen-
tationszentrum, AKH Wien
Medical Documentation Center,
University Hospital Vienna

173 St. Anna Kinderspital
St. Anna Children's Hospital

174 Zentrum für Patho-
physiologie, Infektiologie
und Immunologie
Center for Pathophysiology,
Infectiology, and Immunology

175 Max Perutz Labs,
Vienna BioCenter

176 Zentrum für
Gerichtsmedizin
Center for Forensic Medicine

177 Verwaltungsgebäude,
MedUni Campus AKH
Administration building,
MedUni Campus AKH

178 Zentrum für Anatomie
und Zellbiologie
Center for Anatomy and
Cell Biology

179 Zentrum für Anatomie
und Zellbiologie
Center for Anatomy and
Cell Biology

180 Zentrum für Anatomie
und Zellbiologie
Center for Anatomy and
Cell Biology

181 Zentrum für Patho-
biochemie und Genetik
Center for Pathobiochemistry
and Genetics

183 Blick vom Rathaus
View from the City Hall

243

Kurzbiografien der Herausgeber:innen

MARKUS MÜLLER ist Rektor der Medizinischen Universität Wien (seit 2015), Präsident des Obersten Sanitätsrats (seit 2018), Vizepräsident der Österreichischen Universitätenkonferenz und Mitglied des Supervisory Boards des Universitätsklinikums AKH Wien. Geboren 1967 in Klagenfurt, 1993 Promotion sub auspiciis, Ausbildung zum Facharzt für Innere Medizin in Österreich, Schweden und den USA, Habilitation 1998 (Klinische Pharmakologie) und 2001 (Innere Medizin), 2004 Berufung zum Universitätsprofessor. 2002–2015 Vorstand der Universitätsklinik für Klinische Pharmakologie am AKH Wien; Honorary Fellow des American College of Clinical Pharmacology; Gouverneur, Tel Aviv University (Israel); Adjunct Faculty, University of Florida (USA).

STEFAN OLÁH ist Fotograf, er studierte an der Staatlichen Fachakademie für Fotodesign in München, lehrte von 1995 bis 2017 an der Universität für angewandte Kunst Wien und ist Sprecher der IG Architekturfotografie. Neben seiner künstlerischen Arbeit sowie seiner Publikations- und Ausstellungstätigkeit konzipiert und fotografiert er Bildserien für Institutionen aus den Bereichen Kunst, Kultur und Wissenschaft. Seine umfangreichen fotografischen Projekte haben Architektur und verschiedene Lebens- und Kulturräume zum Thema, sie wurden in zahlreichen Bildbänden publiziert (z. B. *Bunt, sozial, brutal. Architektur der 1970er Jahre in Österreich* oder *Museumsdepots – Inside the Museum Storage*) und sind laufend in Ausstellungen zu sehen. 2019 erschien der gemeinsam mit Ulrike Matzer herausgegebene Bildband *Karl Schwanzer: Spuren – Traces*, in dem Stefan Oláh durch seinen besonderen fotografischen Blick für die erhaltenen Bauten dieses Architekten sensibilisiert.

ULRIKE MATZER ist Kunsthistorikerin, Kulturwissenschaftlerin und Kritikerin, ihre Arbeit ist an der Schnittstelle von Wissenschafts-, Architektur- und Mediengeschichte, Gender Studies und Visueller Kultur angesiedelt. Seit Herbst 2022 ist sie Dozentin im Rahmen des postgradualen Lehrgangs „Theory and History of Photography" an der Universität Zürich, zuvor hatte sie die Gastprofessur für Geschichte und Theorie der Fotografie an der Universität für angewandte Kunst Wien inne. Für ihre Dissertation über frühe Wiener Berufsfotografinnen wurde sie 2021 mit dem Johanna-Dohnal-Förderpreis ausgezeichnet. Seit 2005 hat sie diverse Forschungsprojekte zu Aspekten der Kulturgeschichte Wiens und zu fotohistorischen Themen durchgeführt und ist Autorin zahlreicher Artikel und Kritiken sowie (Mit-)Herausgeberin einschlägiger Bücher.

Short Biographies of the Editors

MARKUS MÜLLER is Rector of the Medical University of Vienna (since 2015), President of the Austrian Public Health Council (since 2018), Vice President, Universities Austria, and a member of the Supervisory Board of University Hospital Vienna. He was born in Klagenfurt in 1967, graduated *sub auspiciis* in 1993, trained as a specialist for internal medicine in Austria, Sweden, and the USA, holds post-doctoral qualifications in clinical pharmacology (1998) and internal medicine (2001), and was appointed as a university professor in 2004. He headed the Department of Clinical Pharmacology at University Hospital Vienna from 2002–2015, is an honorary fellow of the American College of Clinical Pharmacology, a Governor of Tel Aviv University (Israel), and an adjunct faculty of the University of Florida (USA).

STEFAN OLÁH is a photographer who studied at the State Academy for Photographic Design in Munich, taught at the University of Applied Arts in Vienna from 1995 to 2017, and is a spokesperson of IG Architekturfotografie. Alongside his artistic work and publication and exhibition activities, he conceives and photographs pictorial series for institutions in the artistic, cultural, and scientific fields. His extensive photographic projects address architecture and diverse habitats and cultural spaces; they have been published in numerous illustrated books (e.g. *Bunt, sozial, brutal. Architektur der 1970er Jahre in Österreich* and *Museumsdepots – Inside the Museum Storage*) and feature regularly in exhibitions. In *Karl Schwanzer: Spuren – Traces*, which he jointly edited with Ulrike Matzer and which was published in 2019, Stefan Oláh's special photographic perspective enhanced the awareness and appreciation of the remaining buildings of this architect.

ULRIKE MATZER is an art historian, cultural scientist, and critic, who works at the intersection of scientific, architectural, and media history, gender studies, and visual culture. She has lectured on the postgraduate course "Theory and History of Photography" at the University of Zurich since 2022, and was previously a visiting professor for the history and theory of photography at the University of Applied Arts Vienna. In 2021, she was awarded the Johanna Dohnal sponsorship prize for her dissertation on early female professional photographers in Vienna. Since 2005, she has worked on a range of research projects addressing aspects of Vienna's cultural history and of the history of photography and she has also written numerous articles and reviews and co-edited several related books.

Dank

Unser Dank gilt all jenen Mitarbeiter:innen der Medizinischen Universität und des Universitätsklinikums AKH Wien, die ihren Teil zum Gelingen dieses Buchprojekts beigetragen haben. Besonders bedanken möchten wir uns bei Michaela Fritz, Vizerektorin für Forschung und Innovation der MedUni Wien, die unser Vorhaben mit viel Engagement organisatorisch betreut und begleitet hat. Jörg Simonitsch hat als stellvertretender technischer Direktor des Universitätsklinikums AKH nicht nur den Zutritt zu den verborgenen Bereichen des Gebäudes ermöglicht, auch interessantes technisches Detailwissen verdanken wir ihm. Herwig Czech, Professor für Geschichte der Medizin an der MedUni Wien, sowie Johannes Angerer, Leiter der Abteilung Kommunikation und Öffentlichkeitsarbeit der Medizinischen Universität, sei für ihre sorgsame Lektüre des Manuskripts und ihre konstruktive Kritik herzlich gedankt. Daniela Hahn und Franziska Sikl, Archivarinnen im Josephinum – Medizinische Sammlungen GmbH der MedUni Wien, haben uns tatkräftig bei der Suche nach historischem Bildmaterial unterstützt und Scans davon bereitgestellt. Elisabeth Koo, Assistentin der Vizerektorin für Forschung und Innovation, und Klaus Dietl, stellvertretender Leiter der Kommunikationsabteilung, verdanken wir die korrekte Benennung aller fotografierten Gebäude und Räume.

Ein Dankeschön auch an Sybille Hentze, Leiterin der Bibliothek der Universität für angewandte Kunst Wien, die der Autorin während der pandemiebedingten Zutrittsverbote bei der Entlehnung von Büchern behilflich war. Großer Dank gebührt in dieser Hinsicht auch Alain Peano, Paris, für seine Übermittlung französischsprachiger Fachliteratur.

Roman Keller vom Wiener Bildbearbeitungsstudio malkasten verdanken wir die bewährt hohe Qualität der Trommelscans und die feinfühlige Farbabstimmung in der Lithografie. Und last, but not least gilt unser ausdrücklicher Dank Willi Schmid, Wien, dessen Buchdesign unserem Vorhaben die adäquate Form verliehen hat.

Acknowledgements

We would like to thank all those employees of the Medical University and University Hospital Vienna who contributed to the success of this book project. Our special gratitude is due to Michaela Fritz, Vice Rector for Research and Innovation of MedUni Vienna, who provided us with organizational support and accompanied our undertaking with huge commitment. In his role as Deputy Technical Director of University Hospital Vienna, Jörg Simonitsch not only enabled us to access hidden parts of the building, but also shed light on some fascinating technical details. Herwig Czech, Professor of the History of Medicine at MedUni Vienna, and Johannes Angerer, Head of the Corporate Communications Department of the Medical University, must be sincerely thanked for their careful reading of the manuscript and their constructive criticism. Daniela Hahn and Franziska Sikl, archivists of the Josephinum – Medizinische Sammlungen GmbH of MedUni Vienna, supported us energetically in our search for historical images and provided scans of this material. And we would like to thank Elisabeth Koo, assistant to the Vice Rector for Research and Innovation, and Klaus Dietl, Deputy Head of the Communications Department, for ensuring that all the photographed buildings and spaces are correctly named.

We are also grateful to Sybille Hentze, Director of the Library of the University of Applied Arts Vienna, who enabled the author to borrow books while the library could not be accessed due to the pandemic. And similar thanks must be expressed to Alain Peano, Paris, for providing specialist literature in the French language.

Our gratitude is due to Roman Keller from the Vienna image processing studio malkasten for the dependably high quality of the drum scans and the delicate color balance of the lithographs. And, last but not least, a special acknowledgment must go to Willi Schmid, Vienna, whose book design has given our project the appropriate form.

Bildnachweis / Picture Credits

The reproduced material was provided
by the following institutions: Josephinum –
Ethics, Collections and History of Medicine,
MedUni Vienna (figs. C, D, E, F, G, H, K, P, Q);
Wien Museum (figs. A, B, I, J, L, M, N, O).

Impressum / Imprint

Markus Müller, Stefan Oláh,
Ulrike Matzer (eds.)

Medizinische Universität Wien
Spitalgasse 23
1090 Vienna
www.meduniwien.ac.at

Idea
Markus Müller, Vienna

Concept
Stefan Oláh, Ulrike Matzer, Vienna

Acquisitions Editor
David Marold, Birkhäuser Verlag, Vienna

Content & Production Editor
Bettina R. Algieri, Birkhäuser Verlag, Vienna

*Translation from German into English
and proof reading*
Rupert Hebblethwaite, Vienna

Proof reading German
Thomas Lederer, Vienna

Graphic Design
Willi Schmid, Vienna

Image Editing
Roman Keller, malkasten, Vienna
Willi Schmid, Vienna

Printing
Holzhausen, the book-printing brand
of Gerin Druck GmbH, Wolkersdorf, Austria

Paper
GardaPat 11, 150 g; Munken Lynx, 130 g

Typeface
Academica

MEDIZINISCHE
UNIVERSITÄT WIEN

[malkasten]

Library of Congress Control Number
2023937181

*Bibliographic information published
by the German National Library*
The German National Library lists this publication in the Deutsche Nationalbibliografie;
detailed bibliographic data are available on
the Internet at http://dnb.dnb.de.

This work is subject to copyright. All rights
are reserved, whether the whole or part
of the material is concerned, specifically the
rights of translation, reprinting, re-use of
illustrations, recitation, broadcasting, repro-
duction on microfilms or in other ways, and
storage in databases. For any kind of use,
permission of the copyright owner must be
obtained.

ISBN 978-3-0356-2777-0
e-ISBN (PDF) 978-3-0356-2780-0

© 2024 Birkhäuser Verlag GmbH, Basel
Im Westfeld 8, 4055 Basel, Switzerland
Part of Walter de Gruyter GmbH,
Berlin / Boston

9 8 7 6 5 4 3 2 1
www.birkhauser.com

FSC
www.fsc.org
MIX
Papier | Fördert
gute Waldnutzung
FSC® C108696